THE ACHIEVEMENT OF THE AIRSHIP

The Achievement of the Airship

A HISTORY OF THE DEVELOPMENT OF RIGID, SEMI-RIGID AND NON-RIGID AIRSHIPS

GUY HARTCUP

DAVID & CHARLES

NEWTON ABBOT LONDON NORTH POMFRET (VT)
VANCOUVER

To

Iti, my wife, for her
help and patience during the
writing of this book
and to my mother who
originally stimulated my
interest in writing

Library of Congress Catalog Card Number 74-24769

0 7153 6551 7

Set in 11 on 13pt Bembo
and printed in Great Britain
by Latimer Trend & Company Ltd Plymouth
for David & Charles (Holdings) Limited
South Devon House Newton Abbot Devon

Published in the United States of America
by David & Charles Inc
North Pomfret Vermont 05053 USA

Published in Canada by Douglas David & Charles Limited
3645 McKechnie Drive West Vancouver BC

CONTENTS

LIST OF ILLUSTRATIONS

Plates

Line drawings in text

FOREWORD

By Lord Kings Norton, PhD, DIC, F Inst Mech Eng, Hon FRAeS

I think Mr Hartcup in this splendid book has performed a great service to airship history. I have read every word with the greatest interest and while some of the detail, essential in what must be a definitive work, may perhaps occasionally seem hard going for the general reader, he cannot but enjoy the enfolding of a unique piece of engineering history. To the specialist, the book is a godsend, filling gaps in knowledge and comprehension right, left and centre. Fortunately, because the sheer appeal of airships, like the appeal of the great sailing ships, has been sustained in the minds of the more romantic of us, there will be, I think, a great welcome from a more general public as well as for the fruits of Mr Hartcup's researches, which have led him—first, I think among airship historians—to the Public Record Office and to the foreign records in the Imperial War Museum.

There is not much doubt that posterity will accord the highest place in airship history to the Germans. I am always proud to recall that in August 1931 I flew in the *Graf Zeppelin* from Hanworth to Friedrichshafen with Dr Eckener, Captain Lehmann (later to die in the *Hindenburg*) and Captain von Schiller (still active and living in Tübingen). In Friedrichshafen I met the great Dr Dürr and Dr Ehrle. This was just before, through the closing down of the last British airship programme and the wanton scrapping of *R 100*, that I left the airship world for ever.

My professional life has given me two outstanding satisfactions. One is to have been closely connected with the development of the aircraft gas turbine. The other is to have been closely associated with airships. As a post-graduate student at Imperial College in 1922–3, I attended the lectures of Lieut-Col V. C. Richmond, and my imagination was fired by the prospects he saw ahead. In the summer of 1924 he offered me a job as a 'calculator' at Cardington. I left Imperial College to join him there and worked with T. S. D. Collins on the preliminary design of *R 101*. We were joined later by J. F. Baker for a time, by A. F. Pugsley and by Hilda Lyon, as Mr Hartcup relates, and between us we devised systems for calculating external loads and for computing stresses of an accuracy, a comprehensiveness and a complexity never before developed in this area of engineering, though I have no doubt paralleled in the design of *R 100*.

Those were wonderful days. We flew in *R 33* to check our aerodynamic calculations by measuring pressures in flight. We climbed over the giant framework for reasons lost in the mists of nearly half a century. We worked early and late to check and cross check our calculations. We enjoyed ourselves.

Richmond was the leader of the design team; not himself a great designer perhaps, he was a good picker. His chief assistant was F. M. Rope, a brilliant RAF officer who died with so many other of my friends in the final disaster. His was the design genius and I am seizing the opportunity the invitation to write this Foreword gives me, to pay tribute to a wonderful man who has not yet had the appreciation which his immense contribution to airship design deserves.

Of the leading characters in the stress office, all but Hilda Lyon are still with us. I think we must all feel privileged to have found a modest place in the airship saga which Mr Hartcup so meticulously relates. It is a wonderful story, punctuated with tragedy and culminating in disaster, and it is a story which I believe is ended. There are admirable people who are seeking to stage an aerostatic renaissance, as Mr Hartcup tells us in Chapter 10, and I wish them luck, but they are fighting against long odds. I wish they could win because airships have an appeal which still tugs at the hearts of all who were ever near them, however long ago.

INTRODUCTION

Of all the forms of modern transport, the full potentialities of the airship probably have never been realised. From the start, airships have been dependent on scientific development to an even greater extent than heavier-than-air craft. Without hydrogen there was no really efficient form of lift, and light alloys, such as duralumin and aluminium, were essential for the structure of girders for rigid airships. Thus apart from several brave and far-seeing attempts at lighter-than-air flight in the early years of the nineteenth century, the development of dirigible airships—either with a rigid framework containing individual gas bags and supporting control and passenger cars and engines, the hull being protected by an outer cover, or with a gas-inflated envelope with suspended control car engines—had to wait until an efficient internal-combustion engine was available. The revival of the airship today—if it comes—will again be dependent on modern technology.

This is a study of the development of the dirigible airship as opposed to the free balloon. In so far as it examines the special problems of construction and handling, as opposed to the well-publicised and documented disasters of airships, it may provide a guide by which future lighter-than-air developments may be assessed.

One of the earliest experiments proved to be the most successful. This was the rigid airship which realised the dream of a Württemberg cavalry officer—Count Ferdinand von Zeppelin. Within the space of just over a decade, the Zeppelin airships had overcome most of their teething problems and were starting to pay their way with passenger-carrying flights. Their success, it will be seen, was not achieved without a series of mishaps, due less to the imperfections of the ships than to the special problems of handling which had to be solved.

At the same time, other European countries—France, in particular, and later Italy and Russia—began to investigate the possibilities of non-rigid and semi-rigid airships. Although the first attempts with dirigibles in France, such as those of Renard and Dumont, were with non-rigids, it was the semi-rigid sponsored by the Lebaudy brothers, and later copied by the Germans and the Italians, that proved to be the most useful, and was taken up by the army for tasks on the eastern frontier of France.

Semi- and non-rigid airships also began to compete for official recognition in Germany in the early 1900s. The Parseval was an original and effective version of the non-rigid, while the military airship was virtually a copy of the Lebaudy, and a miniature 'crash' programme was stimulated by anxieties about what the French were doing west of the Rhine.

The years 1910–12 were the 'vintage' ones for the airship. For the future of the aeroplane was still problematic, and as for endurance and speed the Zeppelin rigids were for the time being supreme. Another German company called Schütte-Lanz gave a competitive edge, leading to improvements, such as streamlining, in the design of rigid airships. Britain and the United States of America experimented tentatively with non-rigids. Keen rivalry existed between the exponents of the rigid and non-rigid systems. The former believed that their ships had speed and range, while the advocates of the latter believed that rigids were clumsy and dangerous to handle and were forced to shelter in large sheds or hangars when not in use.

During the World War I airship design, especially for the rigid, made great strides in disposable weight, speed and range. In 1914 the greatest distance that an airship had flown was 500 miles. The longest flight during the war was made by the naval Zeppelin *L 59*, which flew 4,200 miles, much of it in a tropical climate, and remained in the air for 95hr. Britain had, in the meantime, belatedly turned to the development of non-rigids, which played an important role in countermeasures to the U-boat threat. But she had not the experience in design to build large rigids in time to operate as 'eyes' for the Royal Navy.

The experience gained by the Zeppelins and Schütte-Lanz's demonstrated that, while rigids were useless as a war weapon, they had great possibilities as long-distance passenger carriers. In this respect they were still superior to the aeroplane. The phase of invention, in which the airship was still an unreliable vehicle, gave way to the phase of exploitation which was marked by the double crossing of the Atlantic by a British rigid, *R 34*, in 1919. During the war the Zeppelins were designed specifically as warships and the crews had been prepared to take risks. The disaster of the British *R 38*, which was to have been bought by the US navy, which had been modelled on the mid-war super-Zeppelin, led to greater emphasis on factors of safety in design, and consequently to heavier airships—a decision which proved to be fraught with grave consequences.

Paying greater attention to the correct ratio of length to breadth in order to reduce, as far as possible, the resistance coefficient, or drag, Britain, after temporarily abandoning airship development, embarked on an experimental programme in which one airship was to be built by the government and the other was supplied on contract by a private company. Such was the genesis of *R 101* and *R 100*. It was intended that they should be the forerunners of regular airship links with the Dominions, and the British development of the mooring mast was held to be the solution to the hitherto intractable problem of handling airships on the ground. But insufficient attention was given to the problem of the airship passing from cool to hot climates, with the consequent effect on its lifting ability. Moreover, political pressure led to the drastic curtailing of the trials of these two experimental ships. Although *R 100* successfully made a double crossing of the Atlantic in a flight to Canada, though not without hazard, her sister ship was destroyed by fire after diving to the ground on her proving flight to India. The economic crisis of 1931 finally put an end to British airship development.

Meanwhile, a group of naval officers and engineers in the United States had also displayed an interest in rigid airships and the US Government, in addition to purchasing *R 38*, had commissioned the building of a Zeppelin (later named *Los Angeles*) as compensation for an airship which should have gone to the USA at the end of the war, but was instead scuttled by the Germans in 1919. The US navy had also built a rigid airship of its own—*Shenandoah*—modelled on a war-time Zeppelin. But that ship, mainly on account of lack of experience, rather than to faults in construction, broke up in mid-air. It did not catch fire, though, as it was inflated with helium, of which the USA possessed the principal source. Like with the British inquiry into the *R 38* disaster, the Americans deduced that much stronger construction was required in future. Moreover, a small number of Zeppelin engineers and technicians had been encouraged to emigrate to the USA to form the nucleus of the Goodyear Zeppelin Corporation, which built two large naval rigids primarily for long-range reconnaissance to be supplemented by aeroplanes carried in the airships.

Following *R 101*, the American rigids diverged from the Zeppelin practice of constructing the framework of their rigid airships as lightly as possible with wire bracing, and instead built heavy unbraced transverse frames, the function of which is described in Chapter 1. Unfortunately, the airship crews lacked experience, and human factors rather than structural defects were responsible for the disasters to two ships, *Akron* and *Macon*. Although rigid airship development was not specifically abandoned, the threatening international situation led the US army and navy to concentrate on heavier-than-air craft.

Luftschiffbau Zeppelin, on the other hand, had a small corps d'élite of naval officers with wartime experience in airship piloting. Behind them the airship designers were responsible for a steady, unspectacular, development in technique from 1916, when the first long-range ships were built, through the rest of the war years, to the post-war *LZ 126* (*Los Angeles*)—the first German airship to fly the Atlantic, the *Graf Zeppelin*, and the much larger ships *Hindenburg* (able to carry 70 passengers) and *Graf Zeppelin II*. The latter two ships were to have been inflated with helium on account of the *R 101*'s destruction by fire. These were the first, and so far the only, transoceanic passenger-carrying airships, and it was a tragedy that *Hindenburg* was destroyed by fire while landing at Lakehurst, New Jersey. At least *Graf Zeppelin*, though undersized, not only made a spectacular round-the-world flight and engaged in scientific research over the Arctic, but carried some 13,000 passengers without loss, mainly across the South Atlantic, and flew a million miles. Her sister ship, *Los Angeles*, was also in active operation for seven years under American command, engaged in less spectacular, though none the less valuable, tasks.

However, the skilful German designers did not have to solve the problems posed by the heavier, though non-inflammable, helium, as Nazi Germany was prohibited from using the gas lest she use her airships for military purposes, and if rigid airship construction had continued probably would have been compelled to modify the traditional light design.

Meanwhile, the semi-rigid airship enjoyed a brief period of fame in Italy, mainly due to the efforts of Umberto Nobile, who made a flight over the North Pole. But a subsequent expedition ended in disaster. Nobile, out of favour with the Fascist Government, went to the Soviet Union to guide that country's expanding airship programme.

The Soviet Union and the USA have been the only countries to use airships recently. Following the example of Britain in World War I, the USA made use of non-rigids in countermeasures against the U-boat during World War II, and continued to use them for military purposes until 1961. The Russians have used, and are using, semi-rigids, though not rigids as far as is known, in the under-developed areas of Siberia and on their eastern frontier.

In regard to future airship development, is the rigid airship, like an antediluvian monster, an anachronism in the fiercely competitive field of aeronautics? Or is it an alternative form of aerial transport—a large VTOL aircraft, able to operate without the large runways on which aeroplanes are dependent, and free to cross land-water boundaries? The future may well see a revival of the large rigid airship as a freight, rather than as a passenger, carrier, for it is in this field that it is most likely to rival its old adversary—the heavier-than-air craft, now jet-propelled. One can only speculate on the design of a rigid airship of the future. While it is likely that the familiar plump shape of the 1930s will be the same, the size will have to be far greater to contain sufficient lifting gas (presumably of helium), for in order to be competitive a payload of some 400–500 tons must be carried. The hull again might be built with longitudinal girders and transverse frames using non-corroding alloys, or it might be built on the monocoque principle. Nylon fabrics would be used for the outer cover, and impermeable synthetic fibres for the gas-cell linings. Power would still be provided by some form of orthodox transport engine (probably a gas turbine) driving propellers, though in the not-so-distant future, current engine designs could well be superseded by ones using nuclear power. On account of their vast size, such airships would operate like satellites, taking up and delivering their loads by means of hydraulic lifts, landing only for maintenance. They would, though, travel at speeds of probably not more than 100mph.

ACKNOWLEDGEMENTS

I wish to thank the Royal Aeronautical Society for allowing me to make use of their fine collection of books and records of airships, and, in particular, to the Librarian, Mr Arnold Nayler, for answering my questions on airships, past and present; for helping with the selection of illustrations; and for reading and commenting on the typescript of the book. Also to his assistant, Mrs Dane, for her charm and the skill with which she retrieved volumes from distant parts of the building, usually within the limited span of a lunch hour. I am also indebted to the Library of the Institution of Mechanical Engineers under Mr R. T. Everett and Mr S. G. Morrison; to Mr F. S. White of the Adastral House Library, Ministry of Defence; and to the staffs of the Ministry of Defence Library (Central and Army), and of the Library of the Science Museum, South Kensington.

Thanks are also due to the staff of the Public Record Office, both in Portugal Street and in Chancery Lane; and to the Air Historical Branch, RAF, Ministry of Defence, under Mr L. A. Jackets and, subsequently, Group Capt E. B. Haslam.

I am very grateful to Dr Noble Frankland, Director of the Imperial War Museum, for making available to me the collection of papers belonging to the late Wing Cdr Cave-Brown-Cave, and to Mr D. G. Lance, Keeper of the Department of Libraries and Archives, the Imperial War Museum. Also to Mr H. G. Tibbutt, Departmental Record Officer, Ministry of Defence, for directing me to the voluminous files in the Public Record Office; and to Mr A. D. W. Pimm for providing me with a valuable bibliography of German airship literature; to Dr R. N. G. Atherstone for the loan of his father's diary of the period when he was an officer of R 101; and to Dr Richard K. Smith for detailed information on American naval airships and for putting me in touch with other airship sources in the USA.

A number of survivors from the 'airship era' gave me the benefit of their memories, in particular, Lord Kings Norton, Sir Barnes Wallis, Dr Jerome C. Hunsaker, Sir Alfred Pugsley, Air Marshal Sir Victor Goddard, Air Marshal P. E. Maitland, Mr R. W. Potts, and Mr S. J.

Rosser. The future potential of airships was explained to me with enthusiasm by Mr Frank Hyde, Secretary of the Airship Association, who also read and commented on the final chapter of the book.

Finally, I must thank Mr Roger Watts for his calculations with a slide rule, and once again, Mrs Audrey Tester, for retyping sections of the MS.

Principles of Buoyant Flight: Airship Systems

'The forces of nature cannot be eliminated, but they can be balanced one against the other.' Count Zeppelin

The lighter-than-air craft, unlike heavier-than-air craft, which relies on dynamic lift to remain airborne, rides in the atmosphere like a ship floating in water in obedience to Archimedes' principle. Size in the air is an advantage to the airship, because the greater the volume of gas inflating it the heavier the load it can carry. But on the ground its great bulk is a handicap, for its lack of weight makes it vulnerable to every gust of wind, while the gas is subject to variations in temperature, increasing or decreasing weight, as the case may be.

Hydrogen and helium are the two gases usually employed in lifting an airship, the latter being non-inflammable. Hot air is also practicable, though with much less lifting ability and presenting special problems of pressure control. An airship's lift is expressed in lb per 1,000cu ft. The calculation takes into account the fact that gas, when put into the gas bags is seldom 100 per cent pure, because of impurities in the gas. Barometric pressure and changes in temperature affect the density of the gas. Hydrogen is computed to weigh 68lb per 1,000cu ft. Helium is 7 per cent heavier and weighs 63lb per 1,000cu ft. The size of an airship can therefore be estimated by the capacity, or volume, in terms of cubic feet.

When an airship lifts from the ground, it must be in trim; its gross weight, as opposed to the disposable weight (which, in the case of the rigid airship, means passengers, crew, freight, fuel, ballast, etc) is equal to the lift provided by the gas.[1] There are, however, two kinds of lift. First, static lift obtained by a lighter-than-air gas. As an airship gains height, the weight of the air it displaces becomes less and less as the atmosphere gets thinner, and so the lift diminishes. At the same time gas bags expand, and, in order to prevent them from bursting, valves are fitted which automatically start releasing gas at what is called pressure height. As releasing gas in this way is wasteful, particularly in the case of helium, the gas bags of a rigid ship are only partially inflated on leaving the ground, so that on reaching the desired pressure height, about 2,000ft, equilibrium, or sufficient lift, will have been obtained. Additional height can be obtained by releasing ballast (usually water). Ballast may also have to be released when descending to the ground, for on entering a cold belt near the earth's surface the gas will contract and gain weight.

An airship can also be kept flying by means of dynamic lift, or flying the ship at a positive, or negative, angle to the direction of the wind. The airship's system of horizontal planes, or elevators, is now brought into play—their action is similar to that of flying a kite. This enables the pilot to keep flying when the airship is heavier than air, and he can keep it down when the ship is much lighter than air. The airship can also be steered laterally—like a seaborne ship—by using the vertical rudders attached to the fins. Stability is also provided for by horizontal planes—found in all but the very early airships—combined with the elevators.

Several problems are involved in maintaining the equilibrium of a rigid airship in flight. When driven by petrol engines, the buoyancy of the ship will increase in proportion to the amount of fuel consumed. As an airship must be landed in equilibrium, hydrogen or helium equal in lifting force to the weight of fuel consumed, must be discharged into the air. This is wasteful.

Three methods whereby gas loss may be prevented or reduced have been evolved. Firstly, the use of a water-recovery system in which the water vapour present in the exhaust of the petrol engines is condensed and recovered. As there were many technical difficulties inherent in this method, the possibility of burning hydrogen in an engine designed to use petrol or diesel oil as fuel, was investigated. But little progress was made. Secondly, and more successfully, the Germans in *Graf Zeppelin*, instead of feeding the engines with liquid fuel, used a gas which had nearly the same specific gravity as air. This fuel gas (blaugas) was contained in fabric bags which collapsed as they emptied, and as the space filled up with air no appreciable change in buoyancy arose from fuel

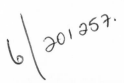

consumption. Certain disadvantages to this scheme will be discussed in a later chapter. Finally, there was the possibility of using engines with an economic consumption of fuel such as the diesel—relatively un-developed for other than road vehicles in the inter-war years—while in the airship of the future, it is probable that gas turbines or nuclear systems (now that reactors have become much lighter) will be used.

Equilibrium is also affected by sunlight falling on the outer cover of the rigid airship causing the temperature of the gas in the gas bags, and of the air contained within the outer cover, to rise independently of the atmosphere. This is known as 'superheating' and will increase buoyancy —in the case of a ship of 2 million cubic feet capacity by as much as 2 tons. It is possible to reduce superheating by making the outer cover more efficient in reflecting sunlight, or by absorbing it so that it does not penetrate into the interior of the ship. Superheating may also be reduced by flying the ship fast at a low altitude, or by flying it into cloud.

The most favourable conditions for flying an airship are therefore when the weather is cold and the barometer high. Night time is usually ideal for airship travel.

Airships are essentially gas containers to which are attached various weights: (1) the cars and cabins containing crew, passengers, freight, and engines; (2) the fuel, oil and ballast; (3) the controls. There are three systems of airship construction according to the various methods of maintaining the form of the envelope or outer cover and of suspend-ing the weights from it—non-rigid, semi-rigid and rigid.

The envelope of the non-rigid airship is, unlike the rigid, a single gas container, and its shape is kept by internal pressure. For this reason non-rigids are sometimes referred to as pressure airships. They are equipped with one or more ballonets. These are internal air bags made of fabric and have a capacity equal to from one-quarter to one-third of the envelope. Their purpose is to prevent the envelope from losing its shape as the airship ascends or descends. When the airship is in flight the air enters the ballonets through ducts from a scoop in the propeller stream, or by the action of a blower. As the airship rises, the expansion of the gas drives some of the air out of the ballonets; when the ship descends, contraction of the gas is made good by the expansion of the ballonets. A pressure-gauge records these movements for the pilot.

The non-rigid is subject to shear forces and bending moments, due, in the first place, to the distribution of the weight not corresponding to the distribution of the lift, and secondly, to the reaction of the controls when airborne. The various ways of dealing with weight distribution are reflected in the several types of non-rigid.

In World War I and post-war years non-rigids rarely exceeded 500,000cu ft capacity, but after World War II, the US navy developed ships of up to 975,000cu ft inflated with helium. Thus while in the early days of non-rigids the larger ones were able to remain in the air for about 60hr, though a record of 100hr was established in 1919, by the end of the 1950s they could achieve up to eleven days of uninter-rupted flight. From World War II onwards they were capable of flying up to about 60mph.

In the earliest non-rigids, a framework or girder of aluminium, long enough to distribute the weight over the main part of the envelope, hung below it.[2] A variation of this kind had a short car with a boom extension at either end to form what was virtually a long girder, and this further increased the distribution of the load over the envelope. This type was adopted in some of the early French and British airships. In other early types the weights were suspended from the envelope by ropes attached to suspension patches on the envelope, or to a suspension band on the envelope, which was of almost circular section through-out.

A more sophisticated form of non-rigid was developed by a German army officer, August von Parseval. The weights were hung from a suspension band under the envelope. The load was transmitted to the envelope by trajectory bands running over the top, so arranged to reduce the deformation of shape and tensile strength to a minimum. This system enabled the car to be slung close to the envelope; it main-tained the latter's shape, was easy to construct and could be expanded to ships of up to about 500,000cu ft capacity.

The French exploited the invention of the Spaniard, Torres Quevedo, with the *Astra Torres*, in which the envelope was of a trilobe, or clover-leaf section, one lobe above and two below. The transverse shape was maintained by continuous longitudinal curtains which helped to give rigidity to the envelope. The suspension ropes entered the underside of the envelope through airtight joints on the centre line, branching out into a smaller number of ropes which were attached to longitudinal ropes or strips in the angles between the upper and the lower lobe. In this system overall height was reduced to the minimum, as the attachments were near the top of the envelope and the minimum amount of rigging obstructed the movement of the airship.

The view from the centre of an inflated airship of this kind, assuming one was equipped with an oxygen mask, was impressive; its length of 270ft gave a cathedral-like vista. Above, the ceiling was formed by the horizontal linen curtain laced to the top ridges, and on either side the curtains from the top ridges to the centre line gave the impression of walls, against which could be seen miles of cordage which connected the main suspension wires to the upper ridges and which fanned to them on either side. The unbleached linen curtains made the interior a study in sepia. But the large amount of internal rigging was heavy and difficult to keep in good condition. The *Astra Torres* system was much used by the British in World War I.

The advantages of the non-rigids were that they were simple to build, easily deflated (in emergency with the help of a rip-cord); and they could be packed up into a small space for transport. On the other hand, they were limited in speed on account of the possibility of the ship's nose being blown in, although an umbrella-like system of battens stiffened that area.

Semi-rigid airships were first produced by the French, but were subsequently developed extensively by the Italians before, during, and after World War I when they attained a capacity of over a million cubic feet.

The semi-rigid resembles the non-rigid in that the form of the envelope is maintained by internal pressure, but differs in the method of distributing the load. In the semi-rigid a longitudinal keel girder fitted to the underside of the envelope provides a rigid and, in certain types, a slightly flexible, backbone. It is therefore possible for a semi-rigid to fly at a much lower gas pressure than a non-rigid. A lighter envelope fabric can be used, and sufficient weight saved to compensate for the extra weight of the keel girder. To fly a semi-rigid at speed requires a fully inflated envelope, but it can be brought in to land with a partially inflated envelope. This is made possible by dividing the gas container into compartments by means of transverse fabric bulkheads;

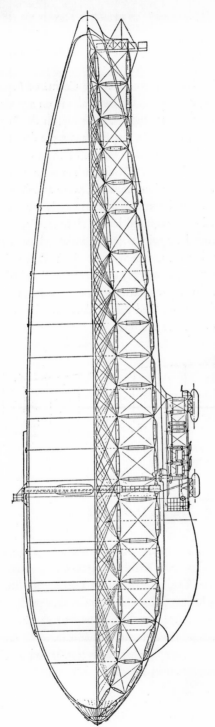

Coastal non-rigid with Astra-Torres envelope

it also reduces the risk of the airship losing lift through an accidental tear in the envelope.

In the French Lebaudy designs, like the German *M* and *Veeh* types, the car and motors were suspended by cables from a girder slung close underneath the envelope (see Figure, page 34). In the Italian Forlanini and Verducio designs, the cabin and engines were directly attached to a keel, which ran along the entire length of the envelope and which was partially enclosed within it. In the Italian military (*M*) type, two jointed booms, or compression members, were attached to the under-side of the envelope, and connected transversely by horizontal struts and braces to obtain the required lateral rigidity. From this structure the car was suspended by wire ropes so arranged as to form a com-pletely triangulated system, which made dismantling easy when the envelope was deflated, and was adjustable to the shape of the envelope during inflation, allowing it to assume its natural form without strain. At the stern, the keel supported the rudders and elevators, while for-ward it helped to reinforce the bow.

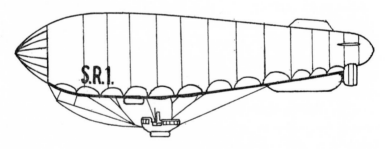

Italian *M* type semi-rigid

In a class by itself, but closely allied to the semi-rigid, is the metal-clad airship.[3] Several pioneer airship designers, including the Austrian, David Schwartz, the Russian, Konstantin Tsiolkovski, and the Ameri-can, Ralph Upson, believed that thin aluminium sheeting was superior to the normal cotton cover to which dope or varnish was applied (in the case of the non-rigid the cover had, of course, to be gas-proof). The view was that a metalclad ship was stronger, lasted longer, and was better able to resist bending moments and shearing stresses during flying. These advantages were denied by the traditional airship designers. They claimed that fabric covers, if properly doped, were in every respect, such as durability, equal if not better than metal sheeting and pointed out that the latter was vulnerable to puncturing and less easy to repair, while the easy generation of heat within the metal cover would present problems. However, the possibility of metalclad airships on the monocoque principle may well be reviewed should there ever be a revival of the airship.

Of all airship systems, the rigid type is the most advanced in respect of disposable lift; range (inter-war rigids were capable of flying up to at least 5,000 miles without refuelling, and today there is the promise that nuclear engines now under development or in an advanced state in the design offices of two or three countries could make an airship entirely independent of the ground except for maintenance); and number of engines, so that the failure of even two does not endanger the airship's safety. Moreover, the ship's static lift will keep her up, and loss of lift can be compensated for by discharging ballast. All parts of the ship can be inspected during flight, which means repairs can be made, for instance, to the outer cover or engines while airborne.

The structure of a rigid airship has so far consisted of a number of polygonal transverse frames to which longitudinal girders were attached, the girders initially being of aluminium and later of duralumin.[4] The gas bags, numbering 15–17, were located between the transverse frames. In all the Zeppelin ships these were braced by steel wires. In their early airships the British and Americans copied the German system, but in the later American designs, and in one of the British (R 101), a wide, unbraced transverse frame was used.

The advantage was, firstly, that it provided extra strength to the hull; and, secondly, that it held the pressure of the gas bags. A major problem in a rigid airship proved to be the fact that changes in altitude and temperature caused the gas bags to fluctuate in size. When the gas bags expanded, or when the ship pitched, or when there was unequal pressure caused by deflation of a gas bag, the girders were subjected to considerable pressure, most of which was borne by the transverse frame. An additional advantage of the unbraced frame was that it gave access for the crew to the interior of the hull. The principal disadvantage of the unbraced frame was that it occupied valuable gas space, thus depriving the ship of lift. For this reason the Zeppelin designers rejected it, but provided extra strength to their largest ships by inserting an axial girder running through the gas bags, and which also provided a walkway for inspection purposes.

Finally, the spaces between the longitudinal girders were crisscrossed by steel bracing wires. Over them was stretched the outer cover, made of cotton, but doped to make it weatherproof and resistant to sunlight. It is possible that airships of the future will have monocoque hulls and dispense with the system of girders.

The gas bags were originally enclosed by two nets, one, a wire mesh and the second of ramie cord, both of which were connected to the longitudinals. Later, circumferential wires were substituted for the nets, running continuously round the hull and fixed to the longitudinals. In some ships the bags were held in position by a catenary wire running through the centre of the ship, later being replaced by the axial girder.

As airships increased in size and speed, strength of structure and reduction of drag became essential. In the early rigids a keel which served the purpose of strengthening the hull, accommodating the fuel and ballast tanks, and supporting the engines, projected below the hull. As design improved this keel was enclosed within the hull. It held passenger quarters in commercial airships. The original long cylindrical shape of the hull was succeeded by one of a plump shape running in a more or less continuous curve, thereby reducing drag and making the ship less vulnerable to external stresses.[5]

The stern of the airship containing the fins, rudder and elevators evolved from complex to simple forms. The fins became streamlined with the remainder of the hull, while the rudders and elevators changed from the box type to simple, balanced surfaces controlled by wires attached to wheels in the control car where they were operated by hand. Also in the control car were toggles for opening the gas and water-ballast valves, and the navigational instruments. The car was originally attached to one of the engines, but eventually became part of the hull.

In early ships, the engines were suspended from the hull in cars, the propellers being fixed on the side of the envelope and driven by gears and long transmission shafts. In hydrogen-inflated airships this was

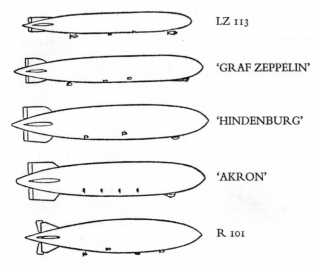

Side elevation of rigid airships (1918–32) to show
development of fineness ratio

dangerous, and transmission faults often occurred. Subsequently the propellers were driven direct from the engine. The helium-inflated American rigids, however, permitted the engines to be installed in the hull, the propellers being fixed on brackets to the sides. Only the Germans succeeded in developing a really useful airship engine, able to go both forward and in reverse like a marine engine. When, in order to eliminate the danger of fire, and to economise in fuel consumption, diesel engines were employed, the Germans again proved more successful than the British.

The bogey of fire, so frequently associated with airships, should be dispelled at this point. Properly designed ships inflated with hydrogen were not susceptible to fire. Accidents that occurred were due to inexpert handling. No rigid airship has been destroyed by lightning while in the air, the frame acting as a lightning conductor. Outside war casualties, only two Zeppelins out of the total of 119 built and inflated with hydrogen were destroyed by fire during flight—excluding *Hindenburg*, which was probably destroyed by brush discharge, or static electricity.

CHAPTER 2

Non- and Semi-Rigids (i): Franco-German Rivalry

'At the beginning of the year 1909 the mystery and craft of flying was still known only to the few.' Sir Richard Glazebrook

It is not surprising that the development of the dirigible airship should have taken place in the stimulating scientific and artistic atmosphere of France of the nineteenth century. But it was made possible by the experiments of Henry Cavendish (1731–1810), a pioneer in the study of gases, and Joseph Black (1728–99), professor of chemistry at Edinburgh, which proved that a balloon inflated with hydrogen would rise in the air. Going a stage farther, the French physicist, J. A. C. Charles (1746–1823), discovered how to make hydrogen by using sulphuric acid, iron filings, and lead. His friends, the Robert brothers, in the meantime, discovered how to make a balloon fabric impervious to hydrogen by impregnating silk with rubber.

The problems of actual flight now had to be tackled. Most of them were solved, though only in theory, by one man—Jean Meusnier, soldier and savant, who rose to be a general in the French army and who was killed in the fighting before Mayence in 1793. Meusnier, in 1784, grasped the essentials of the modern airship; the envelope was to be egg-shaped rather than spherical in the manner of contemporary balloons; the ship was to be propelled by three airscrews or propellers; ballonets were to maintain the shape of the envelope while the airship was ascending or descending; and the cover had to be both impermeable to gas and resistant to rain and sun. Meusnier is rightly called the father of the dirigible.[1]

Meusnier's propellers could not be turned without some form of light engine. Substitutes were tried out, such as the oars which were used by the Robert brothers in 1784. They forgot, however, to allow for expansion of the gas as the balloon ascended (they were using hydrogen), and were saved from disaster by their patron, the Duc de Charles, who, with great presence of mind, pierced the envelope with the point of a small flagstaff. The steam engine offered the first effective means of locomotion. Henri Giffard, inventor of steam injection, propelled his torpedo-shaped airship with a 3hp steam engine. On 24 September 1852 he flew for 17 miles, travelling in circles at a speed of about 5mph.

During the siege of Paris in 1870, when passengers and mail were carried by free balloons, Dupuy de Lôme, a naval engineer, and inventor of the ironclad, was asked by the Government to make a steerable balloon. Two years later, following the principles of Meusnier, he completed a dirigible which was to be driven by an enormous two-bladed propeller. Instead of using steam, which was dangerous, the engine was to be turned by eight sweating labourers. They managed to drive the ship against a stiff breeze about 12° from a normal straight drifting course.

The internal combustion engine was the answer. In October 1883 the scientist Gaston Tissandier and his brother, Albert, flew for a short distance in an airship driven by an electric motor powered by accumulators. The propeller was two-bladed and 9ft in diameter.

By the 1880s then, all the elements of a modern airship had been used —ballonets, ballast, lightweight engine. The next stage was for an airship to return to its point of departure. Capt Charles Renard, in charge of the aeronautical establishment at Chalais Meudon (which had been in existence since the end of the Napoleonic wars), designed and built *La France*, a non-rigid craft, 168ft in length, with a maximum diameter of 27ft and a capacity of about 65,000cu ft. She was to be driven by an electric motor of 9hp connected to a wooden tractor propeller 23ft long fixed to the front of the car. A sliding weight altered pitch. On 12 September 1884 Renard, with a brother officer, Capt A. C. Krebs undertook his first ascent. *La France* made five circuits—a total of 5 miles—at the modest speed of 15mph, returning each time to her point of departure.[2] The following year, with an improved motor installed, she showed off her paces to the Minister of War. She made a round trip from Meudon to Paris. The dirigible was now proved to be a practical form of aircraft. Five more flights were made, each time returning to the place of departure. It did not go unnoticed by a Count Zeppelin in Württemberg. Renard, who was a prolific inventor, not only in the aeronautical field, continued to experiment at Chalais Meudon, but a successor to *La France*, called *General Meusnier*, was never completed. The premature death of Renard in 1905 deprived France of a great scientist and aeronaut.

A reliable type of engine to drive the airship against a headwind was still required. That it was possible was demonstrated by the persistent, though foolhardy, experiments of Dr Karl Woelfert. He was a clergyman turned professional aeronaut who, in 1888, was the first to propel a balloon with a small petrol engine, which he had acquired from Gottlieb Daimler. This primitive engine contained a bunsen burner fed with vapourised petrol from a small pressure tank. It proved to be a lethal adoption, for Woelfert insisted on slinging his car close beneath the envelope; in June 1897 when he ascended from the Tempelhofer Field, Berlin, the petrol tank ignited; within seconds the airship crashed blazing to the ground, killing Woelfert and a companion.[3]

But the man who really exploited the petrol engine (and motoring was now becoming fashionable) was Alberto Santos Dumont, a wealthy young Brazilian, and a keen aeronaut. Dumont came to Paris in 1898, and, with the aid of a small team of reliable mechanics, began to build the first of a fleet of baby airships. He was a showman, mildly eccentric, yet brave and perceptive enough to see that the light petrol-driven motor was the answer to the propulsion problem. In his first airship, which was not a success, he used a 3½hp De Dion tricycle engine which weighed only 66lb. Dumont used to steer, single-handed, above the chimney pots of Paris and would park his balloon by tethering it to a lamp-post. His most notable achievement was in October 1901 when he won the prize of 100,000 francs (about £6,000) offered by Henri Deutsch de la Meurthe, an industrialist who immediately appreciated the importance of the petrol engine, for the first airship to fly under its own power from St Cloud, circle round the Eiffel Tower, and return to the start line, a distance of 7 miles, in not more than 30min. After several abortive attempts, during which he nearly killed himself when he collided with the Hotel Trocadero, Dumont, in his sixth airship, completed the test and won the prize. It was grudgingly given because he was a few seconds over the stipulated time. This airship, pointed at both ends, was 108ft long and 20ft in diameter, and propelled by a 16hp engine. As in *La France*, sliding weights by altering the pitch drove the ship up or down. A ballonet maintained the shape of the envelope.

The French army accepted Dumont's offer of his airship fleet in time of war, although Renard was sceptical of the value of such small vessels, considering them to be merely 'scientific toys'. But an English officer, Col J. L. B. Templer, was sufficiently impressed by them to start building an airship for the British army. Dumont, who later designed and flew one of the first aeroplanes, though he was not an innovator, had shown that the non-rigid was a viable form of aircraft.[4]

Viable, yes, but still not sufficiently practical. The problem of distributing the weight of the engine and the crew below the envelope had not been solved. Several non-rigids, in particular those of another Brazilian, Augusto Severo (like Dumont working in Paris), and a cavalry officer, von Bradsky-Labour attached to the German Embassy in Paris, came to grief. They and their crews were killed. In the latter case this was because no ballonet had been installed.[5]

Much more methodical than those unfortunate aeronauts and Dumont was the French engineer, Henri Juilliot, who from 1896 had thought about the problem of airship design and then set to work to build an entirely new type of dirigible. He decided to strengthen the envelope by giving it a light metal keel running practically its full length and fairing it in with fireproof fabric. The car below was suspended by six steel tubes linked to the keel, not only distributing the load but conveying the thrust of the propeller to the envelope above. At the stern a rudder and elevator were attached to the keel; in later versions, stabilising fins, the invention of Don Simoni, were fitted to the tail. This airship was the first semi-rigid. Juilliot also appreciated that special care had to be taken with construction, which he entrusted to M. Surcouf, who was to become a skilled airship builder.[6]

Juilliot was sponsored by the enterprising brothers, Paul and Pierre Lebaudy, sugar merchants of Moisson, near the banks of the Seine, south of Paris. *Lebaudy I*, or *Le Jaune*, as she popularly became known, because of the yellow painted calico which was intended to preserve the rubber in the material from the rays of the sun, was 187ft long, her maximum diameter was 32ft, and she had a capacity of 80,000cu ft. She was of an odd, unsymmetrical shape, pointed at both ends, but with the thicker end at the bow. The envelope was divided into compartments

c

to prevent the gas surging when the airship moved up or down. The propeller was fixed amidships over the car and was driven by a 40hp Daimler engine. Her gross weight, without fuel, was 1¾ tons.

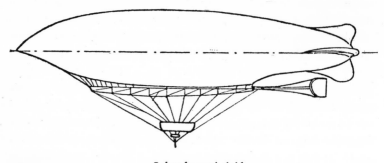

Lebaudy semi-rigid

Lebaudy made her first ascent on 13 November 1902, piloted by the experienced balloonist Georges Juchmès and his mechanic Rey. On 8 May the following year, Juchmès beat Dumont's record when he flew *Lebaudy* from Moisson, 23 miles down the Seine (where recently Monet had painted some of his finest landscapes), to Mantes Gassicourt, which he reached in 1hr 36min. 'I left with Rey, my mechanic,' said Juchmès later, 'and with 120kg of ballast. I did not take more as the heavy rain had weighted the airship to the extent of 90kg. The screws were turning at the rate of 800rpm. We went in the direction of St Martin la Garenne and Mantes.'

The airship circuited the cathedral of Mantes. 'At this point the wind becoming stronger at the height of 250m and I increased the revs of the screw to a thousand a minute,' Juchmès continued. 'I thus moved easily against the wind and steered for the Chateau de Rosny. On arriving above the park, I manoeuvred the ship in every direction. It obeyed its helm perfectly. Then I steered for the balloon shed at Moisson. The airship was put into the shed without any trouble.'[7]

On 3 November 1903 Juchmès and Rey flew *Lebaudy* to Paris, covering 30 miles in 1hr 40min. The airship alighted on the Champ de Mars, where she was secured by workmen dismantling the Paris Exhibition of 1900. She spent the night in the Gallerie des Machines and was admired by a crowd of Parisians. The return journey to Moisson was marred when, on landing, *Lebaudy*, caught by a gust of wind, ran into a tree. That collision deflated her envelope. The machinery was undamaged. The ship was rebuilt, but a similar mishap occurred the following year. She was now enlarged, her volume being increased by 11 per cent, and renamed as *Lebaudy II*. The possibilities of using her for 'sporting' purposes, or as an aerial yacht, were investigated. By the end of 1904 she had already carried, without mishap, just under 200 passengers.

The army had now become interested and the Lebaudy brothers agreed that their airship should undergo trials to discover whether it was fit for military purposes. What was its radius of action? Could it be moored in the open? Was refuelling and reinflating possible in the field? *Lebaudy II* was therefore flown from Moisson to Châlons sur Marne in easy stages, starting on 3 July 1905. She behaved perfectly, arriving at Châlons three days later, having covered the distance of 122 miles in the total time of 6hr 45min. Unfortunately there was again a mishap. A sudden storm tore the airship from its moorings and lodged it against a line of trees. The envelope was deflated, but the car and machinery survived.

Lebaudy II was then reconstructed at Toul, a fortress town near the eastern frontier. There an artillery workshop was turned into a hangar in which *Lebaudy II* was reinflated. During October and early November 1905 a series of exercises were carried out to find out whether the airship was of any use in siege warfare. Photographs were taken; dummy bombs were dropped (though aerial bombing had been prohibited for a period of five years by the International Peace Conference at the Hague in 1899); speed and altitude trials were made; and an altitude of 1,500ft was reached. The results convinced Juilliot that his airship had nothing to fear from artillery fire, for he believed that the envelope could sustain damage from 200 bullets without coming to harm. Last, but not least, the minister of war and a number of high-ranking officers were taken for rides in the airship. *Lebaudy II* was finally deflated at Toul, having made over 70 ascents since construction. At the beginning of 1906 the Lebaudys gave their airship as a patriotic gesture, to the nation.

The army, now evidently convinced of the value of airships, commissioned its first dirigible in 1907. Named *La Patrie*, she was larger than *Lebaudy II*, being 196ft long with a maximum diameter of 35ft; her capacity was 105,000cu ft and she carried a 50hp Daimler engine with two steel propellers on either side. Control was provided by horizontal and vertical planes. The car, braced up close to the envelope, contained a crew of four. *La Patrie* was to be stationed at the frontier town and fortress of Verdun, and, on 24 November 1907, she flew there from Châlons, a distance of 174 miles in 6hr 45min; that was virtually a world record, as the month before the third Zeppelin had made a number of circuits round Lake Constance and had remained airborne only a little longer.

La Patrie, crewed by army officers, now embarked on a series of exercises over Verdun. These were cut short when she had to make a forced landing after the mechanic's overalls caught in a flywheel of the motor and put it out of gear. On 30 November 1907, in a high wind, *La Patrie* broke loose from the handling party of 150 men. She now made a remarkable, but involuntary, journey. Crossing northern France, she was first blown westwards down the English Channel, and then over Ireland. She made a brief descent to the ground in Co Down, losing one of the propellers before rising again. She was last seen on 1 December by a trawler off the Mull of Kintyre.[8]

Patriotic feeling had been generated by the Moroccan crisis and Deutsch de la Meurthe, who had taken to building airships of his own, immediately offered his non-rigid, *La Ville de Paris*, to the army in place of *La Patrie*. Meanwhile, the army, undeterred by the mishap, ordered another semi-rigid which was to be called *La République*. She was similar in design to *La Patrie* but with a smaller capacity of 70,500cu ft. Equilibrium was maintained by shifting weights. Her maiden flight in September 1908 lasted for 6½hr—longer than any airship had flown to date. She also was intended to be used on the eastern frontier. In September 1909, while returning from manoeuvres, disaster occurred, for a piece of metal flew off one of the propellers. That punctured and deflated the envelope. The dirigible crashed to the ground. The crew of four army officers were killed.

What was virtually a race between French and German airships had now begun. The policy of the French was to build 20 airships by the end of 1912; later the number was cut to 18. During the years 1909–11 four more semi-rigids were built—*La Liberté* (with wooden propellers), *Capitaine Maréchal*, *Lieut Salle de Beauchamp*, and *Lebaudy IV*.

At the same time two other firms were constructing non-rigids. Surcouf, of the Astra Company, who had built the first Lebaudy, and his engineer, Victor Tatin, now turned to the non-rigid design of Renard and built for de la Meurthe the *Ville de Paris*. This had inflated ballonets or cylinders at the stern instead of fins. They not only had the advantage of being part of the airship, but were lighter than rigid fins, which were difficult to fix to the envelope and tended to depress the bow. This ship flew, in January 1908, from Paris to Verdun to take the place of *La Patrie*. Her length was 180ft and her volume 112,000cu ft. The car hung well below the envelope, running along its full length, and thus presented a less streamlined appearance than *Lebaudy* or *Lebaudy II*. The new suspension avoided the buckling to which *La Patrie* was prone. A 70hp engine drove a large two-bladed tractor propeller, 19ft in length, and which was thus able to work in undisturbed air. But the transmission shaft was subject to vibration.[9]

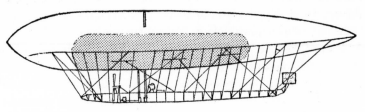

Clément-Bayard non-rigid (*Adjutant Vincenot*). Shaded area—ballonet

C. S. Rolls, balloonist as well as pioneer motorist, has left the following account of *Ville de Paris*. 'What struck me more than anything else was the complete control the captain had over the movements of the ship. He could make her do exactly what he wanted, either turn, or go up or down, slacken or increase speed as required. No ballast or gas [sic] was necessary. We moved up or down to the desired level by merely inclining the planes [elevators]. At one moment we came to within a few inches of the ground, and then, with a touch of the machinery, we moved up to a height of 750ft. The whole ship, balloon and platform, seemed to form one solid block. We were able to walk to and fro on the platform as though on the deck of a ship.'[10]

Between 1906 and 1913 Astra built 16 ships. Five were bought by Russia, Spain and Belgium; the remainder went to the French army, the principal one being *Adjutant Reau*. But the most important development of this company was the acquisition of the design of the Spanish engineer, Signor Torres Quevedo (see page 23). The Spanish army built the first of these clover-leaf-shaped airships before the designer decided to associate himself with the French.

Surcouf also built a non-rigid for M. A. Clément, the wealthy motor-car manufacturer. Subsequently this firm produced nine non-rigids under the name Clément Bayard, between 1910 and 1913, of which four were exported to England or Russia. Of those purchased by the French army, perhaps the *Adjutant Vincenot* was the most notable. She had a capacity of 320,000cu ft, was propelled by two 120hp engines, and achieved a speed of 36mph. The suspension was similar to that of the ships built by Surcouf. She carried a crew of seven. She was actively engaged in the opening phases of World War I, being used both for reconnaissance and for bombing. In 1914 she held the record of endurance for airships, being airborne for 36hr 20 min.[11]

Finally, the old-established Zodiac Company, under Maurice Mallet and the Compte de la Vaulx, which for many years had been building balloons and had recently turned to aeroplanes, began in 1909 to build small airships exclusively with a view to their sporting use. *Zodiac III*, acquired by the French army, with a capacity of 77,000cu ft, was a typical example. The Zodiac Company was to increase its productivity during the war.[12]

What did the French high command intend to do with these airships? Essentially, their role was reconnaissance, and they were divided into three classes—long- and short-range reconnaissance (*croisseurs* and *vedettes*), and scouting at close quarters to the enemy (*eclaireurs*). But there was a shortage of *croisseurs*, which the building of a rigid airship —*Spiess*—did little to remedy. The army distrusted the rigid; it was too vulnerable, cumbersome, and expensive to build. France was a great land power; there were no stretches of water to cross requiring aircraft to possess reserve powers of endurance; and the army believed that the reconnaissance role could be carried out more efficiently by heavier-than-air craft (in 1912 France possessed about 200 aeroplanes). But since the Germans apparently believed in airships, it was necessary to continue to build non-rigids. In any case, the test of war had not yet come. No one had any idea of how important the air arm would be.[13]

The significance of the French lead in the development of airships was not lost upon the Prussian general staff. It had not hitherto been particularly receptive to the possibilities of aerostation (the principles and technique of lighter-than-air flight). An airship detachment (later raised in status to battalion) had existed since 1887, but, as in other European armies, it was mainly concerned with the improvement of the captive balloon. (The army paid some attention to the experiments of Dr Woelfert because of the use of the Daimler petrol engine.) Nor did it show much sign of interest in the more revolutionary ideas of Count Zeppelin.[14] In 1893 the King of Württemburg, under whom Zeppelin had served as a colonel, wrote to the Kaiser and told him of Zeppelin's proposal for a rigid airship. But nineteen years' badgering were to elapse before the Prussian military authorities took the rigid airship seriously. The mishaps to the early Zeppelins, which are described in Chapter 4, do not make this surprising.

However, they were interested in the kite or 'sausage' balloon with which the aeronautical detachment were experimenting at the turn of the century. This was an improvement on the spherical balloon because it made use of the wind and it was, therefore, able to ascend more frequently. Two officers, August von Parseval and Hans Bartsch von Sigsfeld, were enthusiastic exponents of the kite balloon. They appreciated that *Lebaudy* could penetrate 100 miles, or more, into German territory. In 1902 they had begun to build a non-rigid, but through lack of funds it was not completed until 1905, and even then the trial flight was postponed.

Parseval wanted this motorised balloon to be able to follow the army in the field; if necessary, it could land in a small space, and it could easily be deflated and packed into a wagon.[15] It would provide the eyes for the army. Parseval's airship made its trial flight on 26 May 1906. It flew for about 1½hr at a speed of 30mph and at a height of 5,000ft. The airship and the patent were purchased several months later by the recently created Motor Luftschiff-Studien Gesellschaft—the Society for the Study of Airships—which enjoyed the active patronage of the

Kaiser. In 1908 a subsidiary called Luftfahrzeug Gesellschaft was formed to construct and sell Parseval airships. Nothing came of a suggestion from the army that Parseval, who had recently retired from the army to devote himself to scientific work, should combine forces with Count Zeppelin.

The envelope of the early Parsevals was cigar-shaped, but later designs had fish-line fins at the stern. The airship evolved as the result of experiments of the great aeronautical engineer, Ludwig Prandtl, in the laboratory at Goettingen. It was 150ft long, its maximum diameter was 54ft and it had a capacity of 81,200cu ft. Power was provided by a single NAG engine. The car was permitted to swing 13ft below the envelope, in the manner of the kite balloon, by an elaborate system of rigging; the pitching due to the alterations of the propeller thrust was automatically checked by the shifting of the point of gravity. There were two ballonets, one at the bow and one at the stern, connected to a blower located in the car. The ship could be kept trim merely by pumping air from one ballonet to another. The horizontal fins provided aerodynamic control and steering was performed through the rudder below.

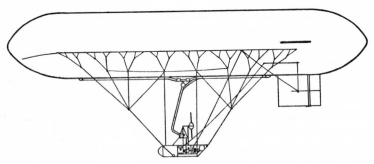

PL 2 Parseval non-rigid

As the Parseval designs became larger, the shape of the envelope became more streamlined. A new system of suspension was invented by Rudolf Haas, one-time employee of the Schütte-Lanz Airship Company. These so-called 'trajectory bands' were made of hemp and passed up the sides and over the top of the envelope in a series of ellipses, thus allowing a more uniform distribution of load, and also preserving the shape of the envelope. *PL 17* built in 1912 was the first of the new type. The letters PL denoted an airship of Parseval design. A roman numeral indicated that the ship had been acquired by the army.

From 1909 to 1914 23 Parsevals were built. As the airship passed the stringent tests of the Prussian army (which were that it should remain airborne for at least 10hr, rise to a height of 5,000ft, and be capable of being transported by road or rail), six were now purchased for military use. Eight were bought by foreign governments, including Austria, Great Britain, Turkey, Japan, Italy and Russia. Four were built for civilian organisations. One of these (*PL 6—Stollwerk*) was taken over by the German navy. It had made 250 flights and had carried 2,300 passengers. The Clouth fabric firm became associated with Parseval, and built a non-rigid stiffened on the underside with wooden lathes.

At the same time the Prussian army itself decided to build airships; it was also taking an interest in heavier-than-air craft. As Zeppelin had been experiencing difficulties with his rigids, and the French were gaining the lead with their semi-rigids, Maj Hans Gross, commanding the airship battalion, was instructed to build a semi-rigid on the lines of the *Lebaudy*. He was financed by the Prussian Parliament. The military, or *M* ship, inaccurately known as the *Gross* ship, was the result. It was designed by the former naval engineer, Nikolaus Basenach.[16] First, he built a small experimental ship which provided a prototype for the *M I*, constructed in 1908, and reconstructed in 1912. She had a volume of 176,500cu ft. At the end of 1908, *M I* flew for 13hr without interruption. She was able to communicate with the ground by wireless telephone. (Wireless communication between a balloon and the ground had just begun in England; in 1912 the British non-rigid *Beta* established wireless communication with a ground station.) *M II* was built in 1909, but was destroyed by fire in September 1913. In these ships the suspended keel was divided into three jointed sections supporting the car and the fins. Power was provided by two 75hp Körting engines.

M III, built in 1911, was both larger (she had a capacity of 388,000cu ft) and more powerful. Two more engines were added, each driving

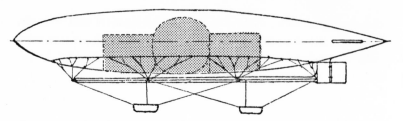

Prussian *M* type semi-rigid. Shaded area—ballonet

two coupled propellers. During her trials she attained a speed of 36mph —just 6mph faster than the existing rigid Zeppelin.

Like the French, the Prussian army intended the airship to be used primarily for reconnaissance, in spite of much speculation in the popular press—both German and foreign—about the possibilities of long-range bombing attacks. The airship had, for the time being, the advantage of endurance as compared with the aeroplane; another advantage was that the airship could be equipped with wireless. Previously staff officers had to drop their despatches, contained in pasteboard containers, at prearranged points. But, again like the French, there were several questions to be answered. Were airships practical in warfare? Were they too slow? Were they too vulnerable to anti-aircraft fire? (Anti-aircraft weapons had already appeared on the scene.) Aeroplanes were able to take evasive action more quickly, though they were not able, as yet, to fly higher than airships. Then, if airships were practicable, which system was the best—non-rigid, semi-rigid, or rigid? In the autumn of 1909, a special exercise, the first of its kind, was held in the Cologne area.[17] Taking part were two Parsevals (*P I* and *P II*), the *M II* and the latest army Zeppelin (*Z II*); the latter had already made a flight of over 20hr duration.

The exercise revealed the inherent limitations of airships. Firstly, they were subject to the vagaries of the weather. *M II*, for example, had to be transported to the exercise area by rail from Berlin because of strong headwinds. The Parseval types were hampered by the autumn mists, and so were forced to fly at ground level in order to find out their position. Secondly, the airship was not yet mechanically reliable. The Zeppelin met with engine trouble and was forced to stay on the ground while repairs were made. The army was not very impressed with the rigid because of the large number of men required to handle her on the ground. On the other hand, the Parseval and *M* ship were too slow and too dependent on favourable weather conditions. Yet in spite of all these drawbacks the value of airships for reconnaissance was not lost on the soldiers. They now wanted airships with improved performance, rather than a succession of new models, and designers that would conform to the army's requirements.

There was, in fact, no lack of proposals, for several other firms had recently been set up to supply airships for military or commercial purposes. Of particular interest was the large non-rigid (395ft in length and maximum diameter 47ft), and with a capacity not far short of 500,000cu ft, known as the Siemens-Schuckert, which was built in 1911. Not unlike a semi-rigid, she had a keel made of specially reinforced fabric; from it were suspended three cars, two of which contained the engines and the third the crew and passengers. She contained two important innovations; one was a mooring component let into the bow; and the second was the division of the envelope into gas compartments which was intended to keep the ship airborne in the event of the envelope being punctured. The Siemens patents were taken over by the army for inclusion in the *M* ships.

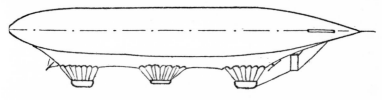

Siemens-Schuckert non-rigid

Similar in construction to *M IV* and the Italian Forlanini (described on page 47) was the *Veeh* airship, built in 1913, which was driven by a rather inefficient engine. The Brucker firm built the non-rigid *Suchard*, with which it was planned to cross the Atlantic, starting from the Canaries. The flight was never attempted. Finally, between 1910–13 the Ruthenburg firm built three small non-rigids similar in size to the early British airships.

Returning to the military aspect of aeronautics, airships and aeroplanes (which were by now developing rapidly) took part in the Kaiser's manoeuvres of 1911. The following year the high command at last made up its mind to concentrate on the rigid airship in preference to the other systems. It had become clear that the greater endurance, range and speed of the Zeppelins, in addition to their ability to rise above the existing range of anti-aircraft fire, had been proved, while another type of rigid (the Schütte-Lanz) had appeared, and had been accepted by the army. Moreover, the aeroplane was becoming more efficient than the non-rigid airship, at least over land, though it could not yet compete with rigid ships.

Yet the non- and semi-rigid in Germany had not been eclipsed—*P IV* and *M IV* ordered by the Prussian army were completed and accepted in 1913. The latter eventually went to the German navy. Meanwhile, non-rigids were still exported to foreign powers. Two Parsevals were bought by Russia, and one each by the armies of Austria, Turkey, Japan, as well as by the British and Italian navies.

CHAPTER 3

Non- and Semi-Rigids (ii): Tentative Experiments by Other Nations

The Italian motor industry had developed rapidly in the first decade of the twentieth century. It was not surprising, therefore, that the light petrol-driven engine put Italy into the small group of countries that were developing aeronautics. However, the first airship in Italy was built privately by Count Almerico da Schio.[1] Small in size, it differed from the French non-rigids in that it was not equipped with ballonets, but had an elastic envelope similar to the first British army airship described on page 52. *Italia*, as she was named, made her first ascent on 21 June 1905 at Schio, near Venice, in the presence of the King and Queen of Italy. The flight lasted for 35min, but the airship did not return to her point of departure. A few more flights were made before she was deflated.

Airship construction has always been an expensive business and so the state has usually had to provide the money. In Italy, then an emergent-nation state, the War Ministry quickly appreciated the value of the French semi-rigids. In 1906 it instructed the newly formed Brigata Specialisti of the Corps of Engineers, under Capts Arturo Crocco and Ricaldoni, to build a military semi-rigid airship.[2] Known as *P* (*Piccolo*) *1*, it had a capacity of 147,000cu ft and was 180ft long. On 31 October 1909 *P 1* flew 130 miles from Lake Bracciano, near Rome, to Naples in order to impress officers of a French naval squadron then in port; she returned to base two days later. *P 1* and *P 2* were larger (154,000cu ft). They had an articulated keel and steel battens to stiffen the bow. The car, shaped like a boat, was fitted with two 75hp Fiat engines, one on each side, and reversible propellers which made the airship more manoeuvrable on the ground. Five airships of this type were built for the army and were allotted to corps.

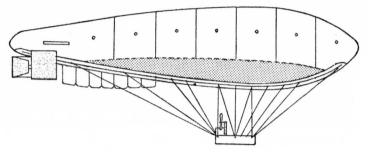

Italian *P* type semi-rigid. Shaded area—ballonet

P 2 and *P 3* were the first airships to take part in war, that by Italy against Turkey in 1911–12. They arrived in Tripoli in December 1911, and early the following year began to fly sorties over the desert—the same ground that was to change hands so often in World War II. Photographs of troop concentrations and other targets were taken. Small bombs were dropped on enemy encampments. On one occasion an airship was refuelled and regassed from a ship at sea. Some 130 flights were made, covering a distance of 6,250 miles without mishap. But enemy opposition consisted only of spasmodic fire from the ground.[3]

In 1912 the first *M* (medium) type was built. Intended for use in the war against Turkey, but never so used, this semi-rigid proved to be a most useful military airship and took part in World War I. The first *M* ships had a capacity of about 420,000cu ft and were also built with an articulated keel. Like the *P* type, the keel changed to a triangular shape at the stern and was covered to serve as a lower fin. Power was provided by two 200hp engines. Up to 1914 two of these airships were built for the Italian navy and one for the army. The navy used them for scouting; the army ship was able to carry a ton of bombs and is reputed to have reached an altitude of 17,000ft. About 22 *M* ships were built up to the end of World War I,[4] one of them being purchased by the Royal Navy (see page 125).

The Italian military airship effort was based on sound scientific principles; Crocco, for example, was one of the first to make a detailed model of an airship and fill it with water for the purpose of determining forces in the suspension system. A wind-tunnel provided useful information.

A private firm also began to construct airships—the Sociéta Leonardo da Vinci in Milan. Its moving spirit was the aeronautical engineer, Enrico Forlanini, who, as early as 1897, had designed and built a steam-driven model helicopter. In 1909 Forlanini built his first experimental semi-rigid.[5] It had a capacity of 421,000cu ft, was 263ft long, with a maximum diameter of 59ft. It was driven by two 85hp engines and it had a lift of 4 tons. The maximum range was 2,400 miles.

Forlanini's airships differed considerably from the military ones. The gas bag was joined to an internal rigid girder which ran from bow to stern. Fitted to the girder were the car, elevating and stabilising planes and rudders. The circular envelope consisted of a double skin with an intervening air chamber which served as ballonet. This arrangement not only made the outward appearance of the envelope perfectly regular, but isolated the gas bag from the effects of the sun and atmospheric disturbances. A fan kept the air circulating in this inner space and there were also vent holes at the top of the cover. The gas bag itself was divided into eleven compartments, each of which was provided with valves, gauges, and supply pipes for the gas.

The keel not only carried the weight of the car but resisted the bending moments of the envelope. It had a triangular cross-section with three longitudinal lines of columns braced in the three planes by cross wires and rigid struts. The internal suspensions secured to the fabric were brought together at a common longitudinal axis and from this the lift of the gas was transmitted by diagonal cables to the top joints of the keel. The latter was therefore rigid and concealed within the envelope. The control car was large and provided good observation; the pilot's position was entirely enclosed by a transparent celluloid material. Behind the pilot sat the observer, and behind him was the engine room and stores.

The second Forlanini, built in 1913, was called the *Citta di Milano*, being paid for by the people of that city.[6] She came to an untimely end. On 9 April 1914, while on a trial flight, she developed a tendency to dip at the stern so the captain made a forced landing. Meanwhile a gust of wind broke the mooring ropes, and dragged the ship into a thicket of mulberry trees. The captain decided to deflate, but before it could be done the ship heeled over towards a crowd of watching peasants who had refused to stand back, or even to put out their

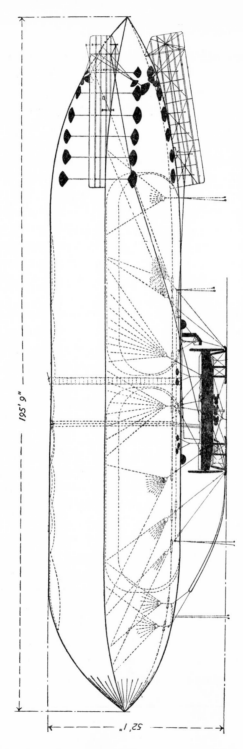

195' 9"

52' 1"

Forlanini semi-rigid (F 5). The envelope contains two gas bags indicated by the dotted lines near the top while the two cylindrical-shaped areas shown by dotted lines in the lower half of the envelope are ballonets. In the centre of the ship is a vertical shaft with steps leading to a machine-gun post on the top of the envelope cigarettes. The ship caught fire and exploded; in a few minutes she was burnt out. About eighty people were injured.

The British navy had, meanwhile, ordered a Forlanini similar to the one destroyed, but as it had not been completed by the outbreak of war the Italian army took it over.

No mention of Sir George Cayley (1773–1857), an English north-country squire, in a history of the development of airships would be remiss. Cayley's influence on aviation has belatedly been recognised to be extremely important.[7] But he also at one time believed that 'elongated balloons made on a very large scale, and of firm airtight materials, may be driven through calm air, by engine power, at a velocity approaching the railroad pace, and, by their buoyancy, carry, whether stationary or in motion, a considerable cargo. Hence, on a grand scale, balloon floatage offers the most ready, efficient, and safe means of aerial navigation.'

Despite the publication, and quite wide circulation, of four papers on airships, Cayley's ideas had little, if any, influence on aeronauts. Nevertheless, he showed that he understood the principle of the ballonet, the function of propellers, the importance of streamlining, and the workings of a light engine, and he was the first to propose a semi-rigid airship, the shape of which would be kept 'by light poles attached to it'. Finally, Cayley understood that size favoured the airship rather than the heavier-than-air craft.

During the nineteenth century two airships were built in England, quite uninfluenced by Cayley. In 1848 Partridge's airship appeared with sail-like planes for steering and three propellers driven by compressed air. Two years later, Hugh Bell's airship, like Partridge's made an unsuccessful flight at Vauxhall.

At the turn of the century English aeronauts were watching events across the Channel, in particular the revolutionary petrol engines developed by Daimler which at last made the propulsion of airships against headwinds practical. Two Londoners, Stanley and Percival Spencer, tried to emulate the exploits of Dumont over the streets and roof tops of Paris. In 1900–2 they built two small airships in Highbury, both under 100ft long and driven by a 4hp petrol engine which, they claimed, had far less chance of igniting the balloon than the engines used by Dumont.[8] Like other non-rigids of that period, the envelope was pointed at both ends and the pilot stood in a light bamboo-and-steel car suspended from the balloon. The Spencers made a number of ascents from the Crystal Palace in south London, as well as from Brighton and Blackpool, providing an alternative attraction to free ballooning, which was such a feature of Edwardian England. But the Spencers's engine lacked sufficient power. An attempt to fly from the Crystal Palace and circle St Paul's Cathedral was defeated by a head-wind.

A similar ship to that of the Spencers was built by a South African named W. Beedle. Instead of using a rudder he attempted to steer it with an elementary form of swivelling propeller. Nothing came of Beedle's ship as such, but his move to Cardiff had quite important repercussions. It was there that Beedle met a young man called E. T. Willows, who became so obsessed with airships that he gave up a career as a dentist and was morally supported and financed by his father to the brink of bankruptcy. Willows has some claim to being called the 'Father of British Airships'. for quite independently he designed and built six small non-rigid airships, and he personally flew most of them. His most important contribution to airship development was to improve on Beedle's swivelling propeller, which was subsequently used in a number of British and American rigid and non-rigid airships.[9]

In Willows's first airship, built in 1905, one propeller was used for propulsion and one for steering. Built practically single-handed this ship was only 12,500cu ft in capacity and was powered by a 7hp Peugeot engine. It was followed by a second with a capacity of 20,000cu ft, which was later enlarged to 32,000cu ft; it was 68ft long. A long steel-and-bamboo boom beneath the ship prevented it sagging in the middle, and thus made it almost a semi-rigid. In this ship Willows flew solo over Cardiff, and from Cardiff to Cheltenham. But his first tour de force came in August 1910 when he made the first British long-distance cross-country flight by airship from Cardiff to London—by night. He began by crossing the Bristol Channel and then set course for London followed by his father driving a car (which broke down). After 10hr flying Willows reached London, but he overshot his destination—the Crystal Palace—and early on a Sunday morning a startled gardener in Catford found himself snatching a drag rope on the instructions of Willows overhead. The envelope had developed a slight leak, the result of a stone thrown by a mischievous spectator during ascent.

Not content, Willows in his airship, now called *City of Cardiff*, accompanied by a mechanic, made the first airship flight from London to Paris. They took off on 4 November 1910 and in the early hours of the next morning came down near Douai. After a number of vicissitudes, including a demand by French customs officers for duty on the gas contained in his ship, Willows eventually reached Paris, and, in early December, made two flights over the city.

Willows's fourth airship proved to be most useful, for in November 1912 the admiralty took it over and used it for training. As a result a number of officers who later became distinguished airship pilots learned to fly on it. The army's opinion of the Willows ships was that they were too slow as well as too light for carrying weapons or wireless, or for making long-distance flights. But the idea of swivelling propellers was adapted in later airships (though adding weight to the ship).

Since the end of the South African War the British army had taken an interest in the development of the airship. Having in South Africa painfully learned the importance of obtaining information rapidly, the army turned to the possibilities of using airships as well as the captive or kite balloons in the use of which it was already well in advance of other European countries. The army was fortunate, though perhaps unappreciative of the fact, that the officer who had been in charge of the balloon detachment in South Africa, and who was now in command of the balloon school at Aldershot, was Col J. L. B. Templer of the Royal Engineers.[10] Behind the conventional exterior of the professional soldier was a mind of rare imagination and inventive ability. Templer had, with his use of steam traction engines, foreshadowed the tank and armoured carrier of the future. He had met Dumont in Paris and had been impressed with his little airships. He had also met Charles Renard, but had failed to persuade the latter to show him round the establishment at Chalais Meudon.

Unlike the French military aeronauts, Templer had to beg for every penny from the War Office. In 1902 he failed to get the full amount of £5,000 which he had asked for, but the following year he asked for another £500 and to his surprise it came, 16 days after the request was made: interest was clearly growing. That summer (1903) a special War Office committee asked for an airship which could be steered, proceed against a headwind and maintain its shape while doing so. The envelope should not leak and the airship should be able to climb to 5,000ft without this prejudicing its performance at lower altitudes. So far none of the British airships had been capable of fulfilling these qualifications. By 1905 Templer had completed his preliminary designs and an airship shed had just been completed at Farnborough.

But on the afternoon of 22 July Templer was at Alexandra Palace, in north London, watching the ascent for the first time of yet another airship—a large non-rigid of 235,000cu ft, with three engines, designed and built by Dr F. A. Barton, president of the Aeronautical Institute.[11] The airship ascended with a crew of five. It made a poor showing. Unable to make headway against the wind, it ran before it and landed at Romford. The car overbalanced with the movements of the crew trying to get out, and one end of the ship tipped skywards. Someone ripped the panel to release the gas; the car heeled over and was totally wrecked. Apart from the airships of Willows, Barton's design was the last private airship of any importance.

Nulli Secundus, as Templer's airship was called after a racehorse owned by Edward VII, was a semi-rigid of unusual design. Her volume was 50,000cu ft; she was 122ft long, and her maximum diameter was 25ft. She did not have ballonets because the envelope was able to expand or contract according to the height of the ship. This was because the envelope was made of two layers of goldbeater's skins—so-called because they were used in the process of making gold leaf. They were extremely impervious to hydrogen and lighter than any other balloon material. (An Alsatian family named Weinling who had settled in the East End of London had for some years exclusively provided the army with goldbeater's skins.) The envelope was cylindrical in shape with hemispherical ends. The car was suspended from a kind of harness work of strong silk bands which covered the envelope and efficiently distributed the weight of the car. The latter was constructed of very light steel tubing. As no satisfactory English motor was available, two 40hp Antoinette engines were bought in Paris. The famous S. F. Cody, ex-cowboy, showman, and eventually expert on man-lifting kites and a pioneer aeroplane pilot, was responsible for installation of one engine in the airship, the second engine being used in an aeroplane piloted by Cody.

Another novel feature of *Nulli Secundus* were the two elevators, known as 'aeroplanes', fixed in the framework, one in front and one behind, which were worked in conjunction with one another. They were inclined so as to create a lifting or depressing force on the ship, and so assist in rising or descending. They were subsequently moved to the bow and made to work in tandem.

Trial flights began in early September 1907. But Templer was no longer in command. One of his subordinates was involved in a court martial, and in 1906, the War Office, perhaps taking advantage of the opprobrium to which Templer was subjected, had asked him to resign. Col J. E. Capper took over command of the balloon school and factory, by then located at Farnborough, though Templer continued to act, quite amicably, in an advisory capacity. On 5 October, Capper decided the time had come to gain some publicity for his work by flying over London. (Leader writers and correspondents to the press were asking why England had been left behind in aerostation.) Capper, with Cody as mechanic, and Lieut W. A. de C. King, the balloon instructor, as passenger, set off from Farnborough and followed the line of the present A30 road to London. Having arrived over the capital, they flew over Buckingham Palace, Whitehall and rounded St Pauls (which the Spencers had failed to do); but a strong headwind later forced the airship to land in the grounds of the Crystal Palace. *Nulli Secundus* had been in the air for 3hr 20 min and had travelled a total distance of 50 miles; not a record, however, for both a Zeppelin and the *Lebaudy* had flown longer distances; moreover, much of the early part of the British flight was made with a following wind and the airship did not return to her starting point. The enthusiasm of Londoners turned to mild ridicule when five days later the airship, unable to ascend because of wet and misty weather, had to be deflated in order to prevent her from being blown away. It was generally believed that the airship became too heavy because the goldbeater's skins absorbed rainwater so easily. More likely, the inability of the airship to ascend was due to the low barometric pressure and the cold hydrogen.

From the remains of *Nulli Secundus* a new airship, *Nulli Secundus II* was constructed. She was designed to fly faster and to be more easy to handle in the air. Her capacity was increased to 56,000cu ft, while the ends of the envelope were slightly tapered. The entire envelope, except for the rounded ends, was covered with varnished silk sheeting, supposedly for the purpose of keeping the rain off the goldbeater's skin, as it was believed, erroneously, that varnish could not be applied to that skin. The understructure was redesigned in a triangular, instead of a box-like, form, and it was entirely covered in by silk sheeting in order to eliminate the air resistance of the tubing. The car itself was now shaped like a boat and had a more streamlined appearance. But the most important innovation was the large elevator placed in the front part of the car. This was intended to raise or lower the bow of the ship more easily than before.

In spite of these improvements *Nulli Secundus II* was a failure. After a few flights in July and August 1908, she had to return to base prematurely because of squally weather and was buffeted on reaching the ground. Later it was found that the cylinders of the engine were so badly worn that there was no compression. *Nulli Secundus II* never flew again.

Her place was taken by *Baby*, which was subsequently enlarged and known as *Beta*. Essentially a research ship, she was deliberately made small, 81ft long, just under 25ft in diameter and with a capacity of 24,000cu ft. She had a streamlined, fish-shaped envelope; the machinery and crew of two were carried in a long tubular framework slung underneath the envelope. Instead of the clumsy harness of *Nulli Secundus*, the framework was suspended by cables attached to a series of silk loops threaded around the envelope just below the axis. At the tail there were vertical and horizontal fins inflated with hydrogen. Although the envelope was again made of goldbeater's skin, there was also a ballonet into which air was pumped by a small fan operated by the engine. Power was, firstly, provided by two 8hp, Buchet motors driving a single propeller situated between the chassis and envelope, and later by a more powerful Robert Esnault-Pelterie (REP) engine which driving two propellers enabled the ship to reach 20mph.

The early ascents of *Baby* were not very successful. The steering was unsatisfactory, which led to changes in the rudders and elevators; the management of the ship left much to be desired largely because of

Capper's inability to understand how the ballonet worked in conjunction with the expanding envelope. Due to the lack of money, the engine was also unsatisfactory.

A more technical approach became possible in 1909 when the balloon factory separated from the balloon school and came under control of a civilian, Mervyn O'Gorman, a consulting engineer. The aeronautical advisory committee composed of a number of distinguished scientists, service officers and engineers was also appointed. These changes were due to R. B. Haldane, Liberal Secretary of State for War from 1905, who had a mind of a high intellectual order, unusual in a politician of the day. Haldane, discarding his top hat for the cloth cap of a mechanic, flew in *Beta* in November 1910.

More plentiful funds increased the scope of the balloon factory. At the end of 1909 *Baby* was enlarged under a new name—*Beta*—and provided with a 35hp engine, named after the first British aero-engine designer, Gustavus Green. She was to have a most successful career up to 1911.

At the same time an entirely new and larger airship, *Gamma*, was being constructed. Her capacity was 72,000cu ft and the envelope instead of being of goldbeater's skin was of rubberised cotton made in France. The 80 hp engine was also designed by Green; it was fitted with swivelling propellers on the lines of Willows's ships to facilitate ascents and landings in a confined space. *Gamma*, launched in May 1910, made a night flight to London and back in the following month.

British airships now had to contend with the rapid development of the aeroplane, especially since the aviation meeting at Rheims in August 1909, which followed hard upon Louis Blériot's cross-Channel flight on 25 July. The respective merits of aeroplane and airship were discussed by the Committee of Imperial Defence (CID)—usually not very scientifically. The familiar arguments—that the airship had greater range, possessed better facilities for navigation, had the ability to carry a larger payload than the aeroplane—were rehearsed in London, as, indeed, they were in Berlin and Paris. The Royal Navy, concerned about the success of the Zeppelins had ordered a rigid airship, although the First Sea Lord, Sir Arthur Wilson, strenuously opposed airships. He argued that they were too vulnerable and unable to gain height rapidly without dispensing with a large quantity of ballast.[12] Winston

Churchill, then First Lord, who later made out that he was an implacable opponent of airships, contending that 'this enormous bladder of combustible and explosive gas would prove to be easily destructible', at that stage argued on behalf of airships, pointing out that they could rise dynamically, using their elevators without expending ballast. The swivelling propellers could also be used for this purpose.

Nevertheless, for the time being, the airship had the undisputed advantage of endurance, and as a reconnaissance vehicle it was ideal. The Germans and the French were still building non-rigids. The British press, ever conscious of the mounting rivalry between Britain and Germany, campaigned for bigger airships. In 1910 two French airships were ordered, one by a newspaper. The *Morning Post* purchased a Lebaudy for the army at a cost of £25,000. (The army stipulated that it should be able to ascend to 3,000ft, remain anchored in winds up to a force of 20mph and be able to fly 300 miles in 14hr.)

The Lebaudy, piloted by Louis Capazza, flew from Moisson to Farnborough on 26 October 1910, carrying Juilliot, the editor of the *Morning Post*, and Maj Sir Alexander Bannerman, who had now taken over from Capper at the balloon school. They made the journey in 5½hr, but various faults became apparent during the flight.[13] The compass went out of action and the girder supporting the envelope began to sag. As the steering gear failed on descent the airship landed like a free balloon. On entering the shed, the envelope was damaged as the airship had been given a more generous girth than the British had anticipated. The roof of the shed had to be raised by 15ft. After its first test flight, in the following May, the Lebaudy crashed into a house while attempting to land. McWade, the balloon factory manager, ran to the airship, turned off the petrol and avoided a fire. The wife of the officer to whom the house belonged, dressing for dinner, was startled to see through the window a large airship descending on her. The Lebaudy was not worth repairing.

The second airship was a Clément Bayard and had a hardly more successful career. The *Daily Mail* had built an airship shed at Wormwood Shrubs and the Parliamentary aerial defence committee agreed the Government should pay for the airship. The Clément Bayard had a capacity of 247,000cu ft, and was powered by two 120hp engines. During the cross-Channel flight it attained a speed of 33 mph. But the

British appeared to have come off worst in the deal. The envelope was found to be leaking and the ship generally was in a poor condition. The makers wanted £25,000, but the War Office offered £12,500 and another £5,000 was agreed by the aerial defence committee. The long, girder car with which the Clément Bayard was provided, almost put it in the semi-rigid class and led to later developments of semi-rigids, but the British scrapped the ship as it had performed no useful service.

Up to 1912, British policy had been to keep a watching brief on continental airship development. Now that rigids as well as non-rigids were being bought by the German armed forces, the technical sub-committee of the CID on 22 May 1912, recommended that the UK should begin an airship programme. An airship of the *Gamma* class should be built at Farnborough, it was proposed, at a cost of £5,000, while the *Willows IV* was, as already noted, to be used for training. The committee looked to the continent for a larger ship. In the non-rigid class the Parseval was the best. Now that the German authorities believed rigids to be superior to non-rigids, the latter were allowed to be exported. Thus *Parseval 17* (*HM Airship No 4*) came into service in 1913. An *Astra Torres* of 280,000cu ft capacity was acquired from the Astra Company in Paris, and was available for use in coastal reconnaissance. As recorded on page 49, the Forlanini ordered by Britain was requisitioned by the Italian army at the outbreak of war. So was a second Parseval by the German authorities.

At home, the aircraft factory at Farnborough had not been idle. Between 1912 and 1914 three new airships were built—*Beta II*, *Delta* (capable of a speed of 40mph, and thus faster than most contemporary aeroplanes), and *Eta*. They took part in exercises with the army, which had temporarily lost faith in aeroplanes. But in October 1913 the Royal Navy took over responsibility for the military airships (the first naval rigid airship, as will be seen on pages 85–7, had been a failure). At the outbreak of war there were seven naval non-rigids of which, however, the only ones of actual value were the *Astra Torres* type. They were patrolling the Straits of Dover on the night war was declared on Germany (4 August 1914).

Around 1911–12, Russia ranked third of the countries with an airship service. Obtaining information about technical developments in Czarist Russia was as difficult as it later proved to be when the Communists took over. Meagre snippets gleaned from the reports of military attachés, and even balder press reports, form the gist of the following account.[14]

Russia seems to have become interested in airships, like other nations, in about 1908, when *Utschebny*, a non-rigid, was built by Capt Schabsky for the Russian army. Her capacity was 42,000cu ft and she was very similar to *La Patrie*. A larger ship, *Lebedj*, similar to *La République* followed. By 1910 airships were nourished by the officer's aeronautical school at St Petersburg, which had itself grown out of a balloon school, in much the same way as the organisation for the British army airships had developed. At this time the Russians preferred to purchase foreign airships rather than to build their own. They thus bought a Clément Bayard, two Zodiacs and a Parseval. The army's policy was that small dirigibles with volumes from 70,000cu ft to 105,000cu ft were to be employed for scouting and larger airships upwards of 100,000cu ft were to be used for strategic reconnaissance. Several ships in the first category were built at the Ischora Works near St Petersburg, including *Gollubj*, *Sokul* and *Albatros*.

In 1911 Russia had ten serviceable airships. Three of them were stationed in Poland, the remainder were under control of the aeronautical school. No privately owned airships existed. Henceforward aeroplanes were developed at the expense of the lighter-than-air craft contingent.

Japan's interest in airships grew out of her victory over Russia in 1905 and the recognition of her claim to be militarily on a par with Western nations. Two kite balloons took an active part in the siege of Port Arthur. Five years later an Englishman named Hamilton imported a small non-rigid and, in 1909, this stimulated the creation of the provisional military research society.[15] The first two Japanese airships were built by Isabura Yamado. They were more advanced than Hamilton's design, with an ellipsoid shape and a fixed vertical fin at the stern. A peculiarity of Yamado's airships was that the engine was contained in a separate pod in front of the car. Both ships were wrecked on landing. Meanwhile the army and navy had jointly built a non-rigid which flew 2·8 miles in 10min.

The Japanese army also bought (see page 44) a Parseval (*PL 13*). She was shipped out by sea. In March 1913, five months after flying over a grand naval review at Yokohoma, she struck a roof while attempting to land. The car and engines were salvaged and incorporated into a new airship called *Yuhi (Beautiful Flight)*. She was completed in April 1915. But she did not fulfil the promise of her name. After taking part in an air review over Tokyo and two cross-country flights the army concluded that her operating and maintenance costs did not justify further employment. So she spent the rest of her days as a 'hangar queen', with one final flight in July 1917 to test an aerial compass. That date marked the end of the army's interest in the airship.

The navy, however, appreciating the value of airships as long-range scouts bought and copied non-rigids of the *Astra Torres* and *SS* types from France and Britain. They saw but limited service. After World War I the Japanese navy turned its attention to the semi-rigid (see page 232).

Before World War I three non-rigids were built by Thomas S. Baldwin, balloonist, parachutist, and tightrope walker. The last was bought by the US army in 1908. Otherwise the armed services evinced little interest in airships,[16] possibly because of the spectacular progress then being made by heavier-than-air craft. But an army airship, built on the lines of the Santos Dumont ships, and equipped with a Glen Curtiss engine, which was called *Californian Arrow* achieved a world speed record in August 1908 of 20mph. By 1911 the US army had decided that airships were not worth investing in.

About twelve privately owned airships flew in the United States from 1907–13. In July 1907 three of them took part in a unique airship race held during the World Fair at St Louis, Missouri. Technically, the most ambitious airships were *America I* and *II* designed by Melvin Vaniman[17] for the business man Walter Wellman. Wellman and Vaniman aspired to be the first to fly over the North Pole. *America I* was a non-rigid, 184ft long, 52ft in diameter and with a capacity of 285,500cu ft. Power was given by two engines, each driving two bevel-geared propellers; a third engine was kept in reserve with duplicate propellers. An unusual feature was the special drag rope, the standard equipment for a free balloon. As the lifting capacity of the airship decreased and it descended, the flexible drag rope would prevent it from falling into the sea or crashing on to the ice, as more and more of the rope rested on the ground. This device was called an equilibrator; it was hollow and filled with provisions and supplies for the journey; it was encased with leather and covered with steel scales to withstand the effect of constant dragging. For flights over the sea the equilibrator took the form of a series of steel tanks strung on a steel cable which passed lengthways through each tank. The tanks contained ballast in the form of a reserve petrol supply.

In 1909 the Wellman expedition ascended from Spitzbergen, but after 30 miles the drag rope fell off. The attempt to reach the Pole was abandoned.

Undaunted, Wellman and Vaniman now made a bid to cross the Atlantic in *America II*, an airship of 321,000cu ft; the car could be used as a boat in the event of a forced landing on the sea. On 15 October 1910, the airship set off from Atlantic City with a crew of six, one of whom took his cat. Wellman planned his route to pass over well-frequented shipping lanes in case of mishap. After 70hr flying the airship was compelled to force land on the sea on account of engine trouble. They had been spotted by the steamer *Trent* and all were picked up, including the cat, none the worse for their exploit. *America II* had, despite her failure, set up a record of endurance which the rigid airships had not yet beaten.

Unhappily, two years later Vaniman was killed with three companions when a larger airship (*Akron*) he was piloting exploded over Atlantic City. The cause of the accident was never discovered.

What had been achieved by non- and semi-rigid airships in the first decade of the twentieth century? The most significant factor was the efficiency of the newly developed petrol engine. In the second place, the semi-rigid design of Juilliot was outstanding, and it was able to withstand a good deal of buffeting; the Germans acknowledged this by copying Juilliot's design in the *M* ship. The Italians also quickly assimilated the semi-rigid design, and for their strictly military purposes it was probably the right choice. Until about 1910 the semi-rigid was undoubtedly a more reliable airship than the rigid in regard to speed and endurance, and it was more capable than the contemporary aeroplanes. From now onwards, though, the rigid's superiority in regard to endurance, payload, and speed became more apparent.

As for non-rigids, the Parseval was better built and more scientifically developed than either the French or British non-rigids.

The British were handicapped by a meagre budget, and in the early stages lacked engineers and scientists to deal with problems of aerostation. However, they were ahead of other nations in developing swivelling propellers.

For a few years to come the non-rigids still had the lead over heavier-than-air craft in that they had greater manoeuvring capacity and stability; although by then not as fast as the aeroplane, they could fly in poor weather; they could remain in the air longer and carry a heavier payload; they could be used at night; and observation was better from an airship than from an aeroplane. But, apart from the special needs of the British navy, the non-rigid was soon to be eclipsed; from a military point of view the aeroplane was rapidly proving to be more versatile.

CHAPTER 4

The First Rigids:
Successes and Failures

'Balloon ship, thought for mail, freight, and passengers. Basic idea: large ship with rigid frame with longitudinals and rings. Divided into 18 separate compartments for accommodation of gas bags. Covered on outside with material. Form to simulate bird. Envisaging dynamic flight. Engine installation under the ship.' Diary entry of Count Ferdinand von Zeppelin, 25 April 1874

There seems to be little doubt that the first practical rigid airship was the brainchild of Count Ferdinand von Zeppelin. At a very early stage legend shrouded his activities and ideas. So the truth is hard to ascertain. Zeppelin, born in 1833, served as a cavalry officer under the King of Württemberg (at that time the kingdom was not part of the Prussian empire). He took part in both the Franco-Prussian War and in the war between Prussia and Austria. He was compelled to retire prematurely in 1885, at the early age of 52, because he objected to the interference of the Prussian war ministry in matters relating to officers from Württemberg.[1]

Zeppelin now turned his full attention to aeronautics. His interest has partly been attributed to his visit to America at the time of the Civil War when he is supposed to have seen observation balloons in operation; other sources indicate that he was influenced by the French use of balloons during the siege of Paris in 1870; others maintain that he borrowed his ideas on the rigid airship, either from the Frenchman, Joseph Spiess, or from the Austrian, David Schwartz. The truth is more prosaic. Zeppelin read a paper written by the Prussian postmaster general, Heinrich von Stephan, proposing that mail might be carried by a navigable aerial train with a rigid framework lifted by gas bags, one behind the other. Another motive was that the patriotic feelings of

Zeppelin were undoubtedly stirred by Charles Renard's flight in *La France* in August 1884.

Three years after this landmark in aeronautical history, Zeppelin wrote a memorandum to the King of Württemberg, proposing an airship with a greater range than *La France* which would also be able to carry passengers or freight. On 20 September 1893 the King drew up for the German Emperor a list of possible functions for Zeppelin's proposed airship; in war these might be long-distance reconnaissance, supply carrying, and bombing of military targets; and, in peace, flights over unexplored Africa or the polar regions. The Prussian war ministry set up a commission to examine the feasibility of Zeppelin's airship, but were put off by its probable clumsiness on the ground, its lack of speed, and its vulnerability. But the biggest objection was the great expense which would be involved in construction.

That same year, however, the first rigid airship was actually built by David Schwartz, a timber merchant from the Austro-Hungarian Empire.[2] It was covered by thin aluminium sheeting instead of by a varnished cotton cover. The airship, built at St Petersburg, never flew because of a mishap to the structure while being inflated with hydrogen. During 1895–7, Schwartz, now in Berlin, and supported by Carl Berg, a manufacturer of aluminium, built a second small rigid, 150ft long, 36ft in diameter, with ring frames and longitudinal girders; the envelope was again of thin (0·008in thick) aluminium sheeting. Shaped like a bullet with a conical nose and rounded stern, it was 157ft long, its maximum diameter was 39ft and its capacity was 130,000cu ft. The car was rigidly connected to the envelope by girders which were braced by wires running from end to end of the airship. Power was given by a 12hp Daimler engine fitted with three propellers; two were placed forward and the third fitted between the hull and the car.

On 3 November 1897 the airship made its first ascent. In a high wind the driving belt fell off the pulley of the engine. The airship made a rapid descent. The resulting damage was so extensive that the ship had to be broken up. Metalclad airship construction was abandoned until taken up by the Americans in the 1920s. So much for Schwartz's effort.

Zeppelin, however, was not put off by Schwartz's mishap, or by the death of Woelfert (see page 32). On the contrary, he continued to work on the concept of the rigid airship. He soon discarded the idea of a train of gas bags in favour of a rigid structure enclosing a number of separate gas bags. At the same time he continued to bombard the Prussian war ministry with memoranda on a rigid airship. Each time his arguments were advanced the cautious soldiers thought of some new obstacle—the airship would be too big; the speed at which it would travel would be too slow; it would be unable to reach an adequate height; or they thought the future lay with heavier-than-air craft. Zeppelin had more success in interesting businessmen in his project than he had with the army. In 1898 the Company for the Promotion of Airship Flight was established in Stuttgart, and provided Zeppelin with sufficient money to enable him to start building his rigid airship.

He chose Manzell on the edge of the Bodensee, by the small town of Friedrichshafen, for his site. Instead, though, of building the shed on dry land, he made a floating shed able to swing round, so that the airship would always be launched parallel to the prevailing wind. This usually blew down the lake from the mountains; the Bodensee was not susceptible to cross-winds. Zeppelin also believed that landing on water presented fewer difficulties than landing on terra firma.

Zeppelin was not an engineer, but a practical man, and he worked closely with his designer, Theodor Kober, who was later assisted by the engineer Kübler. Their concept was radically different from the non-rigid airships which derived from Meusnier's idea (and it must be remembered that no semi-rigid had yet been built). In the first place, the size of Zeppelin's ship was impressive. It was 416ft long, shaped like an elongated cylinder with pointed ends, 38ft in diameter, and it had a capacity of 399,000cu ft. The shape was maintained by a framework of flat aluminium girders, but what really gave the ship strength were the vertical, polygonal transverse frames braced with steel wire like the spokes of a bicycle wheel (later frames were cross-braced). They divided the hull into 17 compartments, in each of which was a large fabric gas bag treated with rubber solution to prevent the gas from leaking. Each bag was fitted with automatic release valves. A light outer cover of cotton and wool called 'pegamoid', resistant to sun and rain, was stretched over the frame. A long aluminium girder, or walkway, was suspended below the hull, 346ft long, to which were connected two cars, or gondolas. Each car, also made of aluminium,

Page 65 (above) Rigid airship in construction (R 26) showing longitudinal girders, braced transverse frames and inflated gas bags; (below) transverse frame of rigid airship (R 80) being constructed on floor of shed

Page 66 (*above*) Interior of rigid airship (*R 101*) control car showing rudder, elevator wheels and voice tubes; (*below*) Lebaudy semi–rigid

contained a 145hp Daimler engine which drove a long transmission shaft to two four-bladed propellers fixed on brackets to each side of the hull. A cable was hung from each end of the walkway, along which travelled a weight, causing the ship to pitch. There were no elevators or stabilising planes, but four rudders fixed to the hull fore and aft provided lateral control. Though much modified, this basic design was followed by all subsequent rigid airships.

LZ 1 was ready by the beginning of July 1900. It was the culmination of over 12 years thought and the refinement of many designs by Zeppelin, by now aged 67. (Even at this stage he believed that his airship would eventually be able to fly the Atlantic in about four days.) High winds, and then a very hot day which gave the airship too much lift, postponed the flight, apart from a dress rehearsal for the handling party (the Friedrichshafen fire brigade), until the evening of 2 July.[3] All that day a large crowd had waited impatiently for the ascent on the lakeside as well as in boats and pleasure steamers. Also watching, were the King of Württemberg, Prussian army officers, the British military attaché from Berlin, and the British consul from Munich. The well-known military balloonist, Bartsch von Sigsfeld, supervised the inflation of the gas bags with hydrogen. At last the great airship emerged from her floating shed. The crew consisted of Count Zeppelin himself, Baron Bassus, Eugen Wolff, a well-known traveller, Ludwig Dürr, the young second engineer, and the mechanic Gross.

The ship rose very smoothly, then described a large circle and executed various manoeuvres to test her controls. She had then attained a height of 1,300ft, and flew down the lake towards Immenstaad, covering 3¾ miles in 17min. At that moment the handle controlling the running weight broke and the starboard rudder failed, as part of it hand tangled with the wire carrying the weight. Zeppelin, who gave orders through a speaking tube, decided that the moment had come to descend: it was also getting dark. 'The airship sank slowly,' wrote Wolff later, 'and rested on the water as smooth as a sea gull—no bump, no crash, no rise, no jumping, no sensation whatever. The aluminium boats dipped only two inches into the water and the airship stood full and safe above us. The good landing was due to Baron Bassus who cleverly measured the spending of the hydrogen as we descended.' Another minor mishap occurred when a stake in the water caught in

E

the envelope, and the running weight became entangled in the stump. However, the crew managed to get the airship back on the pontoon and were towed back to the shed. In spite of the misadventures, the flight had been a success, and the qualified opinion of the military observers was that the airship was suitable for both military and civil purposes.

The need to repair the airship provided the opportunity to make improvements; the long walkway was rigidly connected to the hull, thus making the whole structure much stronger. The lateral rudders were replaced by several vertical planes mounted under the envelope and an elevator with horizontal axis was fitted in front of the forward car. The ship was now easier to control.

The alterations were completed by the end of September, but the airship was damaged while being handled in the shed. So the second flight had to be postponed until 17 October. It lasted for 80min and was only cut short by engine trouble. By mistake distilled water had been poured into the petrol tanks. On 21 October *LZ 1*'s last flight was made; she was airborne for only 20min when the framework was damaged. The expense of building and repairing the ship, and of the shed and various items of equipment, had become too much. The Company for the Promotion of Airship Flight was dissolved. Zeppelin himself bought the shed and installations, hoping to resume experiments at a later date.

But no support was forthcoming. The army was lukewarm. It thought Zeppelin's idea was Utopian and it was already looking with interest at the Lebaudy semi-rigid in France which was showing signs of being a useful airship. Zeppelin was forced to dismantle both *LZ 1* and her shed for scrap.

Zeppelin was not beaten. With the aid of Dürr, who had now taken over from Kübler as chief engineer, the airship was virtually redesigned in the light of their limited experience of rigid airship behaviour. Greater control over the airship in the air was necessary, as were more powerful engines, and stronger, though equally light, girders. So impressed was the King of Württemberg by Zeppelin's persistence that he provided money and also launched a public lottery. Zeppelin's experiments had been widely covered by the press and other states in Germany joined in. Aluminium, engines, and balloon fabric were given by manufacturers. It became possible to start assembling *LZ 2* in 1904.

Dürr built his rigid framework out of triangular-shaped, instead of flat, girders, while the transverse frames were simplified to 16 sides instead of 24. Sixteen larger gas bags, instead of 17, were installed. The engines were increased to 85hp. The height of the walkway was increased and the controls were improved. Otherwise the ship's dimensions were slightly smaller than *LZ 1*.

LZ 2 had a short, unlucky life. Completed early in November 1905, her first emergence from the floating shed was disastrous; the water of the Bodensee was too low for the pontoon to carry her and she was towed out by motor boat. The tow rope fouled one of the elevators and gas bags had to be deflated in order to bring the ship's bow out of the water. She eventually made her first ascent on 17 January 1906, but at 1,500ft she began to drift north-eastwards. At Kisslegg the first landing of a rigid airship on terra firma took place—safely. It was all to no purpose, though, for during that night a high wind tore the airship from her moorings—in the same way as *La Patrie*—and broke the girders. A handling party came out from Friedrichshafen and, unforgiveably, broke up the ship. Individual parts could have been saved.

Although *LZ 2*'s short flight fully justified Dürr's improvements, it was still open to question whether the rigid could answer the requirements of flight and landing. Zeppelin, uncharacteristically, was profoundly depressed by the accident and declared he would not build another ship. He was prepared to sell his plant at Friedrichshafen to the army. The Lebaudy had now proved her worth and Gross, of the airship battalion, tried to tempt Dürr to change over and build semi-rigids for the army. On the face of it, it seemed that they were a better choice. At the same time the war ministry was sufficiently impressed with the rigid to ask the Reichstag to finance the construction not only of a new floating shed, but also of *LZ 3*, to which the Reichstag responded by granting 500,000 marks.

A number of changes were made in the new ship. The most important was the introduction of two pairs of large stabilising planes at the stern.[4] They were intended to reduce the pitching movement experienced by *LZ 2*. Although this innovation is assumed to have been the results of a homemade wind-tunnel test by Dürr, the problem of stability had been exercising Renard since 1885, and in 1904 details had been published by the French Academy of Science. But vertical fins were not added, due mainly to Count Zeppelin's obstinately empirical approach, for another two years. The other main change was the extension of the walkway fore and aft.

On 30 September 1907 *LZ 3* made the first of a series of five test flights carried out on consecutive days. On that day she made an unbroken flight around the Bodensee of over 7hr covering 215 miles—a record for airships at that date although within two months, as has been noted, it was to be challenged by *La Patrie*. The army, though *LZ 3* had not yet fulfilled the requirements laid down, in fact, not by the Minister of War but by the Minister of the Interior (a non-stop flight of 340 miles in 24hr), was at last impressed by this performance; but because of the small useful load that *LZ 3* was able to carry (only 2 tons) the ministry suggested that a larger ship should be built. Such was their confidence that the Reichstag voted a further sum of money —for *LZ 4*. The new airship, much more sophisticated than former ones, had a capacity of 530,000cu ft, was 446ft long, 42ft in diameter, and her engines were increased to 105hp each. Her useful lift was 4 tons. A large passenger car was fitted in the centre of the walkway, and there was a platform on top of the outer cover which was reached by a shaft from the keel. On 1 July 1908, *LZ 4* made a 12hr flight over Switzerland. Three days later the King and Queen of Württemberg made their first ascent in an airship.

On 4 August *LZ 4* attempted to make a 24hr flight up the Rhine valley in order to fulfil the Government's requirements. She left Friedrichshafen at 6.45 on a windless morning. By midday she was over Strasbourg and was greeted by church bells and a salute of artillery, but in the midday heat she had become too buoyant and on two occasions when the engines had been stopped to refuel she had risen involuntarily, emitting clouds of hydrogen through the automatic valves, and this made her heavy. Trouble with one of the engines forced her to land on the Rhine at Oppenheim. Although repairs were completed in no time, the ship was too heavy to take off until late that evening when everything removable, and five members of the crew, had been taken off. She passed over Mainz at 11.0 pm, and turned for home. Over Mannheim she was slowed down by fresh engine trouble, but this was again rectified. By 6.30 am on the 5th, *LZ 4* was south of Stuttgart. But further engine trouble, plus the need to refuel and regas, made it necessary to land near the village of Echterdingen. That afternoon a sudden squall lifted the ship from her moorings while a motor was being repaired; the crew managed to jump clear, while the ship went on to strike a tree and then burst into flames.

But though it was beset with troubles and ended disastrously, the flight was an achievement; *LZ 4* had covered 370 miles and had remained airborne for 20hr 45min. The army thought the flight had been valuable, despite the inability to complete the journey, while the public were so impressed that they raised 6 million marks to enable work to begin on *LZ 5*. From apparent disaster the future of the Zeppelin was now far more secure.[5]

Meanwhile the army, though still uncommitted as to which system —rigid or non-rigid—was the best, considered taking over *LZ 3* after she had been modified and given greater capacity. In November 1908 Crown Prince Henry of Prussia expressed official confidence in airships by flying in her to Donaueschingen where evolutions were performed over the Emperor. In February 1909 *LZ 3** became the first army airship. She was stationed at Metz, then a German town, where a shed had been built for her. She made 26 successful flights.

The improvement of Zeppelin's finances made it possible for him on 1 October 1908 to form Luftschiffbau Zeppelin; and in May 1909 *LZ 5* was completed by the new company. She was 530,000cu ft in capacity, 446ft long and 42ft in diameter. Her lift was greater because her gas bags were made of goldbeater's skins, originally supplied by an English firm, instead of rubberised cotton. On 27 May she set off to fly from Friedrichshafen to Berlin and return without refuelling. But on reaching Leipsic, Zeppelin decided to turn back as he appreciated that with the wind against them, the ship would have to refuel at Berlin. After 36hr of flight, and with both himself and the crew exhausted, he made a forced landing at Goppingen, near Stuttgart. His

---

* The works number. Army ships were at first numbered from *Z I*, including *Ersatz* (replacement) ships. After *Z XII* they reverted to the works number (*LZ 34*) until army ships were discontinued. From July 1915 30 was added to each works number, probably for security reasons. Naval airships were numbered from *L 1*; occasionally the sequence was broken.

landing orders were misinterpreted by the helmsman, and the airship's bow collided with a pear tree, much to the chagrin of the helmsman. The girders and fabric were repaired to Dürr's instructions, which showed, firstly, that the rigid framework could withstand bumpy landings on the earth; and, secondly, that emergency repairs could be carried out. The airship then returned to base under her own power. Shortly after, she made an appearance at an international airship exhibition at Frankfurt-am-Main. *LZ 5* was afterwards taken over by the army and became *LZ II*.

A turning point in the future of the Zeppelin airships had now been reached. The sceptics had to admit that the rigid was no longer a Utopian dream. But while the man in the street was enthusiastic (airships coinciding with the feeling of euphoria in which the Germans were then indulging themselves), in official circles there were still doubts. The army was none too happy with *Z I*, which was not as well made as *LZ 4*, and *Z II* did not distinguish herself at the airship manoeuvres in the autumn of 1909. The verdict seemed to be that airships were still not reliable for military operations. This being so, the army did not accept *LZ 6*, although, with a third engine, she was faster than the earlier ships; and she had made the first flight from Friedrichshafen to Berlin, though arriving a day late because of poor weather. The army wanted a fast ship with greater carrying capacity. At the same time no one was sure whether the semi- or non-rigid was not preferable. (The promoters of the Siemens Schuckert non-rigid were at this time making a bid for popularity.) Furthermore, stimulated by the Echterdingen disaster, a rival rigid airship was being built by the newly formed Schütte-Lanz Company with a number of features which were superior to the Zeppelin.

If the Zeppelins were to survive they had to prove that they were a practical form of aircraft. At the end of May 1909, therefore, the Deutsche Luftfahrts Aktien Gesellschaft (DELAG) was founded by Alfred Colsman. He was son-in-law of Carl Berg, the aluminium manufacturer who had supported the experiments of Schwartz, and who was already manager of Luftschiffbau Zeppelin.

One of the first pilots of the new company was a journalist named Hugo Eckener, who had been a student of economics. He had reported adversely on one of the early Zeppelin flights, but on meeting Count

Zeppelin had been converted to the cause of airships, and he was to become not only the world's most skilful airship pilot but the mainspring of commercial Zeppelin operations in the inter-war years. DELAG was important for two reasons. First, it operated the first commercial air service, although not on a regular basis. The airships flew in good weather only with the following cities on their itinerary —Berlin, Leipsic, Dresden and Munich. Second, DELAG proved to be invaluable in training airship crews for the armed services, and it was owing to this corpus of experience that, during the 30 years life span of the rigid airship, Germany undoubtedly maintained the lead.

DELAG's first ship was *LZ 7*, known as *Deutschland*. She was 485ft long, her maximum diameter was 46ft, and she had a capacity of 680,000cu ft. She was driven by three engines of 120hp each, and she reached a speed of 35mph. The walkway had been widened to form a spacious cabin holding 16 passengers; the elevator system was again improved, and the large oval rudder discarded.

But a fresh series of accidents dogged the Zeppelins and added fresh fuel to the doubters' arguments. On 28 June 1910, nine days after her maiden flight, *Deutschland*, carrying a party of journalists from Düsseldorf, was wrecked in a storm in the Teutoberger Wald—fortunately without loss of life. The prime cause of the accident lay in the fact that the airship took off without a weather forecast and after a partial breakdown of her engines was carried towards a storm front. She ran into a sudden gust of wind which threw her up to a height of 3,500ft. By now she had lost a lot of gas which could not be alleviated by discharging ballast or by using the elevators. (Two months earlier, *Z II* had been wrecked in a storm at Weilburg.) At last DELAG was forced to appreciate the need to study weather; to do so was from then an essential feature of Zeppelin commercial airship operations.

The Zeppelin builders were now sufficiently confident not to be put off by losses of ships. *LZ 6* was rapidly lengthened to replace *Deutschland* and became the first passenger-carrying rigid airship. But she, too, met with disaster, after making 36 passenger-carrying flights between 23 August and 14 September 1910. A careless mechanic cleaning out one of the cars at Düsseldorf set her alight.

In the early days of DELAG regular services could not be run because of the lack of sheds. So circular flights were made from Friedrich-

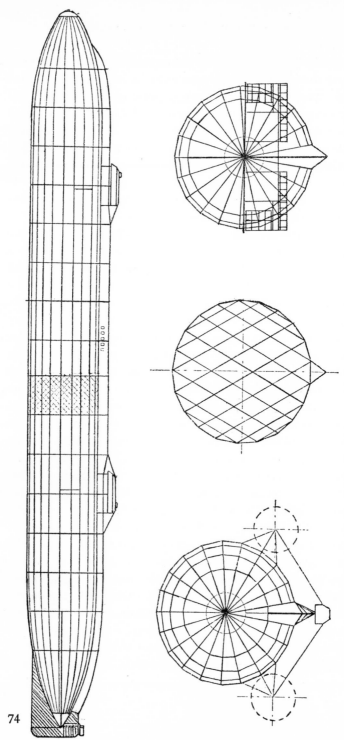

Typical pre-1913 Zeppelin rigid airship with external keel, showing also bow, cross section of hull and stern

shafen, using the same airfield for departure and return. Colsman did not waste time, however, and he built sheds at Düsseldorf and Baden-Oos (the latter more suitable for airship operation, being situated in a valley where the prevailing wind followed the line of the Black Forest). Until a new airship (*Schwaben*) was ready in the late summer of 1911, the service was kept going by the reconstructed *LZ 7* and *LZ 8*, or *Ersatz Deutschland*. The latter was wrecked outside her shed on the windy Dusseldorf airfield. None of the eight passengers aboard was injured. Eckener, who was then a comparatively inexperienced pilot, never made another serious error of judgement.[6]

Schwaben marked another step forward in the evolution of Zeppelin airships. Smaller than her predecessors, she was 460ft long, 45ft in diameter, and her capacity was 592,000cu ft, but her useful lift (over 6 tons) had not been reduced. The rigid airship was now assuming a much more workmanlike shape, with all excrescences removed and the elevators fitted at the stern, at which position they were henceforward retained. The Maybach engines were also greatly improved. *Schwaben* achieved a speed of 43mph—over 10mph faster than *Deutschland*. From July to the end of November 1911 *Schwaben*, with Eckener as captain, made 130 flights, mainly over southern Germany, but also as far as Berlin and the North Sea. On account of *Schwaben*'s success, DELAG constructed airship terminals at Frankfurt-am-Main and Hamburg. Like *LZ 6*, *Schwaben* met her end through an accidental fire on 28 June 1912 outside her shed at Düsseldorf. The accident was due to electricity generated by friction between the rubber material in the gas bags and the framework. In the first half of 1912 two more, larger, ships were built for DELAG—*LZ 11* (*Viktoria Luise*) and *LZ 13* (*Hansa*)—both 460ft long, 45ft in diameter, and with a capacity of 590,000cu ft. *Sachsen* followed in 1913. She had the same dimensions but was enlarged at the outbreak of war for military service.

What was it like to travel in a DELAG airship? The immediate reaction of the passenger was its size and self-sufficiency compared with balloons, aeroplanes, or small airships. Next, the absence of noise and vibration. 'The hum of propellers and motors,' wrote the aeronautical correspondent of the *Scientific American*, 'is as audible as the rustling of trees and the softest speaking voice is audible.'[7] The passengers were installed in a spacious panelled cabin resembling a railway Pullman car. From their tables they looked through large windows at the view below them—'an express locomotive fell behind with its tail of waving handkerchiefs'. Forward was the steward's pantry from which lunch (with wines from the Rhineland) and tea were served. From it a door led along the walkway to the control car. Here stood the helmsman, wearing motoring goggles—Dürr used to insist that on landing a helmsman should be able to feel the wind on his face. At the stern was the washroom, with a partition in which the wireless operator sat. From aft of the walkway members of the crew could climb out through a porthole and inspect the rudders and elevators and make repairs if necessary a thousand feet above the ground. One feature of the voyage was the facilities for passengers to drop a bag with streamers attached containing postcards marked with a special cachet at a selected point.

DELAG did not lose a single passenger from accident during its period of operation from 1910 to August 1914. None of the accidents that destroyed six of the company's airships during this period were in any way due to defects in design or construction, nor did any take place in mid-air. The accompanying table covering this period, though the figures are approximate, gives an idea of the extent of DELAG's operations.[8] The flights of *Deutschland* and *LZ 6* which operated for one and three weeks respectively have been omitted.

Airship	No of flights	Hours	Miles	Fare-paying passengers	Total no of passengers carried
Ersatz Deutschland	62	124	4,090	129	1,778
Schwaben	218	480	17,050	1,553	4,354
Viktoria Luise	489	981	33,950	2,995	9,738
Hansa	399	841	27,750	2,187	8,321
Sachsen	419	741	24,900	2,465	9,837

A flight cost 100 marks, equivalent to £5 sterling of the day, including lunch, per person. Thirty passengers were usually carried at one time, and there was always a waiting list. The crew numbered eight.

One discordant note of the American aeronautical correspondent's description of his flight in *Viktoria Luise* was the observation that the crew were partly composed of sailors and naval officers—a warning of the approaching catastrophe of 1914. The German navy had watched the army's hesitant adoption of rigid airships, finally confirmed in June 1912 with cautious reserve. Admiral von Tirpitz, the commander-in-chief, like senior officers in all navies, was sceptical about new equipment, and, as ever, the decisive factor was limited financial resources available. Yet Tirpitz could not ignore the progress made by the army any more than he could ignore airship developments in Italy, and in Germany's naval rival, England. At least the navy could benefit from the army's mistakes and the sailor was much more at home handling and navigating airships than was the landlubberly soldier. Pressure from the Emperor and from Crown Prince Henry who, after his flight, had become enthusiastic about airships, not to mention vociferous public opinion, changed Tirpitz's mind.[9]

On 24 April 1912 the navy placed a contract for its first airship— L 1 (LZ 14). This naval adoption of rigid airships was an important step forward in the latter's evolution. Speed, greater ceiling, greater lift, and a heavier load were required. Since the air was an element not unlike the sea, the sailors were able to make a practical contribution towards airship design.

L 1 was completed in October 1912 and made her first flight on the 7th. The following month she covered 1,065 miles in 31hr. She was an improvement on earlier Zeppelins and was able to carry a useful load of over 9 tons. On 18 January 1913, Tirpitz obtained the Emperor's consent for a five-year programme of 16 rigids which would put Germany well ahead of other nations possessing an airship service. An airship base was to be built at Nordholz, near Cuxhaven.

This ambitious scheme was never achieved. Two disasters within a matter of weeks, eliminating the cream of the naval airship service as well as the latest airships, left the German navy with only one rigid (L 3) at the outbreak of war. Early in September 1913 L 1 took part in the autumn exercises of the High Seas Fleet. On the 9th, having made the previous day a most successful scouting flight, she was caught in a sudden squall and plunged nose-first into the sea. Fourteen of the crew were killed—the first fatalities involving a Zeppelin airship.[10] The accident was similar to the *Shenandoah* disaster in the USA 12 years later. Just over a month later, *L 2* crashed in flames, after take-off from Johannisthal on her tenth flight, and which, in fact, was to be her acceptance flight .The crew of 28 including a naval architect, Felix Pietzker, who had been pressing the conservative Dürr to make changes, were all killed. The inquiry criticised the close proximity of the engine cars to the hull which had been insisted on by Pietzker. The cars were fitted with windscreens and the draught created by the latter fanned any gas leaking from the hull towards the engines. A single spark from a magneto was sufficient to ignite the hydrogen.[11] In *L 3*, completed in May 1914, the engine cars were suspended well below the hull. It may be that the change in design was not only due to the lesson learned from *L 2*, but was also influenced by the Schütte-Lanz design, to be described later, in which the propeller was fixed to the engine car—a much more practical idea. But the *L 2* accident was for some time the cause of strained relations between the navy and Luft-schiauffb Zeppelin.

L 3 had a greater diameter than *L 2* (49ft) in order to give her more lift, but her length was the same (518ft). She had a capacity of 744,500cu ft and was driven by three engines giving 630hp. She was the first of the *M* class, which formed the core of the wartime fleet of Zeppelins. *Z IV* was the first of the *M* class received by the army.

Luftschiffbau Zeppelin had by now achieved a technique for the rapid construction of rigid airships. This was due largely to the rationalisation of the work. Many of the components were manu-factured locally. The Maybach Company had, since 1909, produced the engines, while there were several offshoots from Luftschiffbau Zeppelin, such as the Zeppelin Transmission Company; the Gasbag Company, set up in Berlin in 1912 to make its own goldbeater's skins; and the Zeppelin Shed Construction Company also formed in Berlin. In course of time, another offshoot, Friedrichshafen Flugzeugbau, began building seaplanes and also, during World War I, the twin engine *G II* bomber, very similar to the Gotha bomber. Employees were well treated and a housing estate (one of the earliest of its kind) was built for them at Friedrichshafen.

By 1913 three ships could be built simultaneously at Friedrichshafen. (It must be remembered that the parallel-sided airships of these days were comparatively easy to duplicate.) An airship shed had been built at Staaken, near Berlin. During the year seven Zeppelins were built—*Ersatz Z I*, *Ersatz EZ I*, *Z IV*, *Z V*, *Z VI*, were taken over by the army; *L 2* went to the navy; *Sachsen*, as already seen, went to DELAG.

Several improvements were incorporated in the *M* (builder's type) ships. Simple vertical and horizontal fins at the tail replaced the complicated system of rudders and elevators. The ship now answered the rudder with only one propeller in action and the elevators were more efficient. These innovations became standard for all subsequent Zeppelins and henceforward only minor changes were made. Military ships were fitted with a machine-gun on top of the hull, the surrounding fabric being covered with fireproof dope. This also became standard equipment for all service ships. A simple bomb-release gear was fitted, but bombing was not at this stage envisaged as a primary role, as only a limited number of bombs could be carried.

The army airships were still not operationally viable. Their low ceiling made them too vulnerable to anti-aircraft guns, and even to rifle fire. They could only be used safely at night. International tension was growing and the German government decided to pay a subsidy to DELAG on condition that the latter's ships should be commandeered by the army at the outbreak of war. In the event the army had six airships available—*Z IV* to *Z IX*—and one Schütte-Lanz.

The Zeppelin design was by no means perfect. If a forced landing had to be made the rigid attachment of the car to the hull transmitted the shock to the framework. The risk of fire was accentuated with the proximity of the engines and propellers to a hull filled with inflammable hydrogen. The box system of control surfaces was very clumsy. As for the shape, the parallel sides and short rounded ends of the Zeppelins, while easy to duplicate, were not aerodynamically effective in reducing drag. This general lack of streamlining would immediately be apparent to the mind of a naval constructor. Such a one was Dr Johann Schütte, of Danzig.[12]

In 1908, Schütte, while admiring the Zeppelin's initial successes, appreciated that it could be improved with better design. Schütte anticipated the shape of the airship that became familiar in the inter-war years. Dürr, however, vigorously denied Schütte's claims to originality. Nevertheless, changes in Zeppelin design occurred significantly after 1911, the date when the first Schütte-Lanz was completed.

Schütte's conception of a streamlined form derived from his experiments in water resistance carried out in 1903–4 at Bremerhaven. He then enlisted the support of Carl Lanz, a Mannheim industrialist, who provided the money to build Schütte's first airship. It had a volume of 734,000cu ft and the hull was built on a helical system using only longitudinal girders which made a criss-cross pattern. Its diameter was greatest in the first third of the length, the cross-section tapering from that point to the stern of the ship, the latter part being of a cruciform shape. The difference between the Zeppelin and the Schütte-Lanz was quite remarkable. The diameter of the latter was 60·3ft, while that of a Zeppelin of similar length (*Sachsen*) was only 48·6ft. The fineness ratio of the first Schütte-Lanz was 1 to 7·1 as opposed to 1 to 9 in the case of the *Sachsen*. The girders of the early Schütte-Lanz's were of wood, mainly because aluminium was hard to obtain but also because Schütte considered wood to be more flexible. A few years later he intended to use duralumin tubing. (Duralumin, an alloy of aluminium, copper and iron, was discovered by Wilm between 1903–9.) The elevators and rudders were built in conjunction with the tapering stern, which itself made steering much easier.

Schütte also designed an elastic suspension system for the cars. This arrangement allowed for a minimum number of struts which were fitted transversely to maintain the car at a given distance from the centre line of the hull. The propeller was fitted to the engine car; the thrust of the propeller was taken by a cable which was led out through the centre of the propeller aft. The advantage of this system was that not only was the machinery simplified, but, with the removal of the projecting side brackets and gears, the danger of fire was minimised (the accident which destroyed *L 2* could not have occurred on a Schütte-Lanz). Finally, Schütte installed electric light and telephones on his airships.

On 17 October 1911 the first Schütte-Lanz made her maiden flight, but she had to make a forced landing after a control cable snapped. She was taken over by the army in December 1912. After her eighty-third flight, one from Königsberg to Berlin on 17 July 1913, she was wrecked by a storm while on the ground. Schütte's second airship, begun in 1913 and completed the following year, had, unlike the Zeppelins an interior corridor, or walkway, triangular in shape. Holding ballast and

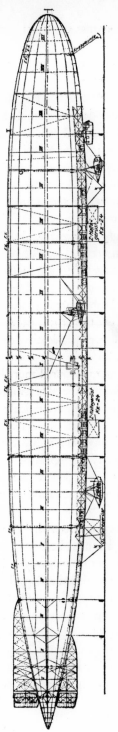

Schütte-Lanz II showing streamlining, internal walkway and suspended engine cars

fuel, it provided an unbroken communication way from one end of the ship to the other. It not only reduced the overall weight of the ship but made it better able to withstand bending moments. Apart from this important innovation, the design resembled the Zeppelin transverse frames and longitudinal girders. Vertical ventilation shafts in the hull dispersed pockets of gas and thus eliminated possible causes of an explosion. (They were not incorporated into Zeppelins until 1916.) The hull contained intermediate transverse frames with the object of reducing the load on the main transverse frames and providing additional support for the outer cover.

By 1915 the wooden girders of the Schütte-Lanz's were to have been superseded by duralumin tubular girders twice as strong as the wooden ones. Schütte reckoned that they were much stronger than the triangular open channel sections used in the Zeppelins. In his later ships he introduced a strong axial cable running through the centre of the ship and the gas bags from bow to stern; it prevented surging by gas bags adjoining one which had been accidently deflated and therefore likely to distort the girders.

Schütte-Lanz airships were favoured more by the army than by the navy because it was found that the glue holding together the plywood structure tended to deteriorate rather quickly in the damp North Sea air. The army crews, being less competent at aerostation, did not pilot their Schütte-Lanz's with any great measure of success. These airships, however, raided London twice, operated against submarines in the Baltic, and flew sorties over Galicia and the Black Sea. Indeed, Schütte-Lanz built 18 ships for the army and navy in the course of the war.

There was keen rivalry between the Zeppelin and Schütte-Lanz companies. For the record, it must be noted that Dürr not only claimed that he had invented the internal walkway and introduced it into LZ 3, but also that Schütte had copied the Zeppelin system of dividing the hull into compartments for the gas bags.[13] Schütte, Dürr contended, wanted his wooden airships to compete with the aluminium constructed Zeppelins, but was forced to admit defeat. Dürr also said that the long, cylindrical shape of the early Zeppelins was dictated by the height of the shed at Friedrichshafen, which was 60ft high—the Schütte-Lanz shed was, in contrast, 70ft high and enabled Schütte to

(*above*) *La République*—semi-rigid; (*below*) Clément-Bayard non-rigid leaving shed

Page 84 (above) M II semi-rigid on flight Cologne–Coblenz; (below) Citta di Milano semi-rigid (Forlanini)

build a slightly fatter ship. Finally Dürr pointed out that even *LZ 1* had electrical signalling equipment.

In 1909, as was seen in Chapter 3, the British, observing the success of the Zeppelins, were forced to take airships seriously. However, the year before Capt R. H. S. Bacon, RN, director of naval ordnance, and who became a member of the aeronautical advisory committee, had proposed to the First Sea Lord, the imaginative-minded Adm Sir John Fisher, that Vickers, the famous armaments and shipbuilding firm, should design a large rigid airship on the model of a Zeppelin. This idea was approved by the Cabinet, and on 7 May 1909, Vicker's tender was accepted, £35,000 being allotted in the naval estimates for the building of a rigid airship.[14] The design and construction was to be the responsibility of the director of naval construction, but Capt Murray F. Sueter, RN, an officer with a technical bent and an aeronautical enthusiast (he was to become a stormy petrel in naval aviation), was appointed to supervise the work on the understanding that he should have no hand in the design.

HM *Naval Airship No 1*, or *Mayfly* as she was irreverently christened by the sceptics because of the delays attending her launching, was the first rigid airship to be built outside Germany—an achievement considering airship design was in its infancy. But the design of *Mayfly* was by no means a slavish copy of the contemporary Zeppelin.[15] Charles Roberton, chief engineer of Vickers, was responsible for her construction. He like Schütte, appreciated the need for reducing drag, though it was unfortunate that he did not consult the recently-formed aeronautical advisory committee. The hull was built of 12 longitudinals fixed to 17 transverse frames. The bow and the stern were tapering (unlike the cigar shape of the Zeppelin) and their dimensions were based on the calculations of an American professor of aerodynamics, Albert Zahm. The ship was 512ft long, 48ft in diameter and the capacity was 640,000cu ft. The girders were of duralumin which doubled their strength and saved nearly a ton in weight. Vertical movement was performed by four sets of horizontal planes situated fore and aft, and there were three groups of vertical planes, or rudders, at the stern. There was an internal walkway which acted as a keel. But there was also a portable keel suspended from the lower longitudinals. Within the hull were 17 gas bags made from fabric produced by the

F

Continental Rubber Co. The upper half of the outer cover was made of silk treated with Ioco—a waterproof dressing combined with aluminium dust. The lower half was of yellow silk treated with Ioco dressing with the object of dissipating heat from sunlight more easily. The airship was fitted with the first water-recovery system. The exhaust from the engines was to be condensed into water passing through about 400ft of thin metal piping into a separator, finally refilling the ballast bags. Power was provided by two Wolseley engines of 180hp each.

The requirements of the Admiralty were commendably precise. The ship was to be used for scouting and had to be able to maintain a speed of 46mph for at least 24hr. She was to alight on the water, moor to a floating mast and so be independent of a shed. She must be equipped with wireless; be able to reach a height of at least 1,500ft; and, finally, there was to be reasonably comfortable accommodation for the crew.

But the designer had difficulty in adapting himself to the medium in which his ship was going to travel—a medium 800 times less dense than water. So he tended to make the ship too solid. The cars, which admittedly had to float, were of Honduras mahogany; in addition to the ordinary supports, the cars had steel wires to hold them in position. The Admiralty, moreover, insisted on adding items of equipment, such as a sea anchor, thereby increasing the weight. But this tendency to gild the lily has been a failing of service departments throughout the technological age.

In May 1911, *Mayfly* was completed in the Vickers yard at Barrow-in-Furness.[16] At 4 am, on the 22nd, she left her shed—which had only 5ft to spare at the sides—and, according to Sueter, hauling her out was like drawing a cork out of a bottle. The crew and the handling party came from the cruiser *Hermione*, stationed in Barrow while the airship was being built. For the next four days *Mayfly* was moored in Cavendish Dock to a floating mast which swung round with the wind, and to which a large sail was fixed to act as a wind break for the bow of the ship. A number of experiments were made, including running the engines, to see how she behaved under semi-operational conditions. An unexpected bonus was a 36mph gale which *Mayfly* rode out admirably. (She was moored by the extreme nose and this attachment was reinforced by steel wires—a naval idea.) The crew of ten lived on board. They had no complaints, except for the hardship of not being able to cook meals or smoke.

But the ship was found to be too heavy. When she returned to her shed the portable keel, which provided strength for the hull, was removed. It was a design change that Sueter was strongly against, and proved to be a fatal alteration. H. B. Pratt, who later became the chief airship designer of Vickers, calculated that without the keel the ship would inevitably break up.

The airship was ready for further trials on 24 September. After she had been drawn out of the shed by two parties of sailors she was taken in tow by a steam pinnace, but while still attached to the hawser held by the sailors a sudden gust caught her; she heeled over and broke her back. No one was injured due to the efforts of Lieut C. P. Talbot who extricated the men from the after car, while Lieut Neville F. Usborne, later to become a devoted exponent of airships, with great presence of mind deflated Nos 7 and 9 gas bags and thus helped to reduce the damage.

Unhappily for Sueter and his small band of enthusiasts, Adm Sir A. K. Wilson, who had replaced Fisher as First Sea Lord, had no faith in airships as instruments of war. Nor had the officer in charge of the court of inquiry set up after the accident—Rear-Adm F. C. D. Sturdee (later to be the victor of the battle of the Falkland Isles).[17] On inspecting the wreck of *Mayfly*, he is reputed to have exclaimed, 'This is the work of a lunatic.' Sueter and the crew were exonerated from any blame, but the structure was found to have been not strong enough. (It was said that while in the shed the bracing wires were continually snapping.) Sturdee wrote to Sueter to say that he had recommended the Admiralty 'not to repair your monster'. There seems little doubt that the removal of the keel caused the airship to break her back.

It is easy to be amused at Sturdee's over-cautious reaction to what was essentially an experiment. But it must be remembered that by 1911 six out of ten Zeppelins had come to grief—not a very reassuring record. Moreover, the naval staff had no conception of the extent to which air power might affect the course of a naval battle. So the airship construction team at Barrow was dispersed. In contrast, the army officers at Farnborough were much more progressive in their views on the value of airships and aeroplanes. Capper, for example, in a lecture given in 1909, foresaw that airships would grow larger in order to increase their range, and that, as far as airships were concerned, the future lay with the rigid. Scouting airships, Capper submitted, would be able to perform their task out of range of enemy ships.

But the persistence of the German and other airship designers on the continent, and the fact that the German army had decided to concentrate on the rigid, caused the British government to think again. In July 1912 Sueter and O'Gorman were sent to Germany to find out what stage of development German airships had reached.[18] They went for a flight in *Viktoria Luise* and were impressed by the strength of the keel, as well as by the way the elevators were able to control the ship aerodynamically. They appreciated the airship's long-range capability, its ability to fly against a 40mph wind, and that it could, in favourable weather, do the work of a number of scouting cruisers.

For the following five years British airship policy was to be subject to vagaries as hazardous as the crosswinds which the airship had to contend with on the ground. The CID recognised that useful experience might be gained by using non-rigid airships, but for purposes of range, endurance and lift, the rigid was unsurpassed. In October 1912 untrue reports of a German airship flying over Sheerness were an added spur to building another rigid.[19] The Government was slowly becoming aware of the vulnerability of military installations to air attack. If the authorities were slow in making up their minds, at least there was no doubt among some of their juniors. In January 1913, Cdr E. A. Masterman, officer commanding the naval airship wing at Farnborough, wrote: 'I consider that, on account of the position I now hold, I might be held to have been guilty of a grave neglect of duty if I did not officially place on paper my firm conviction that the construction of a rigid naval airship should once more be undertaken and that as soon as possible. This is not only my view but is the firmly expressed view of my officers, experts in the Royal Aircraft Factory, Army airship officers, and, in fact, all who have studied the matter.'[20]

On 6 February 1913, at the end of a lengthy discussion in the CID on the respective merits of aeroplane and airship, the Prime Minister said in regard of the latter: 'Solvitur ambulando.'[21] That April the forced landing of *Z IV* at Luneville, on the French eastern frontier, revealed the rapid progress which the Zeppelins had made in recent years. The information was passed on to London. At last, that June, Adm Sir John Jellicoe, now First Sea Lord (who had actually flown in a Zeppelin), decided that the Admiralty could no longer afford to sit back and watch airship development on the continent. It was then that the *Astra Torres* and the Parseval were ordered (see page 57). In the meantime, Vickers had formed an airship department at Barrow. It was now requested by the Admiralty to put forward proposals for an experimental rigid similar to a Zeppelin, and for three non-rigids.

All that Pratt and his colleagues had to go on were photographs of the external shapes of the DELAG ships. Tentative designs of practically all parts of the airship had to be made in order to provide data for the final design. On the other hand, the stress calculations of Eiffel, the French engineer, were used. The Admiralty approved the design for a rigid of 750,000cu ft costing £90,000 and work began in 1914. But in December 1914, five months after the start of World War I, Winston Churchill, First Lord of the Admiralty, agreed with the Board that 'they were not in favour of spending more money on airships'.[22] In February 1915 work was suspended on the new rigid, now known as *Rigid Airship No 9*.

France was the only other country, apart from Britain, to build a rigid airship outside Germany before 1914. In 1912 the Zodiac Company, which hitherto had built only non-rigids, completed *Spiess* for the French army. She was named after Joseph Spiess who designed a rigid airship in 1873, but was not able to construct it. Like the Schütte-Lanz ships, *Spiess* was built of wooden girders.[23] The cars were made of aluminium. In her original form she was 341ft long, 40ft in diameter, and her capacity was 388,400cu ft.

As *Spiess* was found to be too heavy on completion, only one Chenu motor was fitted in the forward car. Her first flight was made early in 1913. She was then lengthened to 420ft and her capacity was increased to 777,000cu ft. She was re-equipped with two Dansette-Gillet motors. The French army's prejudice against rigids has already been noted; they were referred to contemptuously as aerial mastodons or 'bulles de gaz'. *Spiess*, although it made a number of flights in its new form after December 1913, was never used operationally.

In 1913 the Italian airship designer, Crocco, planned to build what for that time was a very large rigid of 1,430,000cu ft. Contemporary

Zeppelins were of little over 700,000cu ft. Most of the material for building the Crocco airship was to have been bought in Germany, but war intervened before construction could begin.[24] During the war the British became interested in this G type airship, as it was known, and which had somewhat similar characteristics to the Schütte-Lanz airships. But the wreck of *L 33* on British soil provided a better model. Italy had, in the meantime, turned exclusively to the construction of semi-rigids.

By 1914 Germany was well ahead of other countries in rigid airship construction and operation. This was due to four factors. Firstly, the vision, courage and persistence of Count Zeppelin. He grasped the essentials of the rigid airship from the start, and, in spite of a daunting series of accidents proved that his idea could be converted into a practical form. Secondly, the excellent organisation of Luftschiffbau Zeppelin and its ancillaries which provided the components. Thirdly, DELAG, with its five airships, had by August 1914, flown 107,740 miles in 3,167hr and carried over 34,000 passengers without mishap, thus proving that airship travel was a safe and reliable form of transport. Fourthly, there had been considerable improvements since the launching of *LZ 1*, much of which was due to the competition of the Schütte-Lanz Company. Some idea of the superiority of the Zeppelin over other rigids of the time is well illustrated by comparing the useful lift of *L 1*, which was 9¼ tons, with *Mayfly* which could only carry 3 tons. By 1914 the capacity of the Zeppelins had more than doubled and so had their speed. In the same year, a Zeppelin (*L 3*) flew for 34hr 59min —not a record, for it has been noted that the *Adjutant Vincenot* remained airborne for another 1½hr.

Contrary to popular contemporary belief, the German armed forces took an extremely cautious view of airship development. Yet they were right to insist on firm specifications, such as ability to reach an adequate height, endurance, speed, useful load, general safety and reliability. They were also right, in the circumstances, to try out the three systems of airship construction. Competition spurred on the development of the Zeppelins. Curiously, when the armed services at last began to take an interest in the rigid, Count Zeppelin himself began to pay more attention to heavier-than-air craft.

But there was a role for the rigid airship in long-distance travel—

though it had to face two further challenges. The first was that it had to prove it could fly through bad weather. The second was the biggest challenge of all: could the airship compete against the aeroplane? Certainly it could not where speed was concerned. 'The only course which was likely to save the airship conception,' wrote Eckener years later, 'was to emphasise the far more extensive—in fact, almost limitless range and loading capacity of airships, impossible for aeroplanes on technical grounds. The aim for airships must be transoceanic traffic.'[25] The test of war brought the airship a long way towards achieving this aim.

CHAPTER 5

The Test of War

'Had I had my way, no airships would have been built during the war, except the little "Blimps" for teasing submarines.' Winston Churchill, *The World Crisis, 1911–14*

'In the beginning of the war, when seaplane flying was quite
undeveloped, [airships] were indispensable to us. Their
wide field of vision, their high speed, and their great
reliability, when compared with the possibilities of scouting
by war ships, enabled the airships to lend us the greatest
assistance. But only in fine weather.' Admiral Scheer, *The
High Seas Fleet in the World War*

The outbreak of war in August 1914 found the German airship service
quite unprepared. The army had at its disposal six Zeppelins (*Z IV–
Z IX*) and one Schütte-Lanz, while the navy only had *L 3*. According
to the pre-war agreement, the army requisitioned the three available
DELAG ships—*Viktoria Luise, Hansa* and *Sachsen*—but only the last-
named was fit for operations. The general staff had not worked out any
strategy for air support of military or naval operations, nor had it
seriously considered the possibility of strategic attacks against targets
far behind the front line. The rigid airship was eminently suited for
long-distance scouting—especially at sea, and, as will be seen, was used
for this purpose. Yet few naval officers had faith in airships or were
aware of their potentialities in 1914. The German reluctance to bomb
targets in Britain was not so much due to squeamishness that they
would be violating international rules of warfare, but that their airships
were not equipped, or the crews trained for such operations. Airships
were not yet able to carry a useful load of fuel in addition to their
bombs, while bomb sights were non-existent and the bombs were
rudimentary; cars were still open, making long journeys most un-
comfortable. Operations were difficult to plan because of the inherent

rivalry between army and navy (the navy eventually took over the army airships in August 1917), and no target priorities were worked out.[1]

Rigid airship operations fall into three categories: first, operations in support of the army; second, strategic operations, and third, maritime operations. The first may easily be disposed of. The German army was not a little embarrassed by the airships it had acquired, and in the early stages of the war missed a golden opportunity to reconnoitre far into French territory to discover troop movements; even bombing attacks on the Channel ports where the British Expeditionary Force was landing might have caused confusion out of all proportion to the scale of attack. What happened, in fact, was that the commander of *Z VIII*, stationed at Trier, in spite of favourable weather, was not allowed to inflate his airship just before war was declared. *Z VI* made a feeble attempt to bomb Liège, using shells, as special bombs did not exist (the first experimental bomb—of 660lb—was not dropped until the middle of December 1914 by the semi-rigid *M IV*). The airship was heavy; the envelope was soon peppered with shells and bullets, causing the ship to crash in a forest near Bonn. Support operations were seriously handicapped by the presence of a staff officer (who knew nothing of the airship's capabilities) to control operations, and who made the airship perform evolutions which could turn out to be fatal. After a month's operations the army had lost four rigid airships, mostly on the Western Front, from anti-aircraft fire. Only *Z IX* (shortly to be destroyed in her shed by British aeroplanes) and the *Sachsen* were now available.

German army rigids made infrequent appearances over the Western Front during 1914 and 1915, but, on the whole, as one Zeppelin commander wrote, 'the High Command forgot all about us. Evidently headquarters no longer had faith in Zeppelins since the loss of the first three ships. We waited for weeks but no orders came'. More use of army airships was made on the Eastern Front, where the great distances made them admirable vehicles for reconnaissance. But, as the months went by and anti-aircraft weapons and their use improved (in any case airships made vulnerable targets), the army airships found it increasingly difficult to carry out their role. In mid-1916 the army decided to commission no more airships and to use those they already had only in poorly defended areas.

The British had long anticipated Zeppelin attacks on their country, and it was for this reason that an attack was made on *Z IX* at Düsseldorf in October 1914. That December British naval aircraft raided Luftschiffbau Zeppelin at Friedrichshafen and inflicted a small amount of damage but leaving unscathed *L 7* then being completed. The outbreak of war had, however, galvanised the factory into a spurt of activity. The DELAG shed at Staaken was converted for airship construction and a new shed, intended for building army airships was nearing completion at Loewenthal, near Friedrichschafen. Meanwhile, using *LZ 26*, originally intended for DELAG, as a prototype, Dürr and his colleagues began to construct airships of over 1 million cubic feet capacity. The war had stimulated the first major innovation of Luftschiffbau Zeppelin[2] for Dürr was conservative in his approach and did not make changes until pressed. His object in sticking to an orthodox plan was, firstly, to produce an airship so perfect in detail that it would maintain a high percentage of its theoretical efficiency, and, secondly, he wanted to retain a standardised frame which would enable production to be rapid and inexpensive.

LZ 26 was the first ship to be built of duralumin. Like *L 2*, the walkway was partially contained within the envelope, forming a keel; the cars were slung well below it and were the first to be enclosed, thus making life much more comfortable for the crew. An enlarged version of this ship—*LZ 38*—of 1,126,000cu ft capacity was completed in April 1915. Ten ships of this *P* class, as it was known, were built for the navy and 12 for the army. The designer was the Austrian Paul Jaray, a recent recruit to the Zeppelin Company. He introduced a more streamlined effect to the hull, though it still had a parallel section in the middle, and it tapered to a sharp point at the stern. Larger bays for the gas bags increased the lift and enabled the ship to climb to 12,000ft, putting it out of range of anti-aircraft gunfire. Four engines provided a speed of 58mph. Two tons of bombs could be carried. As protection against fighter aircraft, machine-guns were mounted on the platform on top of the envelope as well as in the forward and aft cars. This class was the forerunner of the post-war commercial airships.

One novel piece of equipment introduced into some Zeppelins at about this time was a streamlined observation car which could be lowered by means of a winch to some 100ft below the airship. This meant that while an airship could be in or above cloud, an observer in the car below the cloud was able to direct operations, or help in navigation, using a telephone. But most airship commanders disliked the observation car because it increased the overall weight, and as soon as anti-aircraft fire became effective this assumed a very important factor. The Americans adopted this 'spy basket' both for their rigids and for several non-rigids (*TC–13* and *TC–14*) in the 1930s.

The Schütte-Lanz Company may well claim to have anticipated the changes which the war forced on the Zeppelins, but they were slower in production. Nevertheless, *SL 3* was taken over by the navy in February 1915, and was (at that time) the biggest airship in the world, and ahead, by two months, of the first large Zeppelin.

So much for technology. Nothing has been said about the human element and nowhere was this more important than in the untried field of airship operations. Two men, in particular, were outstanding. The first was Capt Peter Strasser, who obtaining his pilot's certificate on 2 March 1914, was in a very short time chief of the naval airship division. He became dedicated to his task and provided the élan vital to naval airship operations. In addition to his powers of leadership he was an intuitive, yet reliable, weather forecaster. When he was killed in the latter stages of the war, morale quickly deteriorated. The second was Hugo Eckener, who by now had become an experienced airship pilot, and able to transmit his enthusiasm and knowledge in bluff and practical terms to novice airshipmen.

With better airships coming off the production line, the chief of the German naval staff urged in January 1915 that an attack be made on London, which he considered to be a legitimate military target. Only military targets outside London were approved, however, due to the Emperor's reluctance to authorise air attacks either on the royal residences or on historical monuments.[3] The first airship attack on England came on the night of 19 January 1915, when three naval Zeppelins dropped bombs indiscriminately and ineffectively over East Anglia. On 29 April the first army airship to attack Britain (*LZ 38*) crossed the sea to fly over Britain and on 31 May *LZ 38* reached London. The East End was the target and £18,596 worth of damage was caused.

In June raids were stepped up, more airships of the *P* class being available. A sharp attack was made on Kingston-upon-Hull. But the short summer nights, the inability of the army and navy to concert operations, and the hesitation of the high command in deciding whether London should be bombed or not, prevented operations on any scale. The Emperor, when Karlsrühe had been bombed by the French and civilians were killed, at last gave his consent to full-scale raids on London—though St Pauls, Westminster Abbey and the royal palaces were by his orders not to be attacked. Operations were intensified in August and continued until mid-October. The most effective raid was an attack on London on the night of 8 September by *L 13*, piloted by Heinrich Mathy, who became one of the most distinguished airship pilots. His airship, alone out of three that set out, reached the target area in the city of London. Twenty-two people were killed and £530,787 worth of damage was caused from fires. A further sharp attack was made on 13 October when a squadron of five Zeppelins was sent against London. Although the financial loss was less than that caused by *L 13* 71 people were killed and 128 injured in and around the metropolis. Probably even more significant was the psychological effect of this new form of warfare which involved civilians far from the battle area. Had the German airships been able to continue their operations at this rate they might well have exercised some effect on the outcome of the war. However, on account of poor weather, and the necessity to provide naval support, London was not attacked again for nearly a year.

Due to the rudimentary air defences airship casualties were small. The army *LZ 37* was destroyed on 8 June by Flight Sub-Lieut R. A. J. Warneford while she was returning to base after fog had compelled the crew to abandon the raid. The navy *L 12* was shot down by anti-aircraft guns after attacking London. Only fragments of this ship were recovered by the British who, ignorant of rigid airship construction, were anxious to capture the airship intact.

But the German airships were no longer able to attack either France or Britain with impunity. Improved anti-aircraft defences, especially on the Western Front, forced them to fly higher, and high altitudes could not be reached until bomb loads had been dropped. The Q class was designed to overcome the difficulties. From December 1915 to May 1916, starting with *L 20*, 12 ships of that class were built.[4] Five went to the navy, seven to the army. Longer than their predecessors, they had a capacity of 1,264,100cu ft. As the distance between the forward and aft cars remained the same, and as the greater part of the increase in length was in the stern, the ship drooped in that quarter in flight. Outer covers were now camouflaged. An attempt was made to quieten the engines. Greater attention to armament reflected stiffening resistance to airship operations. Three machine-guns were installed in the platform on top of the envelope. Swivelling machine-guns were mounted in the stern, which was the quarter from which fighter aircraft usually attacked.

All superfluous items were removed in order to lighten the ship. Some commanders, for instance, refused to allow their crew to carry parachutes. The army removed wireless sets from their airships but, when squadron raids began in 1915, and after attacks had been intensified crews found that inter-ship communication was essential. In this context it should be explained that direction-finding stations were very valuable in helping airships to maintain course, but the enemy could equally well pick up these signals and this was the reason for the loss of an army airship—LZ 77—at Revigny. By the end of the war, more sophisticated direction-finding sets mounted on the airship itself picked up the call-sign transmitted by certain ground stations, and thus enabled bearings to be established without transmitting any signal.

Raids against England continued intermittently throughout 1916, the principal targets being on the east coast; they included Sunderland, Kingston-upon-Hull, Lowestoft, and Great Yarmouth. But this activity only made the British devise better countermeasures. By the spring of 1916 explosive and incendiary bullets were being used in the Lewis machine-guns of the home-defence aeroplane squadrons. Nothing could have been more dangerous for the hydrogen-filled airships. The feelings of the crews may well be summarised by one of them who, after the war, said: 'Had we caught the man who invented that bullet during the war we should gladly have burned him on the great flying ground at Ahlhorn in a stream of blazing hydrogen.'

The need for the airship to ascend higher and more rapidly was therefore vital. For opposition was also increasing from submarines equipped with anti-aircraft guns, as well as from the carrier-borne seaplanes which the British had been developing.

In May 1916 came the second big change in Zeppelin design when the navy commissioned the 'super Zeppelin', or R class.[5] L 30 was the first to be completed. She became available for operations that July. Eight more ships were ready by the end of the year. L 30 was twice as large as L 10 (P class) with a capacity of 1,949,600cu ft, contained in 19 gas bags. She had a useful lift of 27 tons, including 5 tons of bombs. L 30 was nearly 500ft long, 78ft in diameter, and, equipped with six engines, was able to fly at a speed of 62mph. The two extra engines were carried in two small cars slung on each side of the hull amidships. Only the two engines in the rear car still drove propellers fitted to the hull in the old Zeppelin manner. They had been retained from the start of the Zeppelins because of the simple reversing gear always incorporated with the side propeller drive. The development of a new gear drive was considered to require more time than the design and production of a new engine.

The exigencies of war were also stimulating improvements to the Schütte-Lanz airships. The first three ships built in 1915 had a smaller capacity than the contemporary Zeppelins (1,144,000cu ft) and a useful lift of 13 tons. During 1915–16 four ships of the Schütte-Lanz 6 class were built. In 1916–17 ten ships with a capacity of 1,870,000cu ft and useful lift of 20 tons, were constructed. As Strasser disliked the wooden structures of the Schütte-Lanz's, referring to them contemptuously as 'glue-potters', most of them were taken over by the army. Schütte persisted in constructing his airships with wooden girders, only deciding at a late stage in the war to switch to duralumin tube-girders. But no Schütte-Lanz airships were built with this material.

The R class of Zeppelin closely resembled the design of the Schütte-Lanz—a blunt nose, the envelope tapering towards the tail (the fineness ratio of the R class was 1 to 8 as compared with 1 to 10 of the P class) and the parallel portion of the hull was only 105ft long. The employees of Schütte-Lanz claimed that the Zeppelin Company merely copied the former's design, yet the war had brought fresh blood into Friedrichshafen, including the chief calculator Dr Karl Arnstein, and the aerodynamicist Paul Jaray who wanted to make the hull more streamlined. These two men were responsible for the improvements in the R class and in other designs. Changes did mean, however, that it was no longer quite so easy to mass-produce the Zeppelins rapidly. Another drawback, of an operational kind, was that these airships required about a battalion of men to walk them out of and into their sheds. Cross-winds frequently kept them in their sheds and, apart from one uncompleted at Nordholz, there were no revolving sheds whereby an airship could make its exit on a sheltered side.

Using the 'super Zeppelins', an all-out effort against England was made in the autumn of 1916. On 2 September 16 naval and army airships attempted to bomb London. The raid was a complete failure, due largely to bad weather. One of the army airships—*SL 11*—was brought down in flames over Cuffley, Herts, by 2nd Lieut W. Leefe Robinson. The descent of the ship in a great mass of flame not only struck awe into the thousands of otherwise jubilant Londoners watching the destruction of their adversary, but also appeared as a terrible portent of doom to the crews of the other airships still approaching their targets.

The raids continued until the end of the year, but with increasing lack of success. On the night of 1 October 11 Zeppelins were sent to attack targets in the Midlands, but rain, snow and hail made several of them divert to bomb targets in London. One, *L 31*, was attacked and set on fire by 2nd Lieut W. J. Tempest. In his report he wrote that the ship went 'red like an enormous Chinese lantern and then a flame shot out of the front part of her and I realised she was on fire. She then shot up about 200ft, paused, and came roaring down straight on to me before I had time to get out of the way. I dived for all I was worth, with the Zepp tearing after me . . . I put my machine into a spin and managed to corkscrew out of the way as she shot past me, roaring like a furnace.'[6] The captain of the ship—the fearless and inspiring Heinrich Mathy—was found half buried in the ground near the wreck by Potters Bar. He had jumped from the ship rather than be burnt by the blazing hydrogen.

Another airship loss which had even more significance for the British was that of *L 33*. On 24 September, damaged by anti-aircraft fire over the East End of London, she was forced to land at Little Wigborough, on the marshes north of Mersea. In spite of a small fire (most of the gas had escaped) the structure was largely intact and provided an up-to-date model for British designers to examine in detail.

After the last raid of 1916 a further calamity occurred for the Germans. *L 24*, while being walked into her shed, broke her back and caught fire.

In a few minutes the blaze spread to the neighbouring *L 17*. Both ships were a total loss. In 1916 Strasser lost six airships, while the damage that his force had inflicted over the year had been less than that inflicted by a smaller number of ships the year before.

Yet Strasser and his colleagues were not defeated. (Airships demand and obtain total and unswerving devotion from those who serve in them.) They merely insisted on airships able to climb still higher. The *V* class was the result.[7] The first to appear was *L 53*. She became the standard ship for operations over the North Sea for nearly a year. She had a capacity of 1,977,360cu ft. Her length was 644ft, and her diameter 78½ft. As Dürr's aim was to decrease weight as far as possible, he took out the sixth engine, with no significant loss in efficiency, and eliminated accessories to lighten the ship by 3,860lb. He redesigned the hull—nine of the largest frames were spaced 49ft 2in instead of 32ft 9in apart, and reduced the number of gas bags from 19 to 14 though their size was increased, thus giving the ship more lift; there were two layers of goldbeater's skins instead of three. He removed the machine-guns, meaning that the ship had to rely on its climbing ability for defence. He simplified the bomb-releasing gear, and fewer, but heavier, bombs were now carried. Even with a crew of 20 and fuel for a 10hr journey, airships of the *V* class could attain a height of between 16,000 and 18,000ft and were known to have reached a height of 20,700ft. But the new British fighter—the Sopwith Camel—had a ceiling of 17,300ft and could be launched from a battle cruiser or light cruiser.

Main disadvantages of the *V* ships as fighting units were that they were too lightly built to perform evolutions at high speed at low altitudes, which meant that they were no good for scouting at sea—the very task for which there was the greatest need. The new gas bag system had a disadvantage in that if one bag became damaged, the loss of buoyancy could not be balanced by discharging ballast, and the ship could not be kept airborne, even by dynamic means.

For a short time the *V* class of Zeppelins gave the German rigids a new lease of life. This was especially so in the North Sea, where they operated on long-range patrols in conjunction with submarines, then beginning their unrestricted campaign against Allied shipping. Further raids against Britain, particularly on the Midlands, were made. On 19

Page 102 (above) LZ 1 on first flight over the Bodensee; (right) Dr Lüdwig Dürr, principal Zeppelin designer; (below) Hansa—a DELAG airship

October, the last big attack took place. Known as the 'silent raid', for the reason that the anti-aircraft guns had orders not to fire lest they provide route markers to London, but also because the airships' engines were not heard due to the great altitude flown (16,000ft), the attack was nevertheless a disaster. Eleven airships took part in the operation. As the ships climbed to evade the defences before crossing the British coast, they ran into a strong gale. Four were blown far southwards over France and were either forced or shot down. One, *L 49*, forced down behind the Western Front, was captured intact. The crew, exhausted and suffering from height sickness, were soon taken prisoner. *L 49*, as will be seen on page 154, became the model for the first American rigid airship—*Shenandoah*—to be built after the war. The planned big attack was therefore thwarted by the unusual weather conditions and the inability of the crews to carry out their tasks as such high altitudes. But the British realised that 'had the Zeppelins come and gone without let or hindrance, as they well might, the airship menace would, once again, have become a very live one'.

After this fiasco of an operation, the German high command clamped down on airship construction. Heavier-than-air craft were, in any case, in the ascendancy. The Gotha bomber and the 'Giant' bomber, with its four engines, were more effective at strategic bombing, although they still could not equal the range of the rigid airship. Apart from this, British aeroplanes were improving in performance and range; flying boats were operating extensively in the North Sea and carrier-borne aeroplanes in the summer of 1918 executed a decisive attack on the base at Tondern destroying the airships there.

But the airshipmen were determined to go on. The naval staff, still indecisive as to what was the true role of the rigid airship, allowed them to commission the building of yet larger airships with greater speed and higher ceiling, in the vain hope that they would be able to evade fighters and guns. *L 70* was the first of this *X* class of Zeppelin. She was 693ft long, with a capacity of 2,195,800cu ft. She was driven by seven special Maybach MB IVa 'altitude' engines, which gave undiminished speed at high altitudes. She could reach a height of nearly 20,000ft statically and 23,000ft dynamically. Her useful lift was 43 tons and she could carry 8,000lb of bombs on a raid against England.

These technical improvements were to no avail. On the night of 5

G

August 1918, a final, desperate, raid against London was organised, and led by Strasser himself, almost as if in answer to a death wish. While assembling for the attack off the East Coast, the airships ran into trouble. The fighter defences found three airships flying line abreast. L 70 was shot down into the sea. Strasser perished with the rest of the crew. A week later L 53 was destroyed. With the driving force behind them gone there were no more airship raids on England.

There were only two airship raids on Paris—on 20 March 1915 and on 29 January 1916—in each case two airships took part. The most probable reason for this small number of attacks was that the airships, in order to reach their objective, had to cross the most dense concentration of artillery in the world—the Western Front. On the first of the raids on Paris one Zeppelin was brought down by anti-aircraft fire.

Did these long-range operations achieve anything? The official British historian summed up thus: 'In 51 airship raids about 196 tons of bombs were dropped "which killed 557 persons, caused injury to 1,358, and inflicted material damage estimated at £1,527,585".[8] In 52 aeroplane attacks, on the other hand, about 74 tons of bombs were dropped which killed 857 persons, injured 2,058 and caused damage amounting to £1,434,526.'

But for their great vulnerability the airships could have presented a serious threat. If helium had been available to the Germans the story might have been different, though the useful load would have been reduced. As it was 17 rigid airships were lost with their crews, mainly on the raids which have been described above, and, with a single exception, destruction was due to the ignition of hydrogen. Although the material effects of the raids were out of all proportion to the effort put into building the rigids (eg the aluminium might have been better used in making aeroplanes; the production of gas and the manpower tied down in handling the enormous airships on the ground) the pattern was set for strategic bombing which was to obsess military thought in the inter-war period and exercise such a decisive effect on World War II.

But, for the British, even more significant from the military point of view was the diversion of men and materials to home defence. At the end of 1916, 110 aeroplanes were lined up against the airships, while 12,000 officers and men were behind the anti-aircraft guns and searchlights. The high-flying raids of 1917 took the British by surprise (not until September of that year was a single-seat fighter flown at night), but the use of incendiary bullets and the improved performance of the fighters, especially the Sopwith Camel, forced the airships to fly higher, thus decreasing their efficiency, as so much of their useful lift had to be used in carrying water ballast.

The German high command would have been wiser to have concentrated their rigids on scouting at sea and on co-operation with their submarine fleet. Without aircraft the fleets of World War I had to play a game of blind-man's buff. But the naval commanders on both Allied and German sides were slow to appreciate what airships or aeroplanes could do for them. The British, with their well-developed wireless intelligence service, were perhaps less handicapped than the Germans. In spite of the airship's deficiencies, and the extreme vulnerability of the type to the vagaries of the weather, a myth of its value in naval operations grew up, out of all proportion to its actual effectiveness.

Up to the end of 1914, because of fog, storms, or cross-winds which prevented them from being walked out of their sheds, airships were able to operate on maritime operations only on one day in four. Their only active intervention in a surface battle was on 28 August 1914, when L 3 was sent to observe the movements of the British fleet trying to lure the Germans into action. If L 3 had seen Adm Sir David Beatty's battle-cruiser squadron, she might have saved three German light cruisers which were sunk in the action.

During 1915, as noted, the emphasis was on raiding targets in England. On 28 January German airships took part in the Dogger Bank naval action—the first time naval aircraft were used in a fleet action, though they achieved little of value.[9] The Germans lost one cruiser and two others were badly damaged. No British aircraft were on the scene.

There were changes after January 1916 when Adm Scheer became commander-in-chief of the High Seas Fleet. He had an aggressive outlook, and held that in addition to scouting airships should be employed in providing an advanced screen for the battle fleet at sea and escorting cruisers when required. Airships used in conjunction with submarines 'would try to cut off and destroy part of the Grand Fleet', thereby giving the Germans a chance to gain supremacy in the North Sea.

In the Battle of Jutland on 31 May 1916—the only occasion when the two naval battle fleets came into contact—bad weather frustrated airship operations, although the German airships gained what was later found to be an unsubstantiated reputation for useful intervention and led to the often-repeated phrase that a rigid airship was worth eight cruisers.[10] On account of the weather, the High Seas Fleet put to sea without a preliminary reconnaissance, although ten airships were available. By the time the airships had caught up with the fleet, the advanced elements were already in contact. Visibility was very poor and L 14 passed over the two fleets without seeing anything.

A report from Scheer to the airship detachment might well have had disastrous effects for the German fleet because it was intercepted by the British. Unfortunately from the latter's point of view the information gleaned was not passed by the Admiralty to Adm Sir John Jellicoe, the British commander-in-chief. Then in the final stages of the action Scheer misinterpreted L 11's sighting of the British Grand Fleet near Terschelling as pertaining to reinforcements arriving from the Channel. This gave rise to the myth that airships had saved the High Seas Fleet from destruction when, in fact, Scheer had already decided to withdraw. Yet airships did influence this controversial battle, for Scheer's original plan had been to raid Sunderland, and when air reconnaissance was impossible he changed his scheme.

Scheer had now learnt how important reliable and extensive reconnaissance was, and in the next major action which, unlike Jutland, was a cut-and-run raid, an elaborate plan was made for the airships. The objective again was to bombard Sunderland in the hope of encountering the British. One airship force deployed in a screen across the North Sea was to provide long-distance reconnaissance, while a second force was to act as protection to the van and flanks of Scheer's fleet. The operation began on 19 August 1916. But through inaccurate information passed to him from the airships, Scheer gained the impression that the Grand Fleet was withdrawing.[11] The crucial moment came when L 13, captained by an officer inadequately trained in scouting work, reported that an enemy naval force was moving eastwards. Scheer, abandoning the idea of bombarding Sunderland, turned to meet what he imagined to be the British fleet when, in fact, he was withdrawing from it. What L 13 had sighted was the Harwich force which contained no battle-ships. Ironically, *L 13*'s error most likely saved Scheer from being annihilated by a greatly superior British fleet. It was the last major sortie of the High Seas Fleet into the North Sea.

The British were greatly impressed by the German airships' supposedly effective performance in this action. No British rigids were available, and when Jellicoe asked how many airships could have co-operated with his ships, he was told that only ten *Coastal* (non-rigid) airships, with the limited range of 150 miles in favourable weather, could have come to his assistance.

The German rigids were also being used in 1917 to scout for submarines, but they did not penetrate farther than the North Sea. They continued to make reconnaissances in this area for the navy, and to escort minesweeping flotillas, occasionally themselves reporting on the presence of minefields. But by the beginning of that summer their operations were becoming hazardous because of the improved performance of British seaplanes and the arrival of the American-built *H 12* Curtiss 'Large America' flying boat. From May to August three Zeppelins (*L 22, L 43* and *L 23*) were shot down by seaplane or flying boat while on scouting flights.

A year later, in August 1918, Adm Hipper, now commander-in-chief, instructed that seaplanes were to take over all routine flights in the Heligoland Bight. Airships were only to be used when it would be 'of unusual value'.

Life for the rigid airship had become too difficult. Like some ponderous, prehistoric mammoth, it had become all too vulnerable to punier creatures. It is doubtful whether the German rigid airships served a more useful purpose at sea than they had on strategic bombing operations. They had proved a failure in the strategic bombing role, but at sea they had been successful in the reconnaissance role, safeguarding the High Seas Fleet from surprise until longer-ranged British aeroplanes and flying boats proved their superiority. Nevertheless in one respect the rigid airship still held its own, and that was the extreme range at which it could fly. Even at the end of the war a 6hr flight by a Zeppelin from its base in Belgium to, say, Peterhead, in Scotland, could not be equalled by a seaplane.

On one occasion only was this unique characteristic of the rigid airship put to the test. This was an attempt to succour the force under

Gen von Lettow-Vorbeck in German East Africa. By the summer of 1917, his troops had been forced to abandon most of German territory to the Allies, but Lettow-Vorbeck had decided that rather than surrender he would continue the campaign in Portuguese East Africa.[12] In Berlin Dr Zupitza, who had been chief medical officer in German East Africa, was very concerned about the need to send out medical supplies to Lettow-Vorbeck, and suggested that a Zeppelin might do the job. The idea appealed greatly to Strasser, and without waiting for high command confirmation, the German admiralty decided to part L 57, one of the L 53 class, inserting two 49ft bays for gas bags. When completed she was 743ft long, with a capacity of 2,418,700cu ft and a useful lift of 51 tons. She was the biggest airship built to date. Her main drawback was that the engines were inadequate for her size and she was therefore difficult to handle. During a trial flight at Staaken on 8 October, an error of judgement was made by the commander, Capt Lieut Ludwig Bockholt. He decided to take the ship out despite a brewing storm. Realising his mistake, but unable to return to the shed, Bockholt decided to ride out the storm. Lightning seems to have set fire to gas escaping from the valves and the ship was destroyed, fortunately without loss of life.

A second airship—L 59—was immediately assigned to take L 57's place, and by 25 October she was ready for the long-distance flight. As the airship was not intended to return, all her components were earmarked to be utilised in one way or another. The girders were to be used for a wireless mast and for barrack-building; the fabric was to be converted into sleeping-bags; and the keel was laced with leather to be used for boots. L 59 was to carry a total load of 15 tons, including medical supplies, machine-guns and ammunition, sewing-machines, bush knives, binoculars, and so on.

After several false starts because of insufficient ballast being carried, L 59 set off on 21 November on her adventurous journey from Jamboli, in Bulgaria, the most southerly German airship station. Bockholt, though relatively inexperienced, was still in charge of a crew of 21. The airship flew over Turkey—friendly territory—and steered a course between Crete and Rhodes, making then for Egypt where she might expect to meet a hostile reception. In fact her main hazard was tropical storms—the first which an airship had ever encountered. Once the crew thought the ship was on fire, but it was St Elmo's fire, or brush discharge, which appears as a tip of light at the extremity of objects, like a fin, and which was a phenomenon familiar to seamen. So far the ship had responded splendidly.

But, unknown to the crew, the flight was already doomed to failure. On the day that *L 59* left Jamboli Berlin heard (incorrectly, in the event) that Lettow-Vorbeck's defeat and probable capture on the Makonde plateau were inevitable. In the event, Lettow-Vorbeck fought on until the end of the war. Wireless signals failed to reach the airship on account of a thunderstorm near Crete. *L 59* was now following the Nile valley and so well into the tropics. Consequently she had to weather extremes of temperature, for after the heat of the day, when she was over-buoyant, came the chill of darkness when she became heavy. Some 4,400lb of ballast had to be released. The engines were running well, and Bockholt believed he could fly the ship dynamically, but *L 59* was too heavy, due to supercooling, and suddenly dropped from 3,100 to 1,300ft, nearly colliding with a mountain.

At last, at 12.45 pm on 22 November, Bockholt received the countermanding order over his wireless. (The legend grew that the signal had been sent by the British.) At 2.30 pm *L 59* reversed course and began the long journey home. The crew, who had been keyed up by the possibility of reaching their objective, were now gripped by lassitude and morale dropped. But such was their discipline that they kept their watches and maintained the ship. At 3 am on 25 November *L 59* touched down at Jamboli again. She had been in the air for 95hr— almost four days—and had covered 4,200 miles, proving that an airship could fly through extremes of temperature inversions. At the end of the journey there was sufficient fuel on board for another 64hr of flight.

Bockholt and his crew, having survived this odyssey, perished in a futile attempt to bomb Malta in April 1918. The airship was seen by the crew of a German submarine to be descending in a ball of fire. It is thought that the cause of the accident was a fire in a fuel tank, which ignited the hydrogen.

There is no doubt that the German rigid airship, due to the test of war, was greatly improved in design and performance. A comparison of *L 3*, completed in 1914, with the *L 72*—the last of the wartime Zeppelins—shows that the gross or total lift increased from 30 to 66·4 tons; the useful lift from 8·5 to 38·4 tons; the efficiency ratio, ie the ratio of disposal lift to gross lift, from 27·3 to 58·3 per cent; the total horse-power from 630 to 1,470; the full speed at 10,000ft from 50 to 77·6mph; the cruising endurance at 45mph from 20 to 177½hr; and the static ceiling, ie the ceiling reached by static as opposed to dynamic means, from 6,000 to 21,000ft.[13]

Compared with rigid airship development in Germany, the British effort is a story full of error and vacillation, and yet by 1919, due admittedly to the defeat of Germany, Britain was the only country in the world with the capacity to build large rigid airships. But, operationally, her rigid airships achieved virtually nothing. The fiasco of the *Mayfly* made the Admiralty chary of making further experiments with rigids, though it could not ignore developments in Germany. The forced landing of *Z IV* in French territory in 1913 provided information which galvanised it into commissioning Vickers to build *No 9*. A contract was signed in March 1914, but work was stopped by Churchill (First Lord of the Admiralty) in February 1915, on the grounds that the war would soon be over, only to be started again that July when the navy belatedly began to realise the value of the rigid airship as a long-range reconnaissance vehicle.[14] Yet *No 9* was not completed until November 1916 and the ship was not ready for operations until April 1917, having in the meantime been fitted with a 250hp Maybach engine, in addition to three Wolseleys, and the transmission gear and propellers from the captured *L 33*. In the end she was used for training purposes. The first of the successors to *No 9*—the *No 23* class—was not completed until October 1917, while *No 24* and *No 25* were ready at the end of that year, by which time the *Coastal* non-rigid airship could at least perform some of the tasks for which the rigid was built almost as well.

In Germany airships had acquired great prestige from before the war; Count Zeppelin had already become a myth; and Luftschiffbau Zeppelin, enjoying subsidies from the Government, and at the same time the ultimate authority on the design of rigid airships, had so rationalised their construction that a new airship could be launched about three months after the first rivets had been hammered into its girders.

In Britain, control of airships was vested in the Admiralty. Worse still, the control was divided between three departments.[15] The director of air services was responsible for the outer cover and gas bags; the director of naval construction was responsible for the framework; and the engineer-in-chief was responsible for the machinery. This led to all kinds of anomalies. For instance, in the vital matter of lift, the director of naval construction had more say in the matter of weights, the main concern of the engineer-in-chief, than did the director of air services, who, after all, was responsible for the flying of airships.

It was not that the department of naval construction had a hidebound attitude (it nurtured the early tanks and was responsible for the design of the first aircraft carriers), but it knew too little about aeronautics and did not appreciate that it was more important to produce an airship which could compete with the latest Zeppelin than to turn out a number of ships which were too slow, heavy and vulnerable. In any case, policy at the top was so vacillating that the firms involved in rigid airship construction, such as Vickers, Armstrong Whitworth and Beardmore, tended to lose interest, and take up more profitable work. Thus, with the tempo of war making the normal process of research and development almost impossible, British rigid airship construction inevitably lagged behind the Zeppelin's and Schütte-Lanz's, and the German airships were copied whenever that was possible.[16]

No 9 had a capacity of 890,000cu ft and she was supposed to have a range of 1,800 miles. But the navy needed an airship which could 'contend on equal terms with those of the enemy', one which would be used principally for long-range reconnaissance and to provide a screen ahead of the fleet. In the summer of 1915, therefore, three new ships were ordered which became known as the 23 class.[17] They were at least an advance on the uncompleted No 9, and were intended to have a capacity of 1 million cubic feet, be powered by four Rolls Royce engines, each of 250hp, two of which were to mount swivelling propellers to assist in manoeuvring near the ground; while they were to have a disposable lift of 8 tons. Simplified rudders and elevators replaced the box-shaped controls found on No 9.

But the drawback to these airships was that they had insufficient range and lift to enable them to provide adequate support to the fleet. Much of the ship's weight was absorbed by the heavy external keel upon which depended the disposable weights like the fuel and ballast tanks. The scanty information available about German development

derived from the wreckage of *LZ 85* and *LZ 45*, and from interrogation of the survivors of *L 13* destroyed off the East Coast, led naval
constructors to consider building a ship without a structural keel.[18] Their
proposal was vigorously opposed by air officers who were principally
concerned about their ships being able to withstand bending moments
and shearing stresses. In June 1916, however, the naval constructors
won the day, the Admiralty deciding that the last four ships of the *23*
class (the total had by then been increased to eight) should have their
structural keels eliminated (although a walkway still provided accommodation between the cars) and the disposable weights such as engines,
fuel and ballast tanks suspended at the transverse frames.[19] For once a
march had been stolen on the Germans, and it was a pity that greater
priority was not given to the *23X* class, as they were known. They
were the design of C. I. R. Campbell, probably the best of the small
group of naval architects who had been switched to airship design.
They were easy to build, but only two ships were completed (*R 27* and
R 29).

Parallel with this development, the Admiralty ordered in February
1916 two ships with wooden girders (*R 31* and *R 32*) similar to the
Schütte-Lanz's, and their design was, in fact, based on the interrogation
of a Hermann Müller, manager of that firm's girder construction shop,
who had escaped from Germany and placed his services at the Allies'
disposal.[20] Neither *R 31* nor *R 32* was completed in time to play any
part in the war.

The breakthrough, as it might be called, for British rigid airship
design came with the capture, almost intact, of *L 33*, 645ft long and
not far short of 2 million cubic feet capacity with six engines totalling
1,440hp, able to travel at 65mph, and with a disposable lift of over 27
tons. This 'super Zeppelin', although designed in 1915, was so far ahead
of contemporary British thinking that the Admiralty decided to cancel
two of the *23X* class, and to build in their place two ships similar to
L 33, to be known as *R 33* and *R 34*.[21] In June 1917 this number was
increased to five, and, in order to speed production, the work was
divided between Beardmore, Armstrong Whitworth and Vickers. Of
their kind, the ships were well constructed with deeper girders than on
earlier ships doubly braced with extra riveting. Instead of the L-
shaped channel sections—always a problem with duralumin—U-

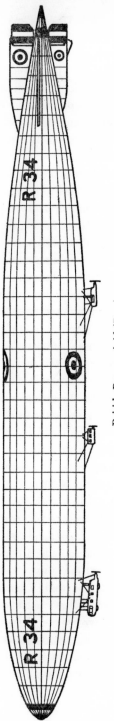

British *R* type rigid (*R 34*)

shaped sections were used; gas bags were prevented from bulging by extra wiring; the hull was of an improved semi-streamline shape; the crew had more cover and better quarters; and the control car was insulated from vibration and almost free from noise. But none of the five ships of the R 33 class was completed before the end of the war. In July 1919, however, R 34 was to be the first aircraft to make a west-to-east crossing of the Atlantic.

At the beginning of 1917 Adm Sir David Beatty, now commander-in-chief of the Grand Fleet, asked when rigid airships would be available to scout for him.[22] The Admiralty replied that they should be ready by April-May at the latest. In fact, the first rigids arrived a year later. But the tide had already turned against the rigid. The aeroplane had proved its superiority as a fighting machine, and a country fighting an all-out war could not spare the skilled labour, the supplies of aluminium, or build the vast sheds that were necessary for construction and shelter. This was even though it was pointed out that less than 350 tons of aluminium were required to complete the whole of the additional rigid airship programme, and that the necessary labour could be found by using women for the most part.

The truth was that the large airship had always been regarded by the Admiralty as a sideshow. In the spring of 1917, Capt David Norris, who had been made responsible for the speed up of airship construction, told the Fifth Sea Lord that if the Admiralty wanted rigids quickly, they would have to give them a much higher priority. That, said Norris, could only be done by one authority at the Admiralty with the power to co-ordinate airship construction, and the ability to bring pressure on slow-moving departments.[23]

The only British rigid actually to take part in an operation was R 29, which located a U-boat off Sunderland and marked its position with a smoke float; the U-boat was subsequently destroyed by surface forces. By the end of the war five rigid airships were in commission, but two were non-operational, and one was in a damaged state. Compared with the German rigids, the R 33 class was inferior, for although on paper they were supposed to have a speed of 60mph, in practice they were only able to achieve 50mph, with a range of 2,215 miles and their useful load was only 26½ tons. Yet R 34 achieved speeds of 70–80mph and was capable of flying 3,000 miles and over.

Nevertheless the few British rigids did help to train airshipmen, a number of whom assisted in the forming of the complement of the post-war ships *R 100* and *R 101*. A tradition of independence from the other services was formed and a more relaxed discipline was adopted when airborne. Although great progress was made during the war with the development of the rigid airship, the rigid's value was minimal from the operational point of view; the inflammability of hydrogen, the only gas available for lift, made the rigid useless as an offensive weapon. The Germans, for their part, never fully exploited the rigid as a scouting vehicle, although the High Seas Fleet needed the Zeppelins to safeguard it from surprise attack. Instead, the requirements for strategic bombing and the countermeasures that had to be taken against fighter aeroplanes and the anti-aircraft gun compelled developments in design which were in complete antithesis to the airship's role as a scout.

When war broke out the Royal Navy had only seven non-rigids in commission. But Adm Fisher, who had been summoned back to serve as First Sea Lord, on the outbreak of war, forward-looking officer that he was, appreciated the value of air power, particularly in relation to the threat of the submarine. In the spring of 1915, he ordered that small non-rigids should be mass produced cheaply and rapidly in order to seek out enemy U-boats. They were to have a speed of up to 50mph, be equipped with wireless, carry 160lb of bombs, and remain airborne for 8hrs or so with a full load.[24]

Fisher's order led to the construction of the first of the three classes of non-rigid airships produced during the war. The genesis of the *Sea Scout* (*SS* ship) is characteristic of British improvisation in the face of an emergency. The initial design, produced in three weeks, was the outcome of a discussion between Wing Cdr Neville Usborne, whose enthusiasm for airships had been whetted after taking part in the building of the *Mayfly*, Sqdn Ldr (later Wing Cdr) Cave-Brown-Cave, a naval engineer officer before being transferred to the Royal Naval Air Service, and Major F. M. Green, engineer in charge of design at the Royal Aircraft Factory. They devised a plan whereby the two-seater fuselage of a *BE2c* aeroplane, minus wings and tail, but with wheels intact, was to be slung underneath the envelope of the *Willows IV* of 20,000cu ft capacity. The suspension of the car, always a problem with non-rigids, was solved by the fixing of what were known as Eta patches (because they were first used on HM airship *Eta*) on the envelope. They consisted of metal D-shaped fittings round which a number of webbing bands were passed and which were spread out fanwise and solutioned to the envelope. In this way the whole weight of the car was equally distributed over the length of the envelope. The bow of the airship was stiffened by an umbrella-like structure of stiff canes covered with fabric to provide resistance against the wind. The propeller was fixed to the front of the car, while the two ballonets were kept inflated by a metal scoop placed in the slip-stream of the propeller.

The finished design came off the board of the drawing office at the naval air station at Kingsnorth, Chatham, which, under the energetic direction of Usborne, was to become the principal 'dockyard' for non-rigids. (Unhappily, Usborne was killed with another officer, while testing an airship-aeroplane combination intended to give additional range to the heavier-than-air craft). An equally important role was played by Cave-Brown-Cave, in charge of the experimental section at Kingsnorth, who became responsible for non-rigid airship design, construction, and trial until the end of the war.

The first *SS* ship never became operational as it was destroyed in an accident, fortunately without mishap to its crew of two. Meanwhile, aircraft manufacturers were asked to submit designs for larger ships of not less than 60,000cu ft capacity. Four designs emerged. One was *Willows VI*, driven by a 90hp Curtiss engine and with the envelope made of ordinary aeroplane fabric, heavily doped. This ship became the prototype of the *SS* ships. But it was not gas-tight, and the design was unsatisfactory. The second was made by Holt Thomas Airships Ltd which had taken on Willows as chief engineer and the envelope was of 70,000cu ft capacity. The car was an adapted Maurice Farman fuselage with the propeller behind, instead of in front, and there was more room for the crew than in the *BE2c*. (Willows later became a rigid airship protagonist, but ill luck, coupled with financial difficulties, pursued him until 1926 when he was killed in a captive balloon which he was using for joyrides in order to restore his finances.)

The third type was from Armstrong Whitworth. It had a Clément Bayard envelope from which was suspended the fuselage of an Armstrong Whitworth aeroplane. It was driven by a 100hp Green engine. Better in accommodation, in its performance it was inferior to the *SS* ship fitted with the *BE2c*. Finally, and the one to be chosen, came the design of Short Brothers, using the *BE2c* fuselage. The early ships were fitted with a 70hp Renault engine; several were sold to the French.

By the end of 1916 49 *SS* ships of various types had been completed. When envelope fabric ran short, Usborne trained the employees of six firms of waterproof manufacturers to cut out fabric. As the war went on efforts were made to make the *SS* ships faster with larger and more comfortable accommodation for the crew. Hence the *SS P* with a 100hp Green engine which was built in 1916. It was superseded by the *SS Zero*, which had a car shaped like a boat, holding a crew of three. Power was provided by a 70hp Rolls Royce engine with a four-bladed propeller fitted above the car. An attempt was made to fit the *SS* ship with twin engines. The so-called official design was dropped in favour of one made by the officers of Mullion airship station, in contravention of Admiralty orders, and fitted with two 90hp Curtiss engines.

It was to the *SS* ship that the name 'blimp' was affectionately given. Several explanations have been given of its origin. The correct one is that Lieut A. D. Cunningham, RN, on a tour of inspection of his *SS* ships at Capel, Kent, one Sunday morning, tapped the side of a taut airship as he stood on the edge of a trench which allowed the car and the envelope to be accommodated within the shed, and off the taut envelope came a resounding 'blimp'. The term 'blimp' later came to be applied universally to all types of non-rigid airship.

The manning of the first *SS* ships was also achieved in an atmosphere of rapid improvisation. Air Mshl Sir Victor Goddard has recalled how as a naval sub-lieutenant he volunteered for 'special and hazardous' duties. He shortly found himself travelling by train to the Admiralty, clutching an envelope containing secret instructions which were to be opened not less than 100 miles from his ship, then at Rosyth. Cutting it open, he found an inner envelope to be opened by the Third Sea Lord and none other. At the Admiralty Goddard met a number of young officers on an errand similar to his own. With difficulty they penetrated to the office of the Third Sea Lord, who, when he had glanced at the contents of the envelope, grunted that he would have nothing to do with it and waved away the crestfallen young men. Who should come on them, clustering in the corridor, but the First Sea Lord himself, obviously in ill humour; it later transpired that he had just handed in a letter of resignation to the First Lord—Winston Churchill. Glancing at the contents of the letter, he said that he was the originator. He swept the group into his office, and in a few minutes the young officers learned that they were to command the first *SS* ships, and set off on their new role fortified by a reading by the First Sea Lord of Drake's prayer.[25]

It was realised by the close of 1915, that the slow speed of the *SS* ships gave time for the German submarines to submerge. Therefore when the U-boats began to operate in force in the south-west approaches the little airships could not reach them. Hence the second main class of non-rigid—the *Coastal*. The first was an improvisation like the first *SS* ship. The envelope was taken from a trilobe *Astra Torres* and the car was made from two Avro aeroplane fuselages with the tails cut off and fastened together. Power was given by two 150hp Sunbeam engines driving a propeller at the rear. A crew of three was carried in the car. The ship could travel at a speed of 52mph. A bigger type of *Coastal* was then built with a capacity of 140,000cu ft and two engines—a 120hp Berliet forward and a 220hp Renault aft. They were later replaced by a 120hp Berliet and a 250hp Fiat. During 1917, with intensified U-boat warfare, the *Coastals* came into their own. Thirty-two were built, of which four were sold to the Russians and one to the French. Nevertheless, their vulnerability was emphasised the nearer they flew to the enemy-occupied coastline. Three *Coastals* were lost in 1916 and two were shot down in 1917, the crew of one being interned.

An improved type of *Coastal*—the *C Star*—of 210,000cu ft capacity, was constructed as a result of a demand for a convoy escort and for anti-U-boat patrols. Its envelope was also modelled on the *Astra Torres* principle. The car was covered with three-ply instead of with fabric. Eventually, the *C Stars* were superseded by the *SS Twin*, noted above.

Flying in these wartime blimps, while less perilous than fighting on the Western Front, none the less was extremely arduous. Engine trouble was frequent and the mechanic would often have to climb out from his cockpit to swing the propeller. One crew member recalls that his flying was usually carried out in very bumpy conditions, and that he was often extremely cold and hungry. 'We only took up chocolate, a 24hr ration of Horlicks malted-milk tablets and a flask of whisky or rum.'[26]

Page 119 (above) Schütte-Lanz 1 in construction, showing helical arrangement of wooden girders; (below) L 53, standard type of Zeppelin for North Sea operations, 1916

Page 120 (*above*) *L 33* brought down by anti-aircraft gunfire at Little Wigborough, Essex. Her wreckage provided valuable information for construction of the British *R 33* class; (*below*) keel and walkway of *R 24*

As there was little chance of rigids coming into service, a non-rigid substitute was designed which would be able to operate on long-distance patrols in conjunction with the fleet, making the third British class of non-rigid to be produced in the war. Known as the *North Sea* type, it was altogether a great advance on its predecessors and, in fact, compared very favourably with the contemporary Zeppelin. Its capacity was 360,000cu ft, twice the size of the *C Star*, and the trilobe envelope was much more streamlined than the *Coastal*; the car, which was closed in, and the engines (two 250hp Rolls Royce) were mounted as separate loads and slung close underneath the envelope by independent systems of rigging. They provided a maximum speed of 60mph.

The *North Sea* was the first non-rigid to have a completely enclosed car 35ft long and 6ft high. It was provided with wide windows and portholes. The front portion was devoted to control and navigation. Here sat the captain and the second pilot, navigating, maintaining height with the elevating wheel, and watching the pressure in the envelope.[27] With them was the coxswain who steered the ship with a wheel which worked the rudders. In the rear part of the ship was a wireless cabin and sleeping accommodation for a crew of ten. The engineers worked in a compartment situated between the engines carried in separate pods one on each side of the car, but accessible to the engineers who could walk to them by means of a gangway supported by wires. As the ship was capable of flying at 30mph on one engine it was possible to stop the other engine if necessary to replace a magneto or do other repairs. The air-gunner with a useless—for the purpose—Lewis gun not only acted as a look-out but also served as cook, stewing or frying food in a pot or pan heated by the exhaust gasses from the engine.

Three or four small bombs of 230lb weight were carried, depending on the amount of fuel required. In the first ship 750gal of petrol were carried in tanks fixed on top of the envelope. In later versions, the tanks were transferred from this exposed position to the interior of the ship, and were carried by independent systems of rigging.

The *North Sea* airships began to operate in April 1918 and were based at East Fortune, near North Berwick, and Longside, near Peterhead. They were required primarily for seeking out and attacking enemy submarines attempting to reach the Atlantic through the passage bounded by the east Scottish coast, on one side, and Norway on the other, and they took part in sweeps with naval submarine-hunting flotillas. Secondly, they escorted coastal convoys from the Tyne to the Orkneys.

But as they were urgently required for those duties, they were put into operation before their growing pains were over. In order to give greater efficiency, the propellers were carried on extension shafts driven by the engines through a universal coupling. After several hundred hours flying, mysterious breakdowns occurred. They were found to have been caused from torsional resonance. Due largely to Lieut-Cdr S. A. Abel, one of two outstanding brothers who later distinguished themselves as engineers with the Bristol Aeroplane Company, the extension shaft was eliminated and the propellers mounted direct upon the engine which had been changed to a Fiat type. Four ships had, however, become operational and had to be grounded until the defect had been rectified.

Full patrols usually lasted from about 12 to as many as 48hr. But frequently a ship was recalled because of rising winds. When escorting a convoy the airship would patrol across the line of advance of the ships to put down any submarine that might be getting into position to attack the convoy. In fact, very little activity by the enemy was seen, and this was, in part, due to the lack of information given to the airships. By the end of the war the *North Sea* airships had greatly increased their efficiency and, in February 1919, *NS 11*, under Maj W. K. Warneford made an endurance flight of 105hr 50min, out-flying a patrol carried out in 1918 by *NS 7* of over 100hr; this was a world record for airships until beaten by *R 34*'s transatlantic flight that July.[28] Unhappily Warneford and his crew were lost in a thunderstorm two days later on a flight from Longside to Kingsnorth.

In February 1919 the non-rigids were ordered to be deflated, with the exception of *NS 7* and *NS 8* which were kept on at East Fortune to train US naval air crews on *North Sea* airships; *NS 14* was purchased by the US navy for their airship service.

At the end of the war, there were 98 non-rigid airships in commision outside the British Isles. They had operated in the Mediterranean.[29] Their main value lay in escorting convoys, where they had the advantage over heavier-than-air craft in that they could keep station more easily. On the other hand, it was said that the airships gave a convoy's position away to a U-boat commander. Yet while they did not actually destroy any U-boats, their presence acted as a deterrent to a submarine commander, who knew that once he had been spotted surface craft would at once be called up to drop depth charges. But for fleet patrols, the non-rigids were less successful; they lacked speed, and until the advent of the *North Sea* type, range as well; they were no match in an encounter with a Zeppelin, and even less with an aeroplane.[30] Attempts were made to increase the range of non-rigids by towing them from destroyers, but those operations were not promising. Again, refuelling at sea was not an easy operation.

Unlike the British, the French used their non-rigids for overland operations during the early stages of the war.[31] The British did, though, attempt to operate, unsuccessfully, a 'spy ship' over the Western Front under cover of darkness. The French army, as noted in Chapter 2, was not enthusiastic about airships, although the French had taken the lead in the development of non- and semi-rigid airships. And considering the great volume of ground fire that could be discharged at the slow-travelling gas bags from the ground made them very vulnerable. So they had to fly at nearly 6,000ft while crossing the front line. Of the small number of airships that flew on bombing raids and reconnaissances, probably the pre-war built *Adjutant Vincenot* had the most distinguished record. Hiding her vulnerability in the darkness, she dropped her primitive bombs on bivouacs and railway junctions.

After the outbreak of war the army ordered three non-rigids of 500,000cu ft capacity. They were *Tissandier* (a Lebaudy), *Pilâtre de Rosier* (Astra Torres), *General Meusnier* (Clément Bayard). Perhaps the most striking feature about these airships was the suspension system evolved by the Zodiac Company. Strong fabric girdles were attached to both sides of the envelope from which the car was suspended. It was thus possible to rig the car close up to the hull, which was long and streamlined.

Casualties to the French army airships mounted up inexorably, though without harm to the crews. In the autumn of 1915 *Commandant Coutelle* and *Alsace* were shot down. In May 1916 *Champagne* was hit, making a forced landing. That June, the venerable *Adjutant Vincenot* was disabled by ground fire, and on 23 February 1917 *Pilâtre de Rosier* caught fire in mid-air and her crew killed by their bombs exploding when the airship struck the ground. But the French High Command had already been persuaded to withdraw all airships from the Western Front. The surviving ships were taken over by the French navy for an anti-submarine and convoy escort role in the south-western approaches, and in the Mediterranean—a task for which they were far more suited.

In place of the rather large types built at the beginning of the war, smaller, handier ships were now designed specifically for maritime warfare. About 20 airships were supplied by the Astra Torres Company, ranging from a capacity of 210,000 to 339,000cu ft. They were able to fly from 8 to 10hr. The Societé Zodiac provided the navy with 6 two-engined *ZD* scouting ships with a capacity of 222,000cu ft and 10hr endurance at full speed. Zodiac also delivered 24 two-engined *VZ* scouts, with capacities ranging from 97,000 to 109,400cu ft and with powers of endurance of 12hr at cruising speed. Their ballonets depended on a small blower for inflation.

A disadvantage of the *VZ* ships was a heavy car which increased the drag. By the Armistice in November 1918, the Zodiac Company had completed the construction of a 326,500cu ft non-rigid fitted with a 75mm cannon for submarine hunting. She was delivered to the US navy under the initials of *ZDUS*. Subsequently she was taken over by the US army and designated *RN-1*, her Renault engines being replaced by Packards. Finally, 8 *CM* class ships were built at the army airship centre at Chalais Meudon, with capacities of 176,000 to 320,000cu ft. Several *T* class ships, equipped with a medium-sized quick-firing gun mounted aft, were built for an anti-submarine role.

At the end of the war, the French navy had 16 non-rigids in commission. Plans were afoot to build a small number of rigids with a capacity of 2 million cubic feet. This was because their existing non-rigids were incapable of carrying out mid-Atlantic anti-U-boat patrols, or of escorting American convoys from the Azores to French ports.

The Italians had concentrated on the building of semi-rigids and continued to use the type throughout the war. Its strong construction was found to be admirable for bombing where height was of prime, and speed of secondary, importance. Unlike the British long-distance patrols, the flights of Italian ships needed to be of comparatively short duration only. Moreover, the low velocity of the prevailing winds in the area of operation enabled the designers to pay less attention to streamlining and fairing.[32]

Semi-rigids were also used by the Italian navy, but British observers considered that the army was more proficient than the navy in flying them. One of the army's most important objectives was the cutting of a bridge over the River Piave during the retreat from the battle of Caporreto. Their airships operated from sheds located not far behind the front, and it is surprising that the Austrian air force did not make more attacks on such obvious targets.

The *M* class, already referred to on page 46, proved to be the most reliable wartime airship. About 22 were built. With its articulated keel, the *M* ship was ideal as a bomb-carrier. (It could carry up to a ton of bombs, a load which was dropped from heights of 13,000 to 14,000ft.) Raids were usually made at night. Two *M* ships were shot down by Austrian aeroplanes, two were destroyed by anti-aircraft fire, and two were burned in their shed as a result of a rare Austrian bombing attack.

One of the *M* class was bought by the British Government as the war came to an end. Known as the *SR 1*, she was flown to England by a British crew under Capt George Meager. This flight, made from Ciampino, in north Italy, to Kingsnorth, although not as spectacular as *L 59*'s flight from Bulgaria to Africa, had a saga-like quality about it.[33] In order to give the ship additional speed, a 220hp Société Piedmonte Automobile (SPA) aeroplane engine was fitted, to complement the two Itala-Maybach airship engines. The flight took three days, landings being made at Marseilles, Lyons, and St Cyr for refuelling and gassing. At one point, south of Paris, the exhaust pipe of the aeroplane engine burned through and fell on to the petrol tanks. Two of the crew climbed out on top of the control car and pushed the blazing mass overboard. Near Rouen the ship ran into thick fog and at one point the first officer, then at the controls, was 'startled to get a very close view of a cow which was apparently about to clamber on board!' Some idea of the troubles with engines even as late as 1918 may be gained from the captain's report that were 'only five stoppages'—due to a carburettor freezing up, moisture in a magneto, defective plugs, a blown-out oilcock, and a blown-out plug.

SR 1 arrived too late to take part in any operations, but was privi-

leged to escort a section of the fleet to a position off Harwich to meet
the first batch of U-boats which had sailed from Germany to surrender.
One feature of this *M* ship was the sleeping berths which were slung
under the girder work within the envelope. On one occasion, eight
passengers were carried in addition to a crew of eight.

Four other types were built by the Italians during the war. First,
there was the *A* class of 700,000cu ft. Like the *M* ship, it was used for
bombing, but it had a short, parallel-sided body; it was driven by two
225hp engines. Only two ships were constructed, and one of them
crashed into the Adriatic. Secondly, there was the *V* class of 500,000cu
ft capacity and with a rigid internal keel. Again, only two were built.
One of them was lost over the Adriatic while on patrol. Thirdly, there
was the small *O* and *OS* class with articulated keel and a boat-shaped
car and with a capacity of 127,000cu ft. It was used for anti-submarine
patrols. One of the *O* class was sold to the USA for experimental purposes. Ten *O* ships were built altogether. Fourthly, there was the *E* or
DE class (Dirigible Exploratore) used for scouting, of which eight were
built.

Finally, although they were never used on operations in World War I,
the first non-rigids of the US navy must be considered. Before 1916 the
US army had evinced more interest in lighter-than-air flight than the
navy, but with the prospect of submarine warfare should America
become involved in a struggle, naval officers turned their attention to
developments in this field. Before America entered the war, and indeed
after, little information on airship matters had percolated into US
service circles, and a British airship officer (Lieut-Cmdr P. L. Teed)
was later to note, 'While the two countries have exactly the same
problems it appears regrettable that they should approach their objective by very different courses through ignorance of each other's
efforts.'[34] So the US non-rigids had to start from a theoretical basis.

The first airship, built on contract for the US navy by the Connecticut Company, was named the *DN 1* (Dirigible Non-Rigid 1), but it
was later called the *A Type Blimp*.[35] In its original state the car was so
heavy that the airship could not possibly have left the ground. Eventually after modifications, *DN 1* was accepted by the navy. Operating
from a floating shed, it made its first flight on 20 April 1917. It was
later damaged by faulty handling and was consequently dismantled.

Before the first flight of *DN 1* US naval designers had decided to model their second airship on the lines of the British *SS* ship. The requirement was that their ship should be able to fly at a maximum speed of 48mph for 12hr when carrying a crew of three. The prototype ship had a capacity of 77,000cu ft (later models were increased to 84,000cu ft) and a 100hp Curtiss engine. It was said to have 16hr endurance capability for patrols. As the prospects of war with Germany became more certain, on 17 February the navy ordered 16 similar ships, primarily for training purposes. This order was reported as to have come like 'a thunderbolt' to the designers, as it made prior research and development impossible. Four manufacturing firms were asked to pool their resources. The Curtiss Aeroplane and Motor Company were requested to make the cars and engines; Goodyear, Goodrich and Connecticut were to be responsible for the envelopes. Goodrich asked for, and obtained, the assistance of Juilliot, the Lebaudy designer, and two of his assistants from Paris.

Goodyear completed the first of the *B Type* non-rigid, as the design became called, in May 1917. But as no shed was available at Akron, the ship was transported to Chicago, where the envelope was inflated with 77,000cu ft of hydrogen in the Goodrich shed. Ralph H. Upson, Goodyear's airship engineer and later developer of the metalclad airship, who, until then, had only navigated free balloons, flew the ship from Chicago to Akron on the night of 29–30 May. That was a distance of about 320 miles. He had to land 10 miles from his destination because he had run out of engine oil. At the time this was a world record for a long-distance flight by a non-rigid airship.

The *B Type* non-rigids were found to be less handy than their British equivalents, though credited with greater carrying capacity and endurance. In the final months of the war the navy designed a *C Type* ship of 172,000cu ft capacity, able to fly up wind more proficiently, with increased endurance to accompany convoys longer (31hr at cruising speed) and fitted with two engines capable of producing a maximum speed of 60mph. Ten ships of this class were built. With peace restored a *C 5* carrying a crew of six, made an abortive attempt to fly the Atlantic in May 1919. After a journey of 1,200 miles from Montauk to St John's, Newfoundland, in 25hr, 50min, it was planned to make a second hop of almost the same distance to the Azores.

Gaseous fuel was to be used so as to maintain equilibrium. But the crewless ship was blown from its moorings in a gale and lost at sea. In December 1921 the naval *C 7* was the first airship of any kind to be inflated with helium.

CHAPTER 6

The Uncertain Years

'There was a public demand for haste and great optimism. Motor car accidents reached a peak, aeroplane crashes to young men flying for fun killed aviators faster than the Germans ever did . . . It seemed inevitable that a succession of airship disasters should occur.' Jerome C. Hunsaker

At the end of World War I Germany knew more about the construction of airships and how to fly them than any of the Allied countries. For those who wanted to develop airships there was a rich vein to be exploited. Just as after World War II, the Allies competed with each other to capture the rocket experts, so after World War I they schemed to obtain German airship technicians.

Ten days before the Armistice in November 1918, 11 rigids were still in commission under the flag of the German navy. Nine more, out of commission, were capable of reinflation.

Germany might be defeated, but the men of Luftschiffbau Zeppelin were by no means despondent. Count Zeppelin had died in March 1917, his dream of transatlantic flight by airship still unfulfilled. That vision had been inherited by the former critic of airships—Hugo Eckener, now business manager and in charge of public relations. Colsman, the able administrator, succeeded von Gemmingen as general manager on the death of the latter in 1924. On the technical side, Dürr was director, assisted by Dr Stahl. Wilhelm Munk headed the experimental section. Jaray was in charge of new designs, while Arnstein was responsible for calculations. It was a formidable team, one unrivalled in any other country.

Funds were not lacking as wartime payments by the German Government, and the subscription of 4 million marks made after the Echterdingen disaster, had been very beneficial to Luftschiffbau Zeppelin. Moreover, the company was closely allied to Deutsche Luftschiff Reederei (the German Airship Navigation Company) and the Maybach Motor Works, which, it has been seen, supplied the engines for airships. In addition the Friedrichshafen Aircraft Company and the Airship Shed Construction Company were also controlled by Colsman. The management of all these enterprises believed that the large rigid airship would complement the steamship as a means of long-distance travel. More important, they had the backing of German banking and shipping companies. They anticipated, initially, an airship service between the capitals of Europe. That would be followed by the opening up of a route from Spain to South America.[1]

It was to inaugurate a route from Berlin to Stockholm that the first post-war commercial airship—*Bodensee* (*LZ 120*)—was built. In designing this ship, Jaray had to conform to the ruling of the Allies that nothing with over a capacity of 1 million cubic feet was to be constructed. She had a capacity of 796,000cu ft, was 433ft in length, with a maximum diameter of 61ft. Four engines gave a total of 960hp and drove the ship at 68mph. Her gross lift was 24 tons and her useful lift was 9·3 tons. She was constructed in the 1907 shed at Friedrichshafen.

As the prototype of the post-war rigid airship *Bodensee* carried the design of *LZ 38* another stage forward. Compared with the wartime Zeppelins, which had a fineness ratio of 1 to 8, *LZ 120* had 1 to 6·5. This was achieved by omitting the usual parallel section in the middle of the ship, a feature which Jaray had always disliked.[2] Another innovation was the combined passenger and control car as part of the framework situated well forward and emerging below the hull. This layout was later copied in *LZ 126* and *Graf Zeppelin*. Jaray also made the rudders so easy to turn that the helmsman, used to making much bigger movements on the older ships, found the new ship difficult to handle. So Jaray, with Dürr's approval, made the rudders smaller and cut off the vertical balance from the vertical control surfaces with which they had been fitted in the first place. In this way he reduced the excessive effect of the rudders, though the leverage on the steering-wheel remained the same. At the same time, however, the ship was lengthened to increase her range and give her a useful lift of 11 tons.

Eckener, who disliked the steering, and who was not a technically minded man, wrongly thought that the better stability was due to the lengthening of the ship. Eckener was also opposed to the low fineness ratio, which he claimed was disregarded in subsequent Zeppelins. But this was not so; there were other reasons for a slight reversion to the old style.

Bodensee made her first ascent on 20 August 1919. By the end of the year, piloted by Hans Flemming, a wartime commander, she had made 103 flights in 98 days from Friedrichshafen to Berlin, carrying 4,050 passengers and 11,000lb of mail, and 6,000lb of other cargo. Some of the mail was flown during a period of heavy snowstorms which interrupted normal postal services. The only mishap occurred on the night of 2 November when, coming into land at Staaken, the engines gave out.[3] The car actually bumped on the ground three times, one member of an improvised landing party being killed and another injured. The ship then rose suddenly, but Flemming steered her clear of the shed. Repairs to the engines were made in mid-air by mechanics used to such events in wartime. By then snow was falling and it became impossible to land at Staaken. The ship flew in the direction of Magdeburg and force-landed safely on a blanket of dwarf fir trees. None the worse for their adventure the passengers were taken, in farm carts, to the village of Wilminstadt. *Bodensee* returned to base the following day under her own power.

Her sister ship, *Nordstern*, completed in the autumn of 1919, was also designed to carry up to 30 passengers. But she was never flown by a German crew.

On 23 June 1919 the German naval airship service, following the lead of their comrades on the sea, scuttled seven rigid airships at Nordholz and Wittmundhafen. So destroyed were *L 14*, which had been in operation since 1915, *L 41*, *L 42*, *L 52*, *L 56*, *L 63* and *L 65*. The crews walked into the sheds where the ships hung suspended with gas bags deflated, as if for a normal day's work. Rapidly loosening the fastenings from which the airships hung, the hulls, deprived of the buoyant gas bags, crashed to the ground in a mass of duralumin girders and wires.

Incensed by the subsequent flights of *Bodensee*, the Allies, on 7 February 1920, told Luftschiffbau Zeppelin that it had violated the peace treaty by manufacturing aircraft parts. Further airship flights were forbidden.

Inevitably relations between the Allied control commission and the German airship people cooled. Colsman, in a letter to Gen Masterman, the British representative on the commission, threatened that if the

Allies insisted on destroying Luftschiffbau Zeppelin's future commercial activities he would ensure that the remaining German airships were scuttled.[4] At the same time he drew attention to the advantages of Anglo-German co-operation in the building of rigid airships, and dismissed the idea that airships now had any military significance—the French still believed that German airships remained as a potential threat.

Nothing came of Colsman's appeal. The British could not contravene the peace treaty, while the Admiralty and Air Ministry argued over the control of air forces in general.

The Germans had rather more success in trying to persuade the Americans. The USA was for several years after the war the only country in the world able to afford to build large rigid airships and she was also the only country with facilities for extracting helium. Not being a signatory of the Versailles Treaty, the USA attempted to negotiate the building of an airship, as the two Zeppelins (L 65 and L 14) promised after the war had been scuttled by the German navy (see page 131). Col W. N. Hensley, of the US army, who had flown in R 34 on her return flight across the Atlantic from America, thought that the prospects for airships looked better in Germany than in England, and reached a secret agreement with Luftschiffbau Zeppelin for the construction of LZ 125. This ship was to have a capacity of 3,532,000cu ft. The transverse frames were actually completed by the end of 1919 (they were seen the following year by Col Richmond, later designer of R 101), when the US Government repudiated the arrangement.

Another venture which quickly foundered was the proposal of an American-German airship;[5] the Americans wanted the ship to be manned by their own nationals and to fly the Stars and Stripes; Colsman insisted on a German crew and a German flag. Attempts were also made by the rivals of Luftschiffbau Zeppelin—Schütte-Lanz—to woo the Americans, but again without success and, in any case, this company did not survive the early post-war years.

These clandestine comings and goings ended abruptly in the summer of 1920 when the remaining German rigids were handed over to the Allies. The French obtained the best of the L 70 class—L 72—which was renamed *Dixmude* and later was destroyed over the Mediterranean (page 164) and the army LZ 113 (soon dismantled). The British took

L 64 and *L 71*. After being flown to Britain both were later broken up as they were in a poor state of repair after two inactive years spent deflated in one of the sheds at Pulham. Nevertheless, much could be learned from their construction.

Japan was given *L 37* which was dismantled for the journey there, but the ship was never reassembled, although a shed was re-erected to house her at Kasumigaura. Belgium, promised *L 30*, was content with receiving vital parts of machinery.

The following summer, the post-war ships were disposed of: *Nordstern* was handed over to the French and renamed *Mediterranée*, while *Bodensee* went to the Italians and was renamed *Esperia*. She served in the Italian navy for nine years, and in an exercise held in 1927 was the only type of aircraft able to operate, the weather being too bad for carrier-borne aeroplanes to take off. In 1931 *Esperia* held the world's airship speed record of 82·40mph. Her career was ended by a clumsy handling party. Italy also took over *L 61* (*Italia*) (she was wrecked while making a heavy landing); and the army *LZ 120* (*Ausonia*), dismantled the same year.

Britain suffered from two handicaps in the post-war development of airships. Firstly, her rigids were based on mid-war designs and, because of vacillations of policy, low priority and lack of facilities (as described in Chapter 6), the *R 33* class did not start coming into service until the spring of 1919. Secondly, the airship was to suffer from the rivalry between the Admiralty and the recently formed Air Ministry.[6] A separate department of state to control and administer the air service had been established following the Smuts report of 1917. Although Gen Smuts had recommended that a unified air force should include lighter as well as heavier-than-air craft, the Admiralty, in February 1918, insisted that the construction and housing of airships should remain under its control, while personnel should be the responsibility of the Air Ministry. This absurd state of affairs prevailed until April 1919, when the Admiralty agreed to relinquish its claim on airships. Rigid airships were too vulnerable to attack from aeroplanes, and they required expensive bases from which to operate. In retrospect, the Admiralty should have encouraged further development of the non-rigid, which had proved so useful in the anti-submarine campaign. But it did no such thing.

The Air Ministry found control of airships something of an embarrassment.[7] Stringent economies imposed by the Government after the war led Air Mshl Sir Hugh Trenchard, chief of air staff, to give priority to the building up to strength of the home-defence aeroplane squadrons. However, in April 1920, the Air Ministry took over from Shorts the aircraft-construction shed at Cardington, and installed there the naval design staff which had hitherto been responsible for construction of the British rigids. Cardington was now designated the Royal Airship Works.

What had the Air Ministry inherited? First to come into service were R 33 and R 34. Each had a capacity of 1,960,000cu ft, a length of 643ft, a maximum diameter of 78ft, a gross lift of 59 tons, a useful lift of 31 tons (well below the latest Zeppelins, which had a useful lift of 50 tons), four engines totalling 1,250hp, and a speed of 60mph on paper but of only 50mph in practice. R 34 was shortly to acquire fame through being the first airship to make a double crossing of the Atlantic. R 33, built by Armstrong Whitworth at Barlow, Yorkshire, took on the less spectacular, but none the less important role of experimental ship for mooring trials and carrying aeroplanes, while, finally, she was used for research in connection with the design of the much larger and more streamlined R 100 and R 101. Two ships of the R 33 class were never completed. They were R 35 from Armstrong Whitworth, cancelled early in 1919, and R 37 which, after partial construction by Short, was dismantled in 1924.

The hook-on experiments by light aeroplanes involving R 33 are worth noting at this point, although they achieved nothing tangible, in contrast to American experiments made a year earlier (see page 243). The ultimate purpose of the trials was twofold—military and commercial. In the former, aeroplanes could be ferried rapidly to a threatened area; in the latter, mails or passengers in a hurry could be slipped from the airship ahead of the scheduled destination. The first experiments were made by Sqdn Ldr R. A. de H. Haigh in October 1925 when he was twice successfully released from the base of R 33 flying a DH 53. This little monoplane was fitted with a hook on the wing which was to engage with the beam of a trapeze suspended below the airship's hull.[8] Trouble was experienced with hooking-on because the engine power of the DH 53 was inadequate for the manoeuvring required.

Further experiments were made two months later, using a more powerful engine, with the result that secure contact was established between aeroplane and airship proving that 'ammunition, fuel, mails or goods could be transferred in mid-air'. In the autumn of the following year two Gloster Grebe fighters were launched by R 33, but with the breaking up of that ship in May 1928 the experiments were discontinued.

Of greater importance, however, was the development of R 36, the first British rigid to be fitted out as a passenger ship. Completed by Beardmore in the spring of 1921, she had a capacity of 2,120,000cu ft, a length of 695ft (she was thus larger than R 33), and a maximum diameter of 78ft; her engines totalled 1,620hp provided a speed of 65mph, while her useful lift before conversion to passenger ship was 32 tons. A combined control car and cabin was built under the hull with accommodation, including galley and two-bunk cabins, for 50 passengers. However, this reduced her useful lift to 16 tons, and when the possibility of her opening a route from England to Egypt was discussed, calculations revealed that only about 2 tons would be available for crew, passengers, mails and ballast.

R 36 made a number of experimental and publicity flights; on one occasion she helped to control traffic at an Ascot race meeting. On 5 April 1921 she nearly came to grief when carrying Air Ministry officials on an extended flight over south-west England. Two fins collapsed, putting out of action one of the horizontal, and one of the vertical, controls. The ship dived from 6,000 to 3,000ft, but Maj G. H. Scott, her captain, stopped all engines, ran part of the crew aft to restore equilibrium, opened up the engines again, and slowly made for Pulham, where he landed safely, thus proving that damage to an airship in mid-air did not necessarily put it in jeopardy.[9]

Not long after she met with an accident while attempting to moor to the mast at Pulham. The long wire to which she was attached swung in a loop, catching an obstacle on the ground. As a result the forward emergency ballast bags were jerked open, and the ship rose rapidly until the wire was taut. The sudden shock caused the bow to collapse. The incident led to improved mooring techniques described later. Meanwhile L 64, which was no longer operational, was rapidly dragged out of her shed in portions during the night so that R 36 could replace her as there was a gale blowing. Though she was repaired, *R 36* never flew again.

The last of the wartime designs was *R 80*. The initial fully stream-lined British airship, she was lovingly designed by Barnes Wallis for Vickers as early as 1916. She was the first ship for which he was solely responsible, and luckily for him he was given a free hand. As Vickers had only a small shed, Wallis's ship had to be smaller than *R 33*. She had a capacity of 1,250,000cu ft, a length of 535ft, a maximum diameter of 70ft, gross lift of 36·5 tons, and a useful lift of 21·5 tons. *R 80*, tech-nically so sound, had a short and unhappy career. On account of lack of skilled labour, and the uncertainty of the future of airships after the war, she was not commissioned until January 1921.

By that date the Air Ministry and the Admiralty, under the threat of stringent reductions in strength, had agreed that the airship service should temporarily be allowed to lapse. When this proposal was put before the Secretary of State for Air, Winston Churchill (as already seen, no lover of airships), he minuted 'and sooner the better!'[10] That August, the airship service was closed down, the rigids that remained being available for private commercial use. A small design staff was, however, kept in being at Cardington.

But there was still one airship at Cardington lying uncompleted. She was *R 38*. Originally designed for the Admiralty in 1919, she was to be the British answer to the Zeppelins of the *L 70* class. Intended to be the first of four similar-sized ships for naval operations, she was to combine speed with a maximum ceiling of 25,000ft—beyond the range of climbing fighters—and she would have the ability to operate for no less than 211hr (over eight days) at a stretch. She was to have a capacity of 2,724,000cu ft, a length of 696ft, a diameter of 85ft, and her six engines would give a maximum speed of 70mph; her total lift would be 78·6 tons and her useful lift 46 tons. Compared with her predecessors, she was a much bigger ship, and this entailed increasing the length of the bays from 32ft 9in to 49ft 2in, like the wartime Zeppelins, and which required the insertion of two intermediate transverse frames. A catenary wire to hold the gas bags in position was introduced and the controls were improved. The control car was much farther forward than previous ships. Altogether she was more streamlined than *R 33*, with more lift and a relatively small increase in weight, about

Page 137 (above) R 29 (23X class); note omission of external keel; (below) BE2C minus tail and wings forming car of early SS non-rigids. Blower for ballonet is fixed over propeller

Page 138 (above) Car of *SS Twin 3* non-rigid crossing East Coast after patrol; (below) *North Sea* non-rigid, the most advanced British craft of this type, leaving the ground

one-third of which was taken up by the engines. But she was still not comparable with *L 70* in regard to useful lift.

The Government's economy drive of 1919 was the main reason for the decision in October of that year to sell *R 38* on completion to the US navy. The Americans then had facilities for building only one rigid —*Shenandoah*—but they hoped to obtain a superior model than their own, and they sent over a crew (known as the Howden detachment) to be trained on a British rigid. For that purpose, *R 80* was reprieved and used by the Americans until *R 38* was ready. *R 80* was finally scrapped in 1925. The remaining ships of the *R 38* class—*R 39*, *R 40* and *R 41* —were either cancelled or their construction was abandoned.

By November 1920, after many delays, only the framework of *R 38* had been completed. There, for the time being, that ship will be left while the one triumph of the British airship service in the immediate post-war years is described.

During March 1919 an invitation by the Aero Club of America for a British airship to cross the Atlantic interrupted a squabble between the Admiralty and the Air Ministry as to which department should be responsible for a transatlantic flight.[11] (British commercial interests had been speculating on the possibility of an Atlantic airship route.) By mid-May the Admiralty had conceded that the Air Ministry should be responsible for commercial airships, and it was decided that *R 34* should make the attempt. As the US services had undertaken to provide landing facilities, it was agreed that an American naval officer should be a westbound passenger and an American army officer should fly on the return journey.

R 34 had only been completed by Beardmore on 14 March 1919. After a mishap in which her port elevator jammed, thus depressing the bow, she made a 56hr demonstration flight of 2,400 miles along the north German coast and over the Baltic between 17 and 20 June. This was intended to intimidate the Germans had they failed to accept the conditions of the peace treaty, but did not take into account the possibility that the airship could easily be shot down. On return, her captain reported that she would be unable to start her trip to America until 1 July, after her engines had been changed and other repairs carried out.

Unfortunately for the airship lobby, Alcock and Brown had flown from Newfoundland to Ireland on 14–15 June, in 15hr 57min in a

I

heavier-than-air craft (although it crashed on landing), and the airship men realised that if they did not move soon their dreams of a long-distance airship service might well come to nothing.

At 1.42 am on 2 July, *R 34*, walked out of her shed by 550 men, ascended in a drizzle from the airship base at East Fortune, on the east coast of Scotland, to start her westward flight across the Atlantic. Officially the flight was inspired by two objectives; firstly, the need to gain experience in long-distance flights, and to gain meteorological information; and, secondly, to show that the fledgling Air Ministry was at least capable, if not better, than the Admiralty in the planning and execution of airship operations.[12]

The ship was captained by Maj G. H. Scott, who had previously commanded *HMA No 4* (Parseval) and later *R 9*, and who had recently been developing a technique for mooring airships (see page 146). The passengers were Brig Gen E. M. Maitland, director of airships, Flight Lieut J. E. M. Pritchard, senior assistant to the director of instruments at Air Ministry, and the American observer, Lieut-Cdr Z. Lansdowne of the US navy (later captain of *Shenandoah*). After starting, a stowaway, a disappointed aircraftman from another ship, was discovered.

After ascent, the ship flew at 1,500ft, crossing the Scottish hills in pitch darkness. Her disposable lift included 16 tons of petrol. Out over the Atlantic three of the engines were shut down because of a following wind and the ship maintained a speed of 34mph, at which 25gal of fuel were consumed per hour. By that night *R 34* had flown over 600 miles in 17hr. Alcock and Brown had made the crossing at three times the speed at which *R 34* was flying, but they at least had the prevailing westerly wind behind them. A major problem on the second day was superheating. The temperature in the gas bags rose to 106° F while the air temperature was 40° F—a difference of no less than 66°. Scott increased height to 4,000ft to cool down the gas. At 7.10 am on 5 July they crossed the coast of Nova Scotia and came down to 800ft to avoid the wind at higher altitudes. The smell of the pine forest came up from below and Maitland, who kept a diary, noted down that the piles of stacked timber looked like bundles of asparagus.

For some time there had been anxiety as to whether their petrol supply would enable them to reach New York, and a signal was sent to the US navy asking for a destroyer to stand by and give a tow should it be necessary. That afternoon the ship was caught in a violent squall and at one moment was thrown 700ft upwards. The petrol situation became so acute that Scott prepared to make a landing at Montauk Point. Luckily, there was a following wind which helped to take the ship to her destination, Mineola, Long Island. At 9.45 am on 6 June, preceded by Pritchard who parachuted out of the airship to supervise landing operations, Scott brought his charge gently down into the hands of the landing party of soldiers and sailors. The time for the outward journey was 108hr 12min for 3,600 miles. Inwardly expressing relief—for only 140gal of petrol was left, or enough for two hours at full speed—the crew clambered out of the control car to receive the welcome of senior US officers. While at Mineola, the ship was grounded during the day for servicing and let up at night on the three-wire mooring system, described on page 145.

After nearly four days, R 34 returned to Britain, leaving shortly before midnight on 9 July; as she left a last mailbag and a case of rum were thrown in through the open window of the forward car—the rum was soon to revive the engineer and mechanics battling with refractory engines. Making for New York, R 34 rose to 1,500ft to give the skyscrapers a wide berth; at 1.0 am Times Square and Broadway were a blaze of light, and the upturned faces of the late-night crowds were clearly visible. She then turned for home. With a following wind the return journey was easier, although one of the engines in the after car broke down when accidentally declutched while running at full power. For that reason Scott decided to make for East Fortune, where the crew's families were awaiting them, instead of flying over London. But while over the Irish coast instructions were received from the Air Ministry to land at Pulham. The ship touched down there 75hr 3min after leaving Long Island. At the end only two of the five engines were running.

The ship had been seriously handicapped by being underpowered; speed was essential to avoid weather fronts and electrical storms; it was also important that the engines should run more economically using up less fuel. Total consumption of the five engines was 71·5gal per hr with full load near the ground falling to 59·5gal per hr at 5,000ft. At the cruising speed load consumption near the ground was 47gal per hr, while at 5,000ft the corresponding consumption was 39·5gal per hr. For the second time a big-end went (as it had on the Baltic flight), and the failure of the lubricating system was the reason for stopping the engines about every half-hour, which was very inconvenient, especially when inversions of temperature were experienced in the early morning and evening.

Superheating caused unexpected problems. When superheating increased, the nose of the ship dipped down at an angle of 6°; the opposite happened when the gas cooled and the tail went down by a corresponding amount. This was rectified to some extent by using petrol from aft in the morning and forward in the evening. Superheating could have been serious on the outward journey; if more than 40° of superheating had occurred at pressure height, petrol, in short supply, would have had to be jettisoned the following evening and the ship might have had to have made a forced landing before reaching Long Island.

All this was due to the fact that the British preferred to retain lifting gas as long as possible. Because as a result the nose of the airship was pitched downwards, speeds were lower and much more fuel was consumed.[13] Again, if the airship became wet and therefore heavy, it was flown up-pitched, the excess need of buoyancy being sustained by upward acting forces on the hull and tail; once more there was a severe loss of speed and increase of fuel consumption. The Germans, on the other hand, when their ship was heavy, sent part of the crew forward, and if the ship was light, sent part of the crew aft. A German ship therefore was flown with a neutral elevator and stable to get steady flight. This procedure led to high speeds and low fuel consumption, and as it was possible to carry a lot of water ballast, the crew were able to valve gas or drop ballast when required. There was, therefore, no necessity to fly with more than 2 or 3° pitch, and this still further reduced fuel consumption.

Nevertheless, the flight of R 34 was an achievement, considering the limited experience of the crew and the inherent limitations of the ship, though the reception given to the returning crew was lukewarm compared with that given to Alcock and Brown. It is of interest to compare the performance of R 34 with that of Zeppelin L 59 during her attempted flight to East Africa, during which, it will be recalled (page 108) she flew 4,220 miles in 95hr. Of course, while *L 59* was an older ship the Zeppelin design was so far ahead of the British that she had a useful lift of 49 tons whereas for *R 34* the comparative figure was but 25 tons. Moreover, *L 59* was carrying 15 tons of stores, but after landing she still had about 11 tons of petrol left, enough fuel for a further 3,700 miles.

Airships had therefore to be improved considerably before they became a commercial proposition. Ships of the *R 34* class would, for instance, have found it difficult to operate with any degree of success, and possibly safety, without intermediate stopping points—in the Azores, or in Iceland, or in Newfoundland. As saving time was the great asset of an airship very little would have been gained by *R 34* over seaborne transport. Nevertheless airships were unable to sustain such record-breaking crossings of the Atlantic as, for instance, that by *Mauretania* of five days 1 hr 49min in 1924.

It could not be denied that the rigid airship would, for some years, represent the only means by which passengers could, in safety, be carried distances of 2,000 miles or over, or at speeds of 60mph, and over. In addition to powers of endurance and relative safety, it had the advantage of size, giving comfort and convenience for passengers, and economy of operation.

A key factor, however, was the handling of rigids on the ground where the majority of accidents, barring acts of war, occurred. The end of *R 34* was a case in point. In pitch dark and driving rain in the early hours of 28 January 1921, she struck high ground (about 800ft) on Guisborough Moor, near Middlesbrough, having lost her way after being recalled from a training exercise. That was some 60 miles from Howden. She lifted clear at once, but with the forward and aft propellers broken off short. In spite of a rising wind she managed to struggle back to Howden using her two centre engines. Worse was to come. Fierce gusts made it impossible to walk her into her shed and the forward car was smashed. She was then put on the three-wire mooring system. But the bridle broke and she was beaten to the ground, smashing girders and puncturing gas bags. In a short while she was a total wreck. If she had been moored to a mast she would probably have been saved.[14]

The airship's most persistent enemy on the ground was the cross-wind. In the early days attempts were made to dissipate its effect by metal screens, but with the increasing size of rigid airships, requiring more space for manoeuvring, the screens had to be placed so far apart that they were practically useless.

Mooring was a big problem. During the war the Germans had attached the bow and other parts of their airships to trolleys running on rails. A landing party, numbering from 100 to 700 men, then walked the ship to its shed, gripping the handrails fitted to the cars. For launching, the trolleys, it was claimed, enabled ships to be taken out of their sheds in cross-winds of up to 25mph without risk of damage.[15] The other German proposal to defeating the cross-wind was the standing shed. A revolving shed was planned but that proved to be too expensive to build.

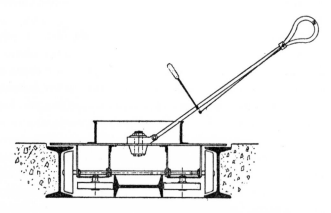

German open trench type of docking rail and trolley

The British experimented with tractors, and even with a tank, which reduced the size of the handling party. On one occasion *No 9* was towed out of her shed in a cross-wind of 30mph.[16] She was buffeted against the side of the shed, but would probably have broken away if the tractor had not been there. The main drawback was that the tractors did not move over the ground evenly. Consequently the structure of the ship's hull was severely shaken.

Mooring systems were believed to be the most satisfactory means of landing rigids and enabled airships to be operated in all weathers, which meant that they could at last run on schedule, and that only small landing parties were required. The first attempt to moor an airship was when the ill-fated *Mayfly* was attached to a floating mast. Wing Cdr Usborne devised the first mooring system on land (for non-rigids) at Farnborough in which the ship was secured to a point on the ground by two wires and steadied by guy ropes. The arrangement, though, was not strong enough for large airships. The three-wire system, mentioned in connection with the flight of *R 34* to America, was first used in 1917 when *No 9* returned from a patrol short of fuel when a strong wind was blowing. The captain decided that it would not be safe to land until the wind had abated, so *No 9* was secured by wires to three bollards situated at the apices of a triangle. From this emergency measure the three-wire mooring system was developed. The three wires were spliced to a central ring and led through blocks at the apices of the triangular base to a swivel block at the mooring point of the ship, close to the bow, and 200ft above the ground. Care had to be taken to ballast up the ship when superheating was anticipated so as to prevent the tail rising to a dangerous angle. The major drawback was that the ship had to be grounded for refuelling, gassing, ballasting and the taking on board of fresh supplies. Apart from this, a very large amount of space was taken up owing to the size of the triangular base required to keep the ship steady.

The obvious solution was a mooring mast. Again, it was Usborne who had experimented with one at Farnborough, and later at Kingsnorth, for mooring non-rigids. It had a revolving cone at the top to enable the airship to swing round with the wind. But the ship still had to land on the ground before being attached to the mast. At the same time, Masterman and Barnes Wallis were experimenting with a mast at the Vickers works at Barrow, and by 1919 a steel-lattice work tower 100ft high had been evolved, and which was constructed at Pulham. The head of the mast rotated around a vertical axis. The bows of the ship were held in a ball-and-socket system, allowing the ship to pivot up and down, but no forward-and-aft movement was possible. *R 24* with a specially strengthened bow, was moored to this mast for periods ranging from 4 to 21 and 42 days. During those tests she rode out a wind of 43mph, thus proving that a properly designed ship should be capable of riding at a mast in any winds likely to be encountered under normal conditions. The great advantage of the mast was that the ship could be serviced from it.

An attempt to fly in and moor to the mast was less successful. The ship, maintaining equilibrium, made a horizontal approach with her engines running astern; two cables were let out, one on either side of the hull and secured to the head of the mast, thus forming a 'bridle'. But the ship began to yaw badly, and it was also realised that she would be subject to changes in temperature and to gusts of wind.

Scott, who was an experienced pilot, therefore devised what became known as the vertical system of mooring. It was the reverse of the Vickers system. On approaching the mast the ship let down a single cable which was attached to a long trailing mast wire on the ground; the latter was then hauled into the masthead until the ship was about 500ft from the ground. Two side guys were then lowered from the ship's bow and attached to bollards forming a ring round the mast. All three cables were then hauled in simultaneously until the ship came in contact with a movable arm at the head of the mast. Throughout the operation, which at the most required no more than two-dozen men, the ship was not subjected to any strain. Of the two systems, the general feeling at the time was that Scott's arrangement was preferable, and it was chosen for mooring R 100 and R 101.

The Germans, on the other hand, who were also experimenting with forms of mooring in the late 1920s, preferred a short, mobile mast.[17] They objected to the high mast on the grounds that with the temperature of gas always subject to change, an airship moored on a high mast presented various risks, although they could be overcome by being constantly alert and making use of the controls. (The British solved the problem by attaching lines from the ship to artillery wheels fitted with control arms which remained vertical when the lines went slack and allowed the ship to swing freely.) Repairs were more difficult to carry out in the air than on the ground. Finally, very little could be done to counter a vertical gust of wind. The Germans therefore devised a low, or stub mast, to which the ship could be moored on landing.

The ship was moored to a high mast (about 80ft high) which ran on rails while, in addition, handling parties took hold of ropes on either side of the bow, the control car and the stern. The ship was also attached by wires to trolleys running on rails on each side of the ship. Another trolley, running on a semi-circular rail, attached to the stern, enabled the ship to ride with the wind. Normally the ship was towed straight into the shed. The principal disadvantages to this system were the downward thrust of winds causing bending moments, and the necessarily large landing parties that were required. For example, when *Graf Zeppelin* landed at Cardington, 300 men were required.

The Americans, while adopting Scott's system in the early stages of rigid airship development, eventually preferred the stub mast. They also devised the world's only shipborne mast (see page 157).

When in July 1921, a British Imperial Conference was held in London several attempts were made to interest the Dominions in the possibilities of an airship route which would link the Empire. The arguments were persuasive. Admittedly, over short routes the airship could not compete with the aeroplane. But when long-distance transport was needed the airship scored heavily with an increase in size. Although the aeroplane was able to fly faster than the airship, it was handicapped by the necessity of having to land every few hundred miles to refuel, or to transfer its load to another plane. A Vickers Vimy bomber flying from England to Australia had made twenty-eight landings for fuel and oil; an airship covering the same journey would require only two intermediate stops.[18]

The airship was also in many ways superior to the passenger steamship. The latter depended (as did the airship) on size to carry powerful engines and the large amount of fuel required to keep them going. Hence a large number of passengers had to be carried to make the service commercially viable. But while with an airship of the largest size the number of passengers and the weight of mails carried would always be small compared with the large steamship, the airship could be run profitably between destinations which would be uneconomical for linking by large liners.

Flying from England at an average speed of 70–80mph it would be possible for an airship to reach Cape Town or Karachi in 4½ to 5 days, whereas the sea journeys then took 14 and 18 days respectively. The air fares would be £100 for India and £120 for South Africa (the first-class steamer fares being approximately £65–70). The total cost (all-in, and including the base) of an airship of 3 million cubic feet capacity, carrying about 80 passengers and 2 to 3 tons of freight, was estimated to be 2s 9½d (13p) per ton mile.[19]

Several schemes were advanced. One by A. H. Ashbolt, the London agent general for Tasmania, and Sir Alan Anderson, a director of the Orient Line, and recently as controller of the Admiralty responsible for airships, was for an Imperial Air Company to which the Dominions would subscribe and Britain would supply the airships then available. Another scheme submitted by M. M. Greenhill required £4 million to finance it, with the Government providing airships and material and, in addition, an annual operating subsidy of £300,000 until the service had established itself. A sub-committee from the conference concluded that from the strategic point of view an airship service should receive serious consideration. But none of the Dominions was prepared to find the money for such a service.

In any case these schemes were Utopian until airships sufficiently large to carry a reasonable payload had been developed. So far research had been concentrated on making them fast and manoeuvrable— qualities more suitable for military than for civil purposes. These qualities characterised R 38.

The completion of R 38 was conducted in an atmosphere charged with antipathy to airships, added to which labour relations at Cardington had been poor due to the cancellation of R 37. Both British and Americans felt that the sooner R 38 was completed and taken over by the latter, the better. Cdr Lewis H. Maxfield, one of the US navy's few experienced airship officers who was in charge of the US crew, stated early in June 1921 that he was prepared to take over the new ship (known by the Americans as ZR 2 under a coding system where a Z prefix stood for all types of lighter-than-air craft, and R for rigid) after 36hr flying, in addition to the British tests, and he did not want those to be more than 50hr. Maxfield was anxious to cross the Atlantic by mid-August at the latest, because September was supposed to be a bad month for airship flying in the USA. British airship officers insisted that a minimum of 150hr flying was required before a ship and its crew could cross the North Atlantic. They felt that the Americans were novices in aerostation and required instruction. The Air Staff, however, supported Cdr Maxfield and the director of training and organisation thought that the trials need not take more than a day, as with *R 36*. It was finally agreed that the Americans should take over the ship by mid-August.[20] It was an inauspicious beginning for a ship which had not yet been equipped to cross the Atlantic and which still had teething troubles with the wiring and engines.

The acceptance trials were also intended to find out how well the new fins and control surfaces behaved. A programme was devised by J. R. Pannell of the National Physical Laboratory. The first flight of *R 38* took place on the night of 23–24 June 1921, and lasted for 7hr.[21] Travelling at just over 46mph, the controls were difficult to operate because the surfaces were overbalanced and the control cables too slack. Overbalancing of the rudders was also not uncommon in battleships. The famous warship *Dreadnought*, for instance, had involuntarily made a number of complete circles during her maiden voyage. The Germans overcame the problem in airships by gearing the impulses transmitted to the stern so that violent movements could not be made.

R 38's second flight, on 28–29 June, lasted for 6hr, and although alterations had been made, the elevators were still over-balanced, preventing the ship from flying more than 51mph. Worse trouble occurred on the third flight, made on 17–18 July, for the ship with an American rating at the helm (Maitland, in command at Howden, where the tests were taking place, had wanted an all-RAF crew until the trials were completed) began to plunge (or hunt, as it was called), diving as much as 500ft (from 2,200 to 1,700ft). Pritchard the officer in charge of airship flying trials from the Air Ministry, who was an experienced airshipman, grabbed the wheel and managed to reduce the hunting to about 100ft, but the strain on the ship was such that an intermediate transverse and a longitudinal girder snapped. The ship, running on two engines, returned at once to base. Pritchard afterwards wrote to Maitland reminding him that the ship had been lightened structurally almost to the point of danger, and also observed that they had been used to flying ships with low speed and small lift near to the ground. The Germans, on the other hand, tested their airships at heights of 7,000–10,000ft.

However, repairs were carried out, and on 23 August *R 38* ascended from Howden for her fourth, and what was to be her last, flight. The crew was Anglo-American (there were 17 Americans) with Flt Lieut

A. H. Wann, RAF, in command.* (The RAF was in charge of the ship until completion of the trials.) Maitland, Pritchard, Maxfield and Pannell with two colleagues from the NPL were also on board. A number of tests were carried out successfully. But instead of making full speed tests before landing at Pulham, the presence of low cloud made Wann decide to cruise out at sea during the night. Further experiments were carried out the following day, but the more important trials did not begin until 4.45 pm. They included a brief full speed run over Kingston-upon-Hull (a rather strange choice of location). Shortly before 5.30 pm R 38 was put through a series of rapid turns (it is said that Pannell was at the helm) which entailed swinging the rudder through a full arc of 50°. Such a manoeuvre had been performed by R 32, a much steadier ship, when the helm had been changed from hard-over-port to hard-over-starboard in 7sec. Such changes of course were more than R 38 could stand, and at 5.37 pm she broke in two, both sections falling into the Humber estuary; due to ignition of petrol the fore part was ablaze. Although passengers and crew were equipped with parachutes, 32 of them, including Campbell, the designer, perished. Wann and three of his crew, and H. Bateman, one of the team from the NPL who was in the stern taking photographs, survived.

The court of inquiry, presided over by Air Mshl Sir John Salmond, contained only two members who had real knowledge of airships—Cave-Brown-Cave (an engine expert rather than one on rigid airships), and A. W. Johns, deputy director of naval construction, who represented the Admiralty. Reporting on 5 September 1921, the court of inquiry found that the structure had failed, first at the top between frames 9 and 10, and pointed out that the design had not been examined by a competent authority before construction started. On the other hand, the court held that although work on the airship in the final stages was rushed, it did not seem to have affected the structure; and, finally, there was no reason to attribute the accident to poor weather conditions.

Following the court of inquiry, the aeronautical research committee set up an accidents investigation sub-committee to 'carry out an investi-

* According to Air Mshl Sir Victor Goddard, Wann had earlier refused to fly R 38 because of the faulty planning of the electrical circuits but would not allow anyone to take over from him.

gation of all technical details which contributed to the . . . accident to H.M. Airship *R 38*'.[22] This committee was composed of a number of distinguished engineers, including R. V. Southwell and L. Bairstow, though without experience of rigid airships. The committee met under Mervyn O'Gorman. The conclusion was that the accident had probably been caused by the structure being subjected to conditions of extreme stress which the calculations had failed to take into account. Like the court of inquiry, they did not consider that the circle of flight was the only cause of the disaster, and they maintained that the factor of safety was inadequate, especially when the ship was put through a series of rapid turning movements. According to the committee, *R 38*'s safety factor was about 1 at the time of the accident. They considered that a factor of 3 was required for such a movement, or when fully pitched, a condition of which *R 38* only gave a factor of 1, there should be a factor of 2·5. In general, the committee held that a more profound knowledge of aerodynamics would be required in future airship design. Stephen Payne, assistant to Campbell, declared that the latter pressed everybody to help him to ascertain what were the dynamic loads—without avail.

The committee's findings marked a significant turning point in British airship development and the new criteria for safety led to the building of very strong hulls, the members of which could be calculated for stresses much more accurately than before. It involved the use of full-scale models and wind-tunnel experiments, and marked a divergence from the methods of Luftschiffbau Zeppelin, which, although also taking into account the theoretical results of models and wind-tunnel tests had, due to their long experience of airship building, a much more empirical attitude. Paradoxically, the Germans had shown that it was possible to build fatter ships with a correspondingly proportionate reduction of aerodynamic bending moments and therefore much safer. But due to restrictions in the size of their only available shed they were unable to build such a large ship. What the British seemed to fail to appreciate was that increased strength meant a reduction in the useful lift, and that a good lift figure was essential if the ship was to be commercially viable.

But the findings of the accidents sub-committee were subsequently contested. J. E. Temple, of Vickers, who had worked out the bending moments for *No 9* from Eiffel's experiments as early as 1914, believed from evidence that had come to his notice that the real cause of *R 38*'s collapse was not a weakness of structure. Temple's view was that the break-up was due to the over-balancing of the rudders, so that while a change of direction was made from hard-on-port to hard-on-starboard the helm was at first quite free, as it was turned it became increasingly harder to move. Suddenly, it would go free again, and it was possible to go over to the extreme position with practically no resistance. The same sequence occurred when the helm was reversed.[23]

Temple also believed that a spring device incorporated in the cables operating the controls had failed, causing slackness, and Hunsaker, the American airship designer, to some extent corroborated this view, when, after talking to Wann, he deduced that the slackness gave a wrong impression on the control car, indicators inducing a false sense of security when the ship was diving.

On the other hand, W. Newman Alcock, by profession a marine engineer but a man who for a number of years made a close study of British airship design, submitted that the accident was caused by the weak intermediate transverse frames, and also that, due to the fact that the engine cars were placed much higher up than in previous ships, *R 38* had to pass through her own slipstream when turning.[24] This increased the external pressure over the lower part of the hull, in turn increasing the load on the lower longitudinals, and the bending moment in the lower members of the intermediate transverse frames. Severe vibration was set up at the mid- and aft-engine cars because their propeller blades passed in and out of the preceding slipstreams, setting up an alternating blow of 200lb ten times a second.

It was, of course, a grave mistake for the leading designer and key personnel to fly in the same aircraft on a test flight. Campbell's death caused a hiatus in the small Air Ministry team of airship designers, and was to have serious repercussions.

Following the *R 38* disaster, the US navy had only one airship available, a non-rigid—*C 7*. However, the construction of two rigids had been planned. Work on the first, then known as *ZR 1*, had begun at Lakehurst in 1919. *ZR 3* did not begin building until 1922. The USA was the only great power which by then still believed in the value of rigid airships as a military weapon. One reason was the Japanese navy, which was rapidly growing both in size and in efficiency. Large rigids with a radius of 5,000 miles, which could be switched from the Atlantic to the Pacific by trans-continental flight were, it was believed, admirable vehicles for scouting. Secondly, as an inducement to building airships, the USA had large deposits of helium—the existence of which in natural hydro-carbon gas had been discovered by the American Dr H. P. Cady in 1903—at her disposal, mainly in Kansas, Texas and Colorado. In October 1914, after Sir Richard Threlfall had suggested that helium might be used to inflate airships, natural gas sources were examined. Threfall correctly deduced that the Germans had no source of helium.

The US army was also interested in rigid airships—and immediately after World War I there was keen rivalry between the two services. In 1920, however, the Joint Army-Navy Board agreed that the navy should be responsible for developing rigids for military and commercial use, and the army for non- and semi-rigids.[25] At the same time, though, both services contained a number of officers who were sceptical about the value of airships. By 1921, opinion had come down in favour of heavier-than-air craft as the best form of air support at sea. But, at least, there seemed to be some sense in the navy's requirement for a long-distance scouting airship and its potentialities were reinforced by the stories currently circulating about the wartime employment of rigids by the Germans over the North Sea.

The US army operated a small number of non-rigids of about 200,000cu ft capacity from Scott Field, Illinois, where a mooring mast for rigids was also built.

In 1921 the army decided to buy a large Italian semi-rigid. This was Roma, designed by a group of engineers who ran the Stabilimento di Construzione Aeronautiche in Rome (see page 231). She was the largest semi-rigid then existing. Her cubic capacity was 1,240,000cu ft, her length 410ft, her maximum diameter 74½ft. Top speed was 68mph and she had a useful lift of 18 tons. She was equipped with the characteristic Italian box-like controls at the stern, and the hull was also fitted with vertical and horizontal stabilising fins. She had an external keel. A crew of 18 which manned her was increased to 25 for long-distance flights. Roma was shipped across the Atlantic, reassembled and inflated with hydrogen. Her Ansaldo engines were changed to the US Liberty design.[26]

On 21 February 1922, while on a test flight at Langley Field, Virginia, *Roma* went out of control, crashed into high-tension wires and exploded. Of a total of 45 on board, 11 were saved. Several theories attempted to explain the cause of the crash. One was that the controls failed; another was that an air duct leading from the scoop to the ballonet became blocked. If the ship had been flying higher, however, it would have been possible to lighten her by discharging ballast. There was one important repercussion, and that was the decision that all service airships were to be inflated with helium. All airships were also required to have jettisonable fuel tanks, and a master switch to stop the engines.

The US army's next venture with a semi-rigid was *R S1*, the first ship to be built by the newly formed Goodyear Zeppelin Corporation (see page 164) with an internal keel.[27] She had a capacity of 740,000cu ft and was 282ft long with a maximum diameter of 70ft. As she was inflated with helium, her useful lift was only 10 tons—considerably less than that of *Roma*. However, after several years, the Army decided to abandon semi-rigids in favour of non-rigids and balloons (see page 242).

Although authorised by the US Government in August 1919, due to the delays imposed by the building of a shed capable of holding two large rigids at Lakehurst, and the transport of girders built in Philadelphia to Lakehurst, *ZR 1* was not completed until the summer of 1923. She was designed by the aircraft division of the naval bureau of construction and repair. The team was under J. C. Hunsaker, the distinguished aeronautical engineer, and included Lieut Garland Fulton (see page 159), the moving spirit behind American rigids, Charles P. Burgess, originally a naval architect, and Starr Truscott, another naval architect. Hunsaker based his design on *L 49* captured by the French, but modifications for increasing the volume were suggested by Campbell. As *ZR 1* was to be inflated with helium, she had to have a greater capacity than *L 49*. Her bow was strengthened for mooring to a British-type mast. The controls were redesigned and strengthened following observations derived from wind-tunnel tests made by the National Advisory Committee for Aeronautics (NACA). After the

Page 155 (above) Bodensee, prototype of the inter-war rigid; (below) LZ 126, later named USS Los Angeles, emerging from her shed on a trial flight before crossing the Atlantic

Page 156 (*above*) R 34 alongside her sister ship, R 33, after her transatlantic flight berthed at Pulham, 13 July 1919; (*below*) USS *Shenandoah* moored to airship tender *Patoka*

R 38 disaster the design was checked by a sub-committee which compared the respective strengths of the *R 38*, *ZR 1* and *ZR 3*.

ZR 1 had a capacity of 2,115,000cu ft; she was 680ft long; her maximum diameter was 78·7ft; and she had five 300hp Packard engines giving a maximum speed of 60mph. She had a range of 2,770 miles in still air at 57mph and could carry a useful load of 33 tons. She had the distinction of being the first rigid airship to be inflated with helium.[28] The helium was extracted from natural gas at Fort Worth, Texas, and transported by rail in compressed form in steel cylinders to Lakehurst.

In November 1922 NACA expressed satisfaction with *ZR 1*'s design, but recommended that she should be thoroughly tested after completion. On 4 September 1923 she made an hour-long maiden flight. On 10 October, after a series of test flights, *ZR 1* was formally christened *Shenandoah*. Now a unit of the US navy under command of Lieut-Cdr Z. Lansdowne, she took part in a series of mooring exercises on the tower at Lakehurst, and tied up to a short mast erected in the stern of the fleet tanker, *Patoka*, the only airship tender in naval history. *Shenandoah* also took part in scouting exercises with the US fleet, but her performance was unsatisfactory. Due to bad weather she lost contact with the 'enemy', and the rainwater which she had collected made her very heavy. She was forced to return to base before the exercise was completed.

The navy intended that *Shenandoah* should fly to the North Pole, but this plan had to be abandoned when the ship, in January 1924, broke loose from her mooring mast in an exceptionally violent gust of wind. The fabric was torn away from the metal framework of the upper stabilising fin (itself 25ft high and 75ft long). Pressure from the wind on the lower fin then exerted a powerful turning movement on the ship. Unfortunately the ball bearings on which the cone holding the airship's bow depended failed so that the ship could not rotate freely. Hence there was a heavy twisting stress on the bow which gave way; the foremost gas bags were also deflated. A skeleton crew which was on board managed to bring *Shenandoah* safely back to base after several hours.

Shenandoah's most outstanding flight took place on 7 October 1924 when she made a trans-continental flight from Lakehurst to San Diego, on the west coast, mooring at several points en route. On return to base on 25 October *Shenandoah* had flown more than 9,000 miles and had been airborne for about 235hr. She did not fly again for some months, the reason being the arrival on 15 October of *Los Angeles* from Germany. As there was insufficient helium for both airships, the gas from *Shenandoah* was transferred to the new ship. In June 1925, however, *Shenandoah* again took part in fleet exercises off the Atlantic coast.

On the afternoon of 2 September *Shenandoah* took off from Lakehurst on what was known as the 'Mid-West Flight', a five- or six-day cruise over mid-west cities and state fairs in response to public demand.[29] It was also the ship's 57th flight. In the early hours of 3 September, after crossing the Alleghenies, she was flying between Cambridge and Byesville, Ohio. Course was changed to avoid a thunderstorm, but the ship made no headway and drifted steadily northwards. She now began to rise. Efforts to check her by depressing the elevators were useless and Lansdowne instructed that covers should be removed from the automatic valves in the event of going beyond pressure height. At about 3,800ft (just below pressure height) the rapid rise was checked for a few minutes, but she then continued to rise rapidly, at the same time rolling and pitching violently. Further attempts were made to valve gas and drop ballast. At about 6,200ft the ship encountered a descending current and began falling at a terrific rate. Further ballast was cast off in an attempt to check her fall. At about 3,000ft she struck another rising current and in a few moments began to rise sharply again. It must have been at this moment that the ship broke her back and rapidly began to disintegrate. First the stern section went, then the control car, with Lansdowne and five others, hurtled to the ground. Thus freed, the forward section rose and free-ballooned to safety about 12 miles away. Lieut-Cdr Charles E. Rosendahl, who had been in the control car with Lansdowne, had been instructed to climb up into the keel to supervise the slipping of fuel tanks; he now took over command of the survivors in the bow. Twenty-nine survived out of a crew of 43. Had *Shenandoah* been inflated with hydrogen, fire would probably have consumed the ship and reduced the number of survivors. Rosendahl was to prove a life-long protagonist of the airship.

The court of inquiry found that the cause of the accident was the collapse of the longitudinal girders, due to an excessive sagging moment, but it did not consider that the ship was in any way deficient in strength according to the standards of the time. The thunderstorm which was responsible for the disaster was not unusual for the time of year, though if more adequate data had been at hand, Lansdowne would have had more forewarning. The crew as a whole were exonerated from blame by the court. Yet German airships had flown through similar weather conditions and had survived. A possible means of avoiding the disaster would have been to have reduced speed, sent more crew forward, and kept the elevators neutral.

The proceedings of the court were exacerbated by the dispute over the control of the air force, then under the army. Gen William Mitchell, a fervent air-power protagonist, but completely ignorant on airships, attempted to twist the evidence in order to denigrate the navy's competence in air matters. In addition, Capt Anton Heinen, a wartime Zeppelin pilot and recently co-pilot of *Bodensee*, who had been recruited by the US navy to help train airship crews, sought to imply that the ship had run into the storm deliberately and that there were inadequacies in the gas valves. Neither of these allegations were substantiated. Undeterred, the court recommended that future rigids should be built to a smaller fineness ratio and their structure should be stronger, with the control car built into the keel. The engines should be more powerful to enable ships to out-manoeuvre storms. A special weather service for the forces was required.

The *Shenandoah* disaster did not halt the development of US rigids, for soon a Presidential board, under Dwight M. Morrow,[30] approved the building of two new rigids of $6\frac{1}{4}$ million cubic feet capacity, though this was no doubt due in large measure to the persuasive powers of Capt (later Rear-Adm) William A. Moffett, chief of the bureau of aeronautics and an officer who had unlimited faith in the value of dirigibles.* His enthusiasm was reinforced by the knowledge and capability of Cdr Garland Fulton.

The purpose of these great airships would be to operate in support of the navy on scouting, reconnaissance, and anti-submarine opera-

* But according to G. Clarke Reynold's *Carrier Admiral*, David McKay (1967), p 34, Moffett, in a conversation with the author, declared airships had no military value, but gave good publicity to the navy.

tions; for the former tasks their range would be increased by five small scouting aeroplanes carried on board and launched from below the airship. Plans for building a new ship actually existed even before the *Shenandoah* disaster and the deficiencies which the latter revealed were soon assimilated. The proposals, however, did not materialise until 1927, when the necessary funds became available, and that they did, was again largely owing to Moffett's persistence. In addition to the rigids, a small metalclad airship was to be built for experimental purposes.

Meanwhile, *LZ 126*, or *ZR 3*, as she was initially called, filled the gap.[31] This airship was to be compensation for the two Zeppelins scuttled by the Germans after the war (see page 131). She was *LZ 126* and she has been wrongly called a 'reparations ship'. Both British and French were strangely reluctant to allow the Americans to obtain the latest type of Zeppelin. But at a meeting of the Council of Allied Ambassadors in Paris on 16 December 1921 approval was given to the American appeal. The British, however, insisted that the airships must be used for civil rather than for military purposes. After much argument the Americans agreed to settle for an airship of a capacity of not more than 2½ million cubic feet, which was the smallest volume whereby an airship inflated with hydrogen could make a transatlantic flight. It would have been impossible for *LZ 126* inflated with helium to have recrossed the Atlantic, even with the advantage of the prevailing west-to-east wind.

LZ 126's keel was laid on 7 November 1922 and she was completed in August 1924. Jaray was again responsible for the design, but he was unable to pursue the innovations which distinguished the much smaller *Bodensee*. In the first place, the German Government was paying Luftschiffbau Zeppelin some 3 million gold marks for the construction and delivery of the ship, and it was therefore incumbent on the designer in those inflationary times to be as economical as possible; and, secondly, the size of the only available shed prevented the construction of a ship with a wide diameter; there was no space for the tackle and ladders required. The fineness ratio of *LZ 126* was 1 to 7·2; she was 24ft shorter but 11ft wider than *Shenandoah*. She had a capacity of 2,624,000cu ft, and was 656ft long, with a maximum width of 90·65ft. Her useful lift when inflated with hydrogen was 35 tons, but this was reduced to 27 tons when inflated with helium. Her total fixed weight was over 40 tons.

Jaray taking note of the failings of *R 38* made the new ship much more rugged. In former Zeppelins the internal keel was triangular in cross-section, the base forming the walkway. The cross-section of *LZ 126* was a 24-sided polygon, but the second side from the bottom was extended downwards; the bottom corner thus formed the apex of the walkway which was triangular in cross-section with its base at the top. A five-sided keel structure was worked into this unusual arrangement at the bottom of the ship. One advantage was that the two upper members of the keel served as main strength members, but also carried local loads such as fuel tanks, ballast bags, and so on, which were formerly carried by special box girders. The bottom centre-line girder was given extra strength, and it made a strong and rigid walkway. The transverse frames were also much stronger with diamond-shaped trusses in the sides of the polygon capable of withstanding compressive loads. There was an improved form of netting for the gas bags, similar to that of *R 38*, in which many wires were secured directly to the joints of the frames in order to relieve the longitudinals of bending loads as far as possible. An axial cable reinforced the wiring of the main frames against unequal pressure in the gas bags. Apart from the top- and bottom-centre lines, there was no distinction between the dimensions of the longitudinals as in earlier ships. The bow was strengthened in order to resist a sudden side thrust such as had torn *Shenandoah* loose from her moorings. The fins were internally braced. A gas cell was placed aft of the cruciform structure. A great deal of attention was paid to making the outer cover weatherproof and resistant to the sunlight. As many as 18 days were spent on doping and lacing one plane.

The combined passenger and control car was similar to that of the *Bodensee*, but was of improved design so that it did not detract from the aerodynamic qualities of the ship (in *Bodensee* and *Nordstern* it tended to act like a forward fin and interfered with the directional control and caused excessive rolling). Twenty passengers could be accommodated in five separate Pullman-like compartments. The quarters of the officers and crew situated along the keel were much more comfortable than hitherto. *LZ 126* was fitted with five 400hp self-reversing VL-1 May-

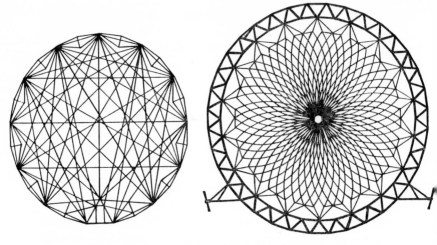

Transverse frames of *Shenandoah* (left) and *Macon* (right)

bach engines to which the propellers were coupled direct. This was a great advance on older ships as it was now possible to dispense with the enormous gearbox.

Completion of the ship was delayed in order to bring the engines to a high state of reliability. On 26 August 1924 *LZ 126* made her maiden flight—the first of five test flights over Germany. In the early morning mist of 12 October she left Friedrichshafen to assume her new nationality. She was under overall command of Eckener, known as the Führer. The watch captains were Lehmann, von Schiller and Flemming—all experienced airshipmen. For some years past, at the express wish of Count Zeppelin, airship officers had studied the winds over the Atlantic and how to make use of them. That training, which had been continued by Eckener, now paid off handsomely. After leaving the French coast at Bordeaux the ship followed the weather map. She avoided the north Atlantic, which was covered by low-pressure areas giving strong westerly winds, and made for the Azores. Here she had to fight against a strong westerly wind. The possibility of running short of fuel arose. Turning northwards, and receiving radio reports from the US navy, Eckener decided to avoid a low-pressure area south of Newfoundland. So he made for Nova Scotia. Then taking advantage of a favourable wind, course was changed towards Boston, and after passing through a belt of fog, *LZ 126* flew over New York and landed at Lakehurst on 15 October. She had flown 5,066 miles in 81hr 17min, and had consumed just over 22 tons of petrol. She still had sufficient fuel to fly to Denver, Colorado.

On 10 November *ZR 3* was formally accepted by the US navy and on 25 November 1924 was christened by Mrs Calvin Coolidge, wife of the President, by the name *Los Angeles*. This naming was not after the city, but meant literally 'angels' in order to emphasise her peaceful function.

Los Angeles had an active life of over seven years, in which she made 331 flights and was airborne for 4,181hr. In 1925 she was engaged in a scientific flight to observe an eclipse of the sun. In 1931 she established an endurance record of 625hr in which she was absent from base and was maintained at mooring masts scattered throughout the country. In operations which had a direct naval bearing, *Los Angeles* in January 1928 landed on the aircraft carrier *Saratoga* and resumed her patrol after re-fuelling. On 3 July 1929 an aeroplane hooked on to the underside of *Los Angeles* in mid-air. In the spring of 1931, when the restriction on *Los Angeles* taking part in fleet exercises was lifted, she operated in a scouting role over the Caribbean. But her performance, like that of *Shenandoah*, was disappointing, and the umpires of the exercise reckoned that in actual warfare she would have been destroyed by enemy aircraft. Her potential value as a military vehicle was thus un-substantiated, but, as a research vehicle for the development of the two new rigids, she performed an invaluable service.

Los Angeles was decommissioned on 30 June 1932, but in December 1934 she was reinflated for a series of experiments with mooring masts. In the course of these tests she stood out at the mast for as long as five months at a time. On one occasion, at an earlier date, *Los Angeles*, while moored to a mast, stood vertically on her nose. The airship's stern, as was the custom, was anchored to heavy wheels, loaded with chain, some of which may have been resting on the ground, preventing the ship from rotating around the mast. The weather was mild. A fresh, cold breeze then struck the ship on the stern, making that part temporarily over-buoyant and thus causing her to rise. However, she quickly resumed equilibrium little the worse for her experience. *Los*

Angeles was finally broken up on 24 October 1939, exactly 15 years after she had been commissioned.

There was one significant aspect to the construction of *Los Angeles*. It was known that after the airship had been completed the sheds at Friedrichshafen would be destroyed under the terms of the Versailles Treaty. Believing this to be the end of German airship construction, Luftschiffbau Zeppelin came to an agreement with the Goodyear Tire & Rubber Company, of Akron, Ohio, and this led in March 1923 to the creation of the ancillary Goodyear-Zeppelin Corporation. The new company assumed the rights to the Zeppelin patents and 12 Zeppelin engineers and calculators led by Arnstein crossed the Atlantic. Thus was established a small corpus of experienced airship builders and designers in the USA. They had not foreseen that two years later the Treaty of Locarno would enable the Zeppelin shed to be preserved. As it happened, however, they made the right choice, for they continued to design airships (of a non-rigid type) long after airship construction had ceased in Germany.

France was the third of the Allied nations which after the war decided to embark on a rigid airship programme. As noted on page 132, the French had received three rigids from Germany. But, like the British at this time, the rigid airship was regarded by the French as a symbol of German militarism. And although France had, as has been seen, pioneered the non- and semi-rigid types, she had so far displayed little interest in the rigid. However, a handful of officers, led by Cdr Jean du Plessis de Grenédan, were enthusiastic about the commercial possibilities of rigid airships.

During the war, a number of non-rigid airship flights had taken place between French North Africa and France. In 1923 it was planned that *Dixmude*, stationed at Cuers Pierrefeu, near Toulon, should test the possibilities of an airship route from France to her colonies in North and West Africa.

At the end of August 1923, *Dixmude* began a series of endurance flights with the intention of breaking existing airship records. These ended with a flight from Cuers to Dakar, 2,500 miles apart.[34] The first long-distance flight, which lasted from 29 August to 2 September, took her over the Mediterranean where she flew along the North African coast, returning to Toulon via Sardinia. It was a testing flight in the literal sense of the word, for the airship flew through a storm, but no damage was sustained, though a large amount of rainwater accumulated on the outer cover and on the cars.

On 25 September *Dixmude* flew beyond the North African coast and over the northern part of the Sahara desert. She arrived back at base, but before touching down flew on to Paris as a triumphant gesture. At the end of the flight she had covered some 5,000 miles in 118hr 41min, an endurance record for rigids that was not broken until November 1935 by *Graf Zeppelin*, as described on page 228. On 17–18 October, *Dixmude* cruised over the French heartland, passing over Lyons, Toulouse, Tours, Nantes and Bordeaux. The next trip was made over the Mediterranean from 21–24 November, while cruising with the fleet. Again the airship had to fight her way through a storm and there is reason to believe that the crew had not yet acclimatised themselves to voyages of such long duration. But du Plessis was confident and undaunted.

On 18 December 1923, *Dixmude* set off on what was to be her last flight. The intention was to make a reconnaissance to In Salah in the central Sahara. Her full complement came to 50 persons, including 10 officers as passengers. A Zeppelin of her size, intended for high-altitude flights, normally carried a crew of 25. On board was fuel for a four-day flight, and water and provisions to last for eight days. It would seem, and German opinion tends to confirm this view, that *Dixmude* was overweight for a flight of this duration, and that less reserve fuel should have been taken. However, she crossed the coast at Bizerta and made for the desert. Early on the 20th, on her return from In Salah—mail had been dropped, but no landing made—du Plessis informed base by radio that two of the crew were ill. That afternoon, he reported that on account of strong north-westerly winds he was making eastwards for the Gulf of Gabes. But a storm was imminent; du Plessis decided to skirt round it by flying up the leg of Italy. At 2.20 am the ship reported that she was reeling in her radio aerial because of a thunderstorm. *Dixmude* must have plunged into the sea off the south-west coast of Sicily about seven minutes later, if reports from the village of Sciacca of a flash and explosion out to sea are to be believed. Three days later fishermen recovered the mutilated body of du Plessis; he was the only member of the crew to be found. Some wreckage was later washed ashore.

The published verdict of the court of inquiry was that the ship had been destroyed by lightning in the storm; mechanical failure was discounted. The only criticism was that emergency landing grounds should have been prepared in the desert where the ship could have sought refuge. But German airship authorities believed, probably correctly, allowing for some prejudice in the matter, that with better leadership and study of the weather, the disaster could have been averted.[35] In particular, the ship was too heavy at the outset of the voyage; inadequate attention was paid to the necessity of erecting mooring masts in North Africa; and finally, they pointed out that it was the worst time of the year in the Mediterranean for an endurance flight of the kind. What the Germans did not know, however, was that the ship had been fitted with defective gas bags, and the accident may well have been caused by hydrogen blowing off into the electrically charged atmosphere. Like *Shenandoah* and *R 38*, the *Dixmude* disaster must, in general, be attributed to lack of experience in handling large rigid airships.

Without the drive of du Plessis, the impetus was taken out of French rigid airship operations. *Mediterranée* continued to fly spasmodically until August 1926. She was then load-tested to destruction. The Zodiac Company carried on building a small number of non-rigids which were flown by naval personnel.

In Britain and America the disasters to *R 38* and *Shenandoah* had been traumatic. In Britain airship construction had stopped and personnel dispersed. The Americans, more confident, obtained *Los Angeles*. But funds were not yet forthcoming to build airships of their own. However, a private company, Goodyear, sensibly induced a number of leading Zeppelin technicians to come to America. France quickly abandoned the rigid airship.

It was concluded, rightly or wrongly, that if airships were to be safe their individual members would have to be much stronger and more scientifically calculated; and it was assumed, perhaps too easily, that insufficient attention had been paid to aerodynamics. Hence the British formed two official bodies—the airship stressing panel, which considered methods of calculating the strains and stresses arising out of aerodynamic forces, and the airworthiness of airships panel, which recommended a number of factors of safety. The Royal Aeronautical

Society provided a valuable forum for the discussion of theoretical airship problems and instituted an annual *R 38* memorial prize essay in which the leading airship designers made important contributions. Study also began on fuels for airship engines which would have a low risk of flammability. Research to make airships stronger was also begun by the US navy.

In Germany, by which is meant Luftschiffbau Zeppelin, as other competition had ceased to exist, the order for *LZ 126* at least kept development going. But here there was some conflict of opinion whether to build fatter, more streamlined hulls, like *Bodensee*, or to retain the traditional light, cigar shape. This problem was resolved by the lack of funds and political dictates, which compelled the Germans to build on traditional lines. The problem which now faced airship designers was how to build a large ship capable of withstanding the external forces acting on the hull, and able to carry fuel and ballast for long journeys, as well as a sizeable enough complement of passengers to make a commercial service viable.

CHAPTER 7

Orthodoxy Versus Innovation

'We are witnessing the greatest adventure in constructional engineering that has happened in our life time.' R. V. Southwell, 1926

During the second half of the 1920s the British and the Americans pushed the development of the large rigid airship another stage forward. At the same time, the Locarno Treaty of 1925 allowed the Germans to begin a new airship programme with the purpose of continuing and extending the passenger service begun by DELAG before 1914.

The economic crisis of the early 1920s had put the development of the rigid airship in the doldrums. Although in Britain opinion had been lukewarm, both towards a commercial airship service and a military or naval role for rigids, by 1923–4 several factors had put the rigid in a more favourable light.[1] Firstly, the improved mooring techniques, discussed in Chapter 6, and secondly, the possibility of employing diesel engines using fuel with a very high flash point, thus allaying the bogey of fire. From the defence point of view, the role of naval scouting was, of course, paramount, but other roles for rigids, such as troop-carrying, aeroplane carriers, and aerial listening posts to give warning of hostile bombers approaching the British coast, were conceived. Now that the home-defence aeroplane squadrons had been built up to strength, the Air Staff was more favourably disposed towards airships, though the pressure tended to come from outside.

The most persistent promoter of commercial airship development in Britain at this time was Cdr Dennistoun (later Sir Dennistoun) Burney, a technically minded ex-naval officer who had invented the paravane—an anti-submarine device—during the war, and who was then Member of Parliament for Uxbridge. Burney knew nothing about airships, but had become obsessed with the idea of launching an airship service linking England to India, with a five-day flight, which later could be extended to Australia and the other Dominions.[2] Burney had associations with Vickers, which had, as already seen, considerable experience in airship building. When in March 1922 the Coalition Government announced its intention of selling the remaining rigids, Burney proposed a partnership between Vickers and Shell. Little short of £5 million was required for a fleet of six ships. Burney suggested that the British and Dominion governments should provide subsidies. However, the Government, no doubt influenced by the lack of enthusiasm of the armed services, refused to bite. But it did appoint a sub-committee of the Committee of Imperial Defence under the chairmanship of Leo Amery, Parliamentary Secretary to the Admiralty, to study the proposals and the general utility of airships.

When the Coalition fell in October 1922 no decision on airship policy had been reached.[3] In the Conservative Government that followed the Secretary of State for Air was Sir Samuel Hoare (later Lord Templewood). Hoare was an air enthusiast. In May 1923 he was advised by Trenchard to encourage a cheaper scheme proposed by Sir William Letts, managing director of A. V. Roe and Co Ltd, in conjunction with Lieut-Cdr F. L. M. Boothby, an experienced airshipman. This was to employ serviceable British airships, such as *R 33* and *R 36*, after re-engining them and converting them for commercial use, on the London–Cairo route which had been used by aeroplanes. (The route from Egypt to India had not yet been investigated.) But Roe decided to pull out on the grounds that it was unable to submit a scheme for finance which would appeal to the Government and the public at the same time. With four British airships lying idle in their sheds public enthusiasm was less than lukewarm. The air staff was more interested in keeping Cardington in being and in using *R 33* for experimental purposes.

Encouraged by Roe's lack of interest, Burney in November 1923 formed the Airship Guarantee Company. Agreement had almost been reached with the Government when there was a general election and the first-ever Labour Government took office in January 1924 under Ramsay Macdonald.[4] At once a fresh gloss formed on airship policy: not for the first time the airship was hauled into the political arena. The new Air Minister was Brig Gen Christopher Birdwood Thomson, a professional soldier who had joined the Labour Party and who, after failing on three occasions to be elected to the House of Commons, had been created a peer. Significantly he had taken for his title Cardington —the home of the Royal Airship Works. Like Burney, Thomson had become an airship enthusiast without practical knowledge of the subject.

When the new Cabinet considered the Burney scheme, Thomson pointed out to his colleagues that not only would a private firm obtain a monopoly in airship construction, but that defence requirements could not be tested satisfactorily and that, in general, there would be an inequitable division between state and private interests. Thomson proposed that the Government should, firstly, recondition R 33 and R 36, and secondly, construct a new ship of 5 million cubic feet capacity at Cardington, where R 38 had recently been completed.

The real battle was, however, being fought behind the scenes between the Admiralty and the Air Ministry, then engaged in a prolonged struggle for control of air forces. The former, its interest in airships revived, unreservedly backed the Burney scheme, especially since, if accepted, the Air Ministry design staff would be pushed out into the cold. The Air Ministry held that if the Government was prepared to finance airship development, the work should remain under Government control; the project would benefit from close contact with the National Physical Laboratory and other Government research centres; and the military and naval possibilities of airships could properly be assessed. Furthermore, it was essential that at the end of the development phase, the existing whole ground organisation such as the Cardington and Pulham stations, and the bases to be built in India and Egypt, should also be under Government control; likewise the Air Ministry should be in possession of the operational and meteorological data for the England–India route. To the charge that the Air Ministry had done little to advance airship development, the answer was that although Burney's company had put some research in hand, no results had yet been obtained.

At a meeting presided over by Air Marshal Sir Geoffrey Salmond, air member for supply and research, on 15 April 1924, the battle came to a head.[5] A decision had to be made whether to approve the Burney scheme, or whether to entrust airship development solely with the Air Ministry. The Admiralty supported the Burney scheme, because, if it was approved, the Air Ministry would relinquish control over airships, while the Air Ministry appreciated that if the Admiralty got its way the independent air service on which so much effort had been expended would be put in jeopardy. Adm C. T. M. Fuller, Third Sea Lord and controller of the navy, openly inferred that the Air Ministry was incapable of building airships and that the only successful British rigids had been designed by naval staff; and that the Air Ministry team at Cardington, consisting of the designer, Lieut-Col V. C. Richmond, hitherto associated only with non-rigids, and their consultants R. V. Southwell and A. F. Sutton Pippard, and the director of flying, Maj G. H. Scott were greatly inferior in knowledge and experience to H. B. Pratt, Barnes Wallis, J. L. Teed and J. E. Temple who had been associated with Vickers. The upshot was that Salmond angrily reported Fuller's 'immoderate language' to Lord Thomson.

The Cabinet was now persuaded by Thomson to agree that the Air Ministry should go ahead for the next three years with research on rigids and should build a new shed for a 5 million cubic feet capacity ship at Cardington; its primary purpose would be naval scouting. (This was another effort by the Admiralty to regain control over airships.) Burney, however, was to be given first refusal to develop a commercial ship for the Air Ministry, and he was also given the option to buy the ship back on successful completion of its trials.

The Labour Government fell before the final decision had been taken. Appreciating that interminable inter-service squabbles must be brought to an end, the second Baldwin administration decided to uphold the scheme of its predecessors both for a government-built airship and for a private enterprise-built ship. A final attempt by the Admiralty to force a reversion to a purely commercial scheme along the lines originally proposed by Burney did not meet with any success.

The vexed problem of which department was going to be responsible for rigid airships was finally settled by the Prime Minister on 25 February 1926 with a ruling that the Air Ministry should be solely responsible. The Admiralty never interfered again. None of its representatives ever sat on any advisory or technical board. The Government airship was built without any reference to a naval role.[6]

Meanwhile, in October 1924 a contract had been signed by the Air

Ministry with the Airship Guarantee Co for £300,000 to build a ship to be known as *R 100*, plus a capital grant of £50,000 for putting the wartime airship shed at Howden, Yorkshire, in order again.[7] The Air Ministry staff had already been working at Cardington for two months on the proposals which the aeronautical research committee had recommended since the inquiry on the *R 38* disaster. The forecast price of the Government ship (to be known as *R 101*) was £200,000, plus overhead charges, which were not disclosed. There was a later increase in the estimated cost to £275,000. In addition, there were grants, amounting in all to some £376,000, for enlarging the Cardington shed, for removing the Pulham shed to Cardington, for a mooring mast at Ismailia, and for a new airship station at Karachi. But by March 1930 the costs of *R 101* had risen to £650,000. She was, however, admittedly an experimental ship, incorporating the fruits of the latest research. *R 100*, on the other hand, being built to a fixed price could not benefit from deviations from the original design.

American airship development suffered less from inter-service rivalry than did the British, for the US army had relinquished any claim to control over rigid airships. With no large colonial empire, requiring a link with the 'mother country', there was little obvious incentive for American commercial companies to show any interest in airship routes. However, the orders for the construction of *R 100* and *R 101* enabled Moffett to obtain funds to build a ship large enough to make a double crossing of the Atlantic without refuelling, one which would have a performance comparable to the British pair. Bearing in mind the loss of *Shenandoah*, a new ship would have to be strong enough to withstand conditions two to three times as severe as those sustained by the former. It was therefore decided that the new ships would need to be of a capacity of $6\frac{1}{2}$ million cubic feet. In June 1926 two rigid airships of that capacity were authorised as part of a five-year naval aviation programme.[8]

Although funds did not become available until 1927, the time was not wasted for preliminary work on a design was pushed ahead. This was reinforced by wind-tunnel experiments on models, and by full-scale tests with *Los Angeles*. Girders and materials were also tested.

Instead of building the new ship in the US navy shed, it was decided to encourage an indigenous airship industry. Bids were called for

Page 173 (*above*) *R 100* at tower and *Graf Zeppelin* landing on visit to Cardington, April 1930. This shows the contrast in design of their respective hulls; (*below*) lounge of *R 101*, vying in comfort with ocean-going liner

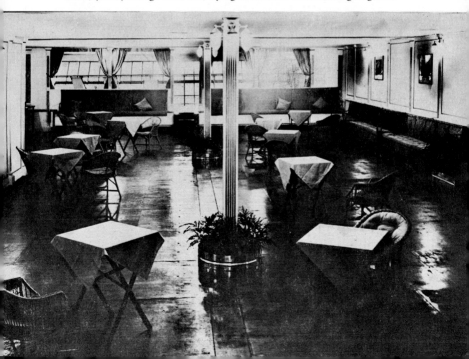

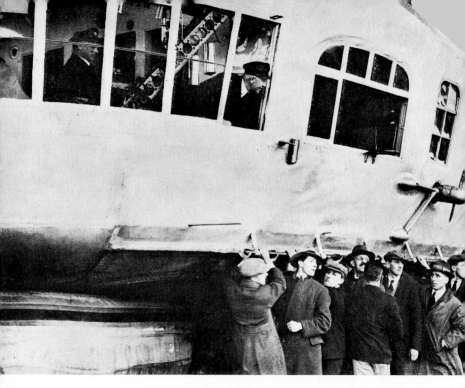

Page 174 (above) Control car of *Graf Zeppelin* about to take off from Cardington with Eckener (right) and Lehmann (left). Note landing bumper under car; (below) His Majesty's Airship *R 101*

through a competition. It was won by the Goodyear Zeppelin Corporation, even though a second chance was given to the Brown-Boveri Electric Corporation, whose New York Shipbuilding Corporation aspired to enter the airship business. Goodyear Zeppelin, had as vice-president in charge of engineering Dr Karl Arnstein, who had helped to design some seventy Zeppelins, including *Los Angeles*. In October 1928 Goodyear Zeppelin agreed to deliver the first of the two rigids to the navy within two-and-a-half years; it was promised the second ship would follow 15 months later. The navy had the option of cancelling the second ship. The first was to cost $2,450,600.

The range and general protection of these ships was increased by their ability to carry five aeroplanes within their hulls. (See page 243 for the first American experiments with 'hook-on' aircraft.) The aeroplanes were equipped with hooks on their upper wings and they were launched and retrieved aboard the airships by means of a trapeze. A decision was made of concentrating on the protective role rather than on reconnaissance, and a fighter, the Curtiss F9c–2, was chosen in preference to a long-range aeroplane. It was not until 1934 that fleet exercises proved that the rigid airship was best employed as a carrier and communication centre for a brood of aeroplanes that could act as its distant eyes. The possibility of equipping the naval airships with dive-bomber aeroplanes was put forward, but nothing came of this proposal.

In May 1926 the ruling which had prohibited the Germans from building airships of a volume exceeding 1 million cubic feet was cancelled by the Treaty of Locarno. Unaffected by the emigration of some of its staff to America, Luftschiffbau Zeppelin was geared to start building again. Eckener and Colsman resurrected the idea of a South Atlantic airship route. And again, the project was financed by public subscription. Airship captains (heroes to the Germans) stumped the country giving lectures, and with the 'Zeppelin mania' still at a high pitch, raised a total of 2·5 million marks. In fact, the total cost of a new ship was about 5·5 million marks. Fortunately, with other countries building airships, there was no question of military requirements. Therefore designers and promoters were able to concentrate on the problems raised by long-distance commercial flights.[9]

The chief requirement of the new ship was that she should be capable of operating a regular service from Friedrichshafen to Brazil carrying mail, freight and passengers. She was to have a capacity of 3,707,505cu ft and to be powered by five VL-2 engines, each with a maximum output of 530hp giving a speed of 70–80mph. She was to be the largest Zeppelin yet built, but still not large enough to be commercially viable. The initial trips were to be of an experimental nature to discover how the ship behaved under the weather conditions it was likely to encounter—line squalls in the North Atlantic; hurricanes, tropical cloud bursts, or thunderstorms on the South Atlantic route.

What sort of men were the airship designers? The team at Luftschiffbau Zeppelin combined a judicious blend of experience and enthusiasm which carried it through the difficult post-war years. Eckener was, of course, the guiding spirit, and a splendid public relations officer. Dürr, the chief designer, was in contrast a retiring man by nature. He could, though, when necessary, turn his hand to a practical job, and do it as well as a skilled craftsman. By the 1930s Albert Ehrle, in charge of general design, was considered by some to have surpassed Dürr as a designer. The other principal members of the team were Fritz Sturm (engines), Förster (stressing), Besch (ground handling), and Schirmer (wind-tunnel experiments).

The attitude of the German team to airship design is usually considered to have been an empirical one. This was not strictly true. In 1921, only three years after the war, the largest and most up-to-date wind-tunnel was completed at Friedrichshafen.[10] But while the British and the Americans had to rely on theoretical knowledge, and on experiments, to bring them to the level of achievement of the Germans, the latter had a considerable body of experience behind them, acquired painfully over the past 20 years. Finally, an important difference between the German and British design staff was that the former periodically flew as members of the crew and thus saw at first-hand how the ship behaved.

In Britain there was a fundamental cleavage between the designers of the wartime rigids, such as Pratt, Wallis and Temple, with their naval constructors' background, and those like Richmond, a designer, and Cave-Brown-Cave, an engineer, who had graduated to rigids via non-rigids. The lack of experienced airship designers made it impossible for two teams of equal ability to undertake the design of the two new experimental ships. This probably contributed to the tensions between, and the isolation in which, the two teams worked: though this aspect was exaggerated by Nevil Shute in his retrospective account of the construction of R 100 in Slide Rule. 'Nevil Shute', then endeavouring to make a mark as a novelist, was N. S. Norway, an aeronautical engineer who was chief calculator to Barnes Wallis at Howden in the design of R 100.[11]

Richmond, the leader of the Cardington design team, had been in charge of the wartime Admiralty airship dope section and thereby earned the nickname of 'Dopey'. Surviving colleagues maintain that, while he had deficiencies as an airship designer, which he admitted, he was a good organiser, he got on well with his staff (though his relations with the officers of the crew, like those of Scott and Colmore, seem to have been unhappy) and, judging from the papers he wrote, he attained a mastery of the technical side of his subject. His chief assistant was Sqdn Ldr F. M. Rope, who contributed much to the originality of the design. In charge of framework stressing was T. S. D. Collins, a naval architect. He was joined first by H. Roxbee Cox (later Lord Kings Norton) from the Imperial College of Science who became the 'calculator', who in turn was followed by J. F. (later Sir John) Baker, a structural engineer, A. F. Pugsley, who became a distinguished aeronautical engineer, and the outstanding mathematician, Hilda M. Lyon, who, like Roxbee Cox, contributed papers to the Journal of the Royal Aeronautical Society, both winning the R 38 Memorial Prize. They were a dedicated team, working long hours. Design and calculations took up two years.[12]

The directorate of airship development also employed a consultant during 1924–6. He was Paul Jaray, who, after completing the design of Bodensee and LZ 126, had left Luftschiffbau Zeppelin at his own wish. Richmond and Scott visited him at his home in Switzerland. His answers to their questions confirmed the British opinion that German airship design was based on empirical formulae rather than on first principles and mathematical analysis. His influence on R 101, apart from his belief in fat, streamlined hulls, would appear to have been slight.[13]

The staff at Cardington, first under Air Comm P. F. M. Fellowes, and subsequently under Colmore, was very isolated from the other elements of the Air Ministry situated in London. The air member for supply and research, ultimately responsible for airships, was not an airship man. 'In the RAF,' wrote T. E. Lawrence after the R *101* disaster, 'there exists a jealous and ineradicable feeling against lighter-than-air ships. We are so pinned to aircraft that we cannot hear a good word of gas bags!'[14] This feeling may have made the Cardington team more stubbornly determined that their airship must succeed, and may well have contributed to the taking of unjustified risks.

At the same time the potentialities of the rigid airship had aroused great interest in engineering circles. Southwell, an outside adviser to the Cardington team, was a firm supporter of the new airships. At the annual conference of the British Association in 1925, he expounded the advantage which size conferred on the rigid airship 'which relies for its "lift" upon its buoyancy, (and) experiences a relatively insignificant handicap in the stresses which it has to sustain . . . By doubling every dimension, we obtain an airship which will carry eight times as much load, and can withstand winds of the same strength as before.'

Meanwhile, at Howden, the wayward, but in many respects percipient, Burney appointed Wallis as his chief engineer, after Pratt had turned the job down. Wallis later achieved fame both as aeroplane designer and as inventor of wartime devices such as the bouncing bomb and the 10-ton block-buster bomb. He had served his apprenticeship in airship design under Pratt, but surpassed the latter in the design of R *80*. He was ably assisted by J. E. Temple, considered by some to be the brains at Howden, who had been his chief calculator for R *80*. As the hull took shape, with the simplest of tools, Wallis has recounted, among other stories, that of the admiral who, when confronted by the interior of the great frame which was to hold the gas bags, exclaimed, 'What a waste of space!'[15] But by the time R *100* was ready to fly, Wallis had already left Howden (on 23 December 1929 accompanied by Teed, a member of his technical staff), unable to work further with Burney, his genius attracted to the greater potentialities of heavier-than-air craft. Burney himself had become disillusioned with airships and had expressed his disappointment in R *100* in a book published in the summer of 1929.[16] His proposal for an elliptical-shaped airship designed to land on water was condemned by the aeronautical research committee.

Finally, it is worth noting that the two British teams were served by the sub-committees of the aeronautical research committee, and apart from those dealing with stress and airworthiness already mentioned, airship development was generally supervised by the airship co-ordinating sub-committee on which the so-called rival airship designers, Wallis and Richmond, sat from time to time. Moreover, Colmore, and Scott made frequent visits to Howden and were personal friends of Wallis for many years.

In the Goodyear Zeppelin Corporation, with Paul Litchfield as its leader, the German influence was naturally very strong, although Zeppelin techniques were not adhered to slavishly. In addition to *Akron* and *Macon*, Karl Arnstein designed what was to be the largest airship shed in the world. Built at Akron, it was 1,200ft long, 325ft wide and about 200ft high and had a semi-cylindrical cross-section which reduced the danger of cross-winds at the entrance. Arnstein said that he would have become a painter had he not decided to be a mathematician (before joining Luftschiffbau Zeppelin, he had been a bridge designer and had made calculations for the restoration of Strasbourg Cathedral); and something of the artist's concern with form was reflected in the airship designer's search for streamlined and functional shape.[17]

In order to understand why several of the great rigids were successful and others were not, some explanation of the major differences between the British, German and American ships, and the extent to which they had been improved upon, in comparison with their predecessors, must be given. The most important factors were weight of structure, useful load, volume, speed and range.

A rigid airship hull had to be strong yet light, capable of sustaining adequate passenger accommodation as well as the essential weight of machinery, ballast and fuel, and it had to have the minimum of parasite resistance. In order to fulfil the last condition both *R 100* and *R 101* were designed with the lowest fineness ratios of any rigid airship—1 to 5·33 for *R 100* and 1 to 5·50 for *R 101*. The nearest to approach this figure was the theoretical streamline shape—*U 721*—with a fineness ratio of 1 to 4·62 designed by the Admiralty airship department during World War I.[18]

The Germans, on the other hand, did not pursue the small fineness ratio of *Bodensee* (1 to 6·5) in the design of *LZ 126* and *Graf Zeppelin* for two reasons; one was that Dürr preferred the long cigar rather than the stubby shape; and the second, as already explained, that the only shed available at Friedrichshafen was too small to hold a larger ship. However, *Hindenburg*, the first post-war airship built for a regular commercial service, had a fineness ratio of 1 to 6·2, similar to that of *Bodensee*, and a new shed was erected specially for her.

Construction of the British and American ship was strongly influenced, it has been noted, by the accidents to *R 38* and *Shenandoah*, *R 100*, for example, had a safety factor of 4, even though the airworthiness panel laid down a factor of 2. The Germans, however, with their greater experience of design, saw no reason to depart from tradition which had proved reliable in their wartime ships, though they were not oblivious of the need for more streamlining and more space for gas capacity. Unlike the British, strength and safety standards were not imposed on them by an outside official committee.[19]

In the design of the Zeppelin hull the main considerations were always to obtain maximum lift, and, at the same time, to provide sufficient strength. The hull had evolved from those early ships built of transverse frames with 17-sided polygons to which were added intermediate frames, then to the stronger post-war 24-sided transverse frames designed, first, for *Los Angeles*, and then for *Graf Zeppelin*, described on page 176, and with provision for a much stronger keel. These transverse frames were braced by cross-wires.[20]

The drawback to the braced transverse frame was that when a gas bag deflated, the end pressure of the full gas bags on each side pressed against the bulkheads. That set up a tension in the cross-wires, with a correspondingly large compression on the stiff rim of the frame, eventually causing it to buckle. To avoid such troubles, and to provide extra strength for carrying a heavier load, *Akron*, *Macon* and *R 101* were built with frames without wire bracing which were much thicker than the conventional Zeppelin frames.[21] In *R 101*, their depth was 10ft 6in; in the American ships it was 8ft. Apart from their strength, the frames permitted the crew to climb up and make a thorough inspection of the ship, and they also provided space for fuel and ballast. The American ships were further strengthened, on account of their great capacity, by two walkways, one on each side of the hull in the

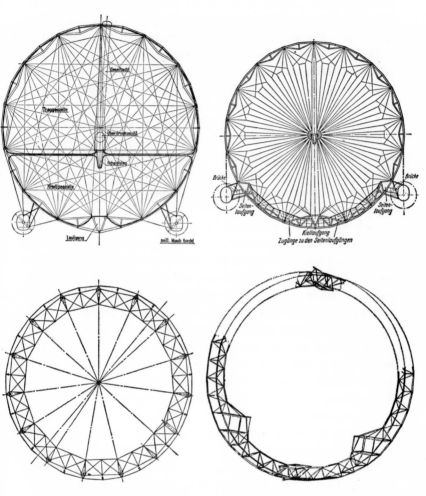

Transverse frames and bulkheads of *Graf Zeppelin* (top left), *Hindenburg*
(top right), *R 101* (bottom left) and *Akron* (bottom right)

Key:
Graf Zeppelin—*Traggaszelle:* lifting gasbag; *Gasschacht:* gas shaft; *Uberdruckventil:*
pressure valve; *Achsialsteg:* axial girder; *Kraftgaszelle:* fuel gasbag; *Laufgang:*
walkway; *seitl Masch Gondel:* engine gondola.
Hindenburg—*Brücke:* bridge; *Seitenlaufgang:* side walkway; *Keillaufgang:* keel
walkway; *Zugänge zu den Seitenlaufgängen:* entrance to side walkways

lower part of the ship, and one running along the top of the hull, in addition to the normal walkway in the keel. Unlike *R 101*, the American ships were also fitted with intermediate transverse frames.

The disadvantage of the deep unbraced transverse frame was that it took up valuable gas space, as much as 4 tons lift, and this added to the weight of the frame, although it might be quite light in design. It was also less efficient than the braced frame in resisting distorting forces such as the lift of the gas at the joints around the circumference when opposed by weights concentrated in the walkway. The Americans solved this problem by placing their weights away from the centre of the ship in the walkways described above. In fact, evaluation of all forces proved that the stresses due to lift and weight were greater than those due to a deflated gas bag.

Both the Germans and Wallis, who had originally intended an un-braced transverse frame for *R 100*, therefore decided to opt for the conventional type of transverse frame; and even the larger *Hindenburg* and *LZ 130* were built with braced frames. The latter were 36-sided polygons and were fitted with supplementary stiffening frames to which the bracing wires were fixed. These wires ran out radially from the 'spine' of the ship which served as a fixed central point, but were not deflected by the supplementary frame before reaching the main frame, so that only the alternate corners of the latter were in tension. In contrast with *R 101* the transverse frame of *R 100* was only 2ft 6in deep, though her longitudinal girders were bigger. Dürr, while ad-miring the unbraced frame of *R 101*, thought that it was too heavy and that it would reduce payload and fuel, thus restricting the range of the ship.[22]

The British and American ships were built with the aim that strength of structure was paramount. In order to estimate their forces accurately, their main members were reduced to the minimum. In *R 101*, there were only 15 longitudinal girders—though they were reinforced by 15 intermediate girders—the main purpose of which was to give additional support to the cover; and to perform this function they could be jacked out to provide extra tension when the cover was slack. *R 100* had 16 longitudinals, but no intermediate members, thus giving the ship a concave appearance; this was all the more pronounced because a system of wiring pulled the cover inwards in a definite curve in order to give it tension. *Macon* and *Akron* had 36 longitudinals, which gave adequate support to the outer cover.[23] Some compensation for the weight of the structure of the American ships was found in the much larger gas bags than those in *Los Angeles* and *Shenandoah*; and there was also additional space for ballast which could be dropped in an emergency; greater engine power (*Macon* had eight 560hp engines as opposed to the five 490hp engines of *Los Angeles*) provided more dynamic lift to overcome an excess of weight over buoyancy.

The Germans, on the other hand, were determined to keep their ships as light as possible without, at the same time, sacrificing a high standard of safety; a safety factor of 2 in the girders; for the controls, bow, engine cars and suspension a higher factor of safety applied. Their skill in handling and navigation also compensated for the light construction of the framework. All the girders were built up from triangular channel sections with stamped lattice bracing. Most of this work had to be done with riveting in situ. The sharp edges of the bracing pieces were always arranged so that they did not face the fabric of gas bags and outer cover. *Graf Zeppelin* had 25 longitudinals, which provided the cover with ample support. In the German ships the gas bags pressed against the longitudinals without harm, protected by cord netting of ramie fibre preventing chafing and unusual stresses, whereas *R 100* and *R 101* suffered from chafing of the gas bags.

Graf Zeppelin had an important new design feature—the axial girder which ran through the ship just below the centre of the hull. This was a development of the catenary, or axial, wire cable connected to the wiring of each transverse frame, and which took the strain off the bulkhead when there was difference of pressure in adjacent gas bags.[24] The axial girder also carried a catwalk, enabling the crew to inspect the 17 gas bags, of which 12 were designed to hold fuel gas. This catwalk was reached by three ladders from the walkway which ran along the keel, and which additionally provided accommodation for the crew and additional strength for the hull. Wallis also designed an axial girder for *R 100*, but it was not big enough to carry a catwalk.

In designing *Hindenburg* Dürr was faced with the problem of accommodating 20 to 30 more passengers and in *LZ 130* of increasing the size in order for the ship to be inflated with helium, for which, since the destruction of *R 101* by fire, there had been an increasing popular

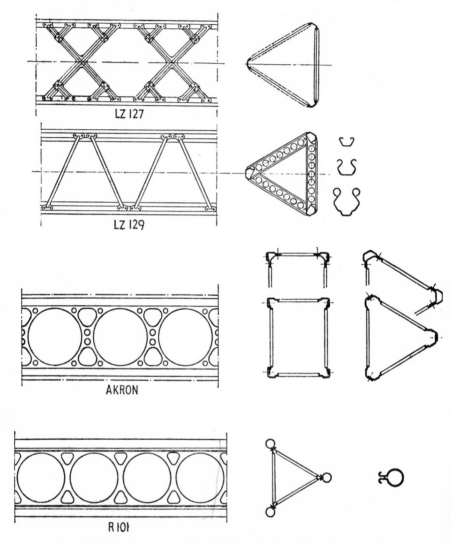

Longitudinal and transverse frame girders showing sides and cross-sections
of *Graf Zeppelin, Hindenburg, Akron* and *R 101*

clamour. Neither Dürr nor the crew wanted to inflate their ship with helium; the former on account of having to increase size, and hence weight, while the latter, after operating with fuel gas in *Graf Zeppelin*, were reluctant to change over to a new system.[25] In fact, apart from certain modifications to the girder channels and bracings, no radical changes proved to be necessary for the bigger ships, although *Hindenburg* was fitted with corner booms of an omega section instead of the usual open section, and they were riveted on two sides to the longitudinals. An axial girder and catwalk were again fitted in *Hindenburg*, intended to be inflated with a combination of hydrogen and helium (double gas bags were installed for this reason), and in *LZ 130*, which was to be inflated solely with helium. In the event, helium was unobtainable for both ships, so that the problem of a heavier lifting gas never had to be faced.

The British made up for their lack of experience in design by displaying considerable ingenuity in facilitating the process of construction. The triangular girders of *R 100* with tubular booms were made entirely of duralumin. Wallis found it impossible to make tubes of adequate diameter which at the same time were sufficiently thin.[26] As the tubes were expensive, Wallis bought the cheaper duralumin strips and made them up into tubes with a special machine. The strip was wound into a helical tube and riveted along the continuous overlap, the bracing piece building the tubes up into girders being stamped out of strips of the same material.

To enable rapid production, the girders of *R 100* were built of only 11 different parts and they did not include variations in thickness which could be obtained by ordering the material in different gauges. A standard joint was used, and although there were 15 different types of joint in the whole structure, all were made from the same parts on a production basis; the only variation was in the joint joining the transverse frame to the longitudinal girder. This uniformity made calculation of the eventual weight much easier.

J. D. North, technical head of Boulton & Paul, the Norwich aeroplane manufacturers, who was a fine engineer, was made responsible for design and construction of the *R 101* girders. Like those in *R 100*, they were triangular-shaped with tubular booms; they also incorporated rustless steel in certain parts in addition to duralumin strip.[27]

Again like *R 100*, there was a simple standard joint, and the ship was assembled as though from the members of a giant Meccano set. Instead of riveting, the finished members were assembled merely by inserting nuts and bolts, though these had the disadvantage of being able to chafe and injure the gas bags.

The wide spacing between the longitudinals of the British ships compared with the Zeppelins caused a great deal of trouble, particularly in *R 100*, in regard to the outer cover. The British also made the mistake of doping their outer covers, in the hope of saving weight, before placing them in position, which was contrary to Zeppelin practice and they deteriorated very rapidly. The outer covers of *Los Angeles* and *Graf Zeppelin*, on the other hand, had good lasting qualities, probably because the dope was applied with much more care. In fact, the cover of *Graf Zeppelin* lasted for five years, only the top part having to be renewed in 1935, yet the cover was subjected to tropical heat as well as to heavy rain and high winds.

A major problem in airship design was to find the best way of transmitting the lift of the gas bags to the joints of the hull structure. In the Zeppelins the gas bags, though enclosed by cord netting, pressed against the slender longitudinals already under strain from bending moments imposed on the entire hull. British airship designers, therefore, were attracted to the idea of an entirely separate system of support for the gas bags attached to the structure only at its joints. The problem was solved in two quite different ways.

Rope devised for *R 101* an ingenious system like a pair of parachutes placed back to back, sharing a common crown which was on the same alignment as the transverse frame when there was no pressure difference.[28] The edges of the parachutes consisted of catenary chains to which the wires running over the surface of the bag were anchored. The ends of these chains were in turn anchored by bridles to the main joints. Owing to the lift of the gas, attachments from the bulkhead to the lower part of the ring were required. The vertical thrust of the forces in these attachments transmitted the lift of the gas within the parachute-like ends of the bags. The lift thus applied to the lower portions of the rings was about 50 per cent of the total. The remainder of the lift was transmitted to the frames through circumferential wires, whose tensions were tapped off by means of bridles attached to the joints in each main panel. Although this type of bulkhead allowed a considerable amount of displacement of buoyancy, it varied progressively with the pitch from zero in such a way that there was always a positive righting movement. Thus it was supposed to avoid the surging which occurred in the case of an ordinary slack bulkhead. Unfortunately *R 101*'s lack of lift made it necessary to modify the gas bag wiring and extra surging was experienced.

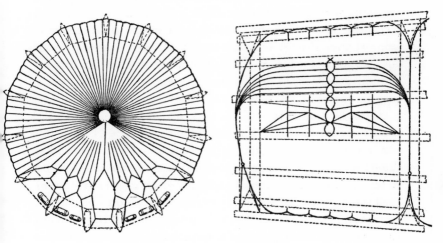

Gas bag wiring system of *R 101*

Wallis considered that the conventional Zeppelin wiring system, in which the wires were stretched hand taut between the longitudinals, was very difficult to adjust; any slackness or irregularity of tension seriously modified the load and consequently modified the lateral forces applied to the longitudinals. In a ship as big as *R 100* there could be no ambiguity in loading. 'The simplest and most obvious way,' wrote Wallis, 'of getting over the difficulty of having to attach wires to the longitudinals is to run them straight from transverse frame to transverse frame.'[29] This meant loss of gas amounting to 4 or 5 tons in a ship the size of *R 100*. Wallis therefore adapted the 'parallel helix' system of mesh wiring, whereby the pitch of the helical wires could be varied in such a way that the resultant shape of the gas bag, seen in cross section, could be adapted to practically any shape desired.[30] The

187

great advantage of this system was that no lateral loads were placed on the longitudinal girders, and that, whatever the adjustment of the gas bag might be, no variation in the magnitude or direction of these forces could occur. The application of this idea propounded many years earlier by Lord Rayleigh foreshadowed Wallis's celebrated geodetic system for the framework of heavier-than-air craft applied later with much success in the Wellesley and Wellington bomber aeroplanes. It will be recalled that the longitudinal girders of the first Schütte-Lanz airship was arranged in a helical system.

Diagonal wires attached to each alternate corner of the transverse frame were installed in *Akron* and *Macon*. In the event of a deflated bag, this netting kept the adjacent gas bags from excessive bulging. Furthermore, it prevented excessive surging when gas bags were equally inflated and surging became likely to cause instability.

The question of the control of the pressure difference between the interior and exterior of the gas bags and of the outer cover of the airship was one of great importance (the failure to find a solution had, as already seen, contributed to the destruction of *Shenandoah*). The gas valves of *R 101*, also designed by Rope, were designed to give a very rapid automatic discharge of gas, so that a rise of 4,000ft a minute was provided for in the event of the ship being rapidly carried upwards in a thunderstorm.[31] These valves were fitted on each side of the hull at the level of the axis of the ship and could be reached easily by riggers passing along a girder. There were no gas valves at the top of the bags, as in the Zeppelin arrangement, because it was thought that the leakage of valves in this position would be more difficult to bring under control. The opening of the valves was controlled by a simple bellows-pressure arrangement, which could be adjusted so that action was either automatic or from a control position. Unfortunately, if the ship was rolling about her centre of gravity (29ft below the axis), lateral acceleration occurred at the position of the relief valves, causing the valves to open slightly when the ship was rolling heavily. There was no time to remedy the defect before the last flight of *R 101*.

The gas bags and gas valves of *R 100* were made by Luftschiffbau Zeppelin, and the system followed that installed in *Graf Zeppelin*. The valves at the top of the bags discharged through cowls in the outer cover; the automatic valves at the bottom of the bags discharged through special trunks between the bags and out through the outer cover. No gas was released into the space inside the outer cover.

Airship engines were intended to be reliable and able to run for long periods without maintenance, but they also added considerably to the dead weight. The Maybach engine was the only really satisfactory airship engine. Yet with an inadequate number of engines, the breakdown of one would have a serious effect on the speed, indeed safety, of the airship. Large single units were likely to cause structural difficulties and compel the use of very large propellers. On the other hand, an airship equipped with too many engines increased the drag, while the number of the crew might have to be increased unnecessarily. In the 1930s the best size for an airship engine was about 800–1,000hp. Propeller speeds of 800–1,200rpm could be handled without recourse to excessively large blades. There also had to be a reliable and quick way of reversing the propeller thrust. This was done by reversing the direction of engine rotation; by the use of gears; or by swivelling propellers. Finally, low fuel consumption was necessary.

With this last-named condition in mind, and to satisfy the requirement of keeping the ship in equilibrium during the voyage, H. R. Ricardo, the distinguished engineer, on the instructions of Burney, began to develop a single sleeve-valve engine operating on a mixture of kerosene and hydrogen. It was intended that two out of the six engines of *R 100* were to burn hydrogen. The problem was how to prevent the combustion of a mixture of air and hydrogen in the pipeline between the gas bags and the engine.[32] As a satisfactory flame trap could not be evolved in time, Burney decided to install in *R 100* six ex-RAF reconditioned 650hp Rolls Royce Condor III engines running on petrol. They were fitted tandemwise in three cars, two of them amidships, with the other aft on the centre line. The after engine in each car was reversible. In the early test flights these engines gave trouble, and the water jacket of one cracked.

The development of *R 101*'s engines, however, led to far greater misfortune. Five Beardmore Tornado 585hp diesel engines (modified from a design originally intended for use on the Canadian railways) were fitted.[33] But only four could provide forward propulsion, for the reason that the steel variable-pitch propellers originally fitted developed such severe torsional resonance that they were temporarily replaced with wooden propellers for the home trials. The fifth engine was fitted with a propeller of negative pitch to provide reversing power when the ship was mooring. The diesel engines' fuel would not only be economic in consumption, but its high flashpoint would minimise the fire risk. From June 1924, when the prototype engines should have been ready, until 1929, one mishap followed another. Shaft resonance, or vibration, cracked an aluminium crankshaft which had to be replaced by a steel one. That increased the overall weight. The substitution of metal by wooden propellers reduced the number of revolutions per minute. Big-end bearings failed; cylinder-heads cracked, due to bad design; tappets and valves failed; there was inadequate oil cooling; and when the engines were started violent shocks occurred.

While it was possible to deal with all these faults (and faults are commonplace in aeronautical research and development) the Cardington team felt that the Tornados should be replaced by Condors before it was too late. This was also the opinion of members of the aeronautical research committee which came to inspect the engines. Two distinguished engineers, Sir John Petavel and Prof Mevill Jones, warned Fellowes, then director of airship development, and Cave-Brown-Cave, director of research, that experimental engines should not be used in the early stages, however desirable a diesel engine might be; while the decision to waste one engine for the purpose of reversing was 'fantastic'.[34] But the air member for supply and research had already decided against the use of petrol engines, presumably on the grounds that they were unsuitable for use in the tropics.

Cave-Brown-Cave wrote to Mevill Jones that the only way, in his opinion, of avoiding the loss of an engine for astern running was to provide astern gear boxes. But that modification would take even longer than alternative engine units to make and instal. He thought that Tornado engines should be used for the home trials, and if they failed to give R 101 speeds of more than 60mph, the Condors should be fitted to prove the airship at high speed. The two reversible Tornado engines were installed in August and September 1930, the second only a week before the final flight.

Across the Atlantic Goodyear Zeppelin had trouble with petrol engines for *Akron* and *Macon*. They had planned for a lightweight, low-

Page 191 (above) USS *Akron* at short mooring mast; (below) *Hindenburg* leaving Friedrichshafen

Page 192 (above) *ZPG 3W* largest non-rigid built to date. Designed for US Navy airborne early warning service. Radome can be seen on top of envelope; (below) *ZMC-2* Metalclad

fuel-consumption, reversible engine, modelled on the Packard six-cylinder-in-line engine. But it could not be produced in time. Instead, each ship was fitted with eight VL-2 reversible Maybach 560hp engines, similar to those of *Graf Zeppelin*. They weighed only 4·5lb per hp, compared with 8lb per hp of the British diesels. As because of helium there was no fire danger, the engines were installed inside the hull; an outrigger for the support of the rigid transmission shafts, bevel gears and propeller was arranged outside the hull. The swivelling propellers could be used for forward and reversing motion, and for vertical thrust by tilting their axes by 90°. As the after propellers had to work in the slipstream, they were changed for three-blade propellers of adjustable pitch.

Opinion was tending in the mid-30s, however, to an improved form of diesel engine as being the best form of propulsion for the airship. After long trials *Hindenburg* and *LZ 130* were fitted with Daimler-Benz diesels generating 1,000hp each. They weighed just over $3\frac{1}{2}$lb per hp and so were much lighter than the British Tornados.[35] The reason for this was that crankcases were made of aluminium as opposed to steel, and, being carried in light duralumin cradles, there was hardly any vibration. On her first flight to America, the engines of *Hindenburg* were started up in 4sec, and, according to one of the Cardington staff who was watching, 'ran beautifully straight away'.[36] Two small diesel engines were installed in the hull on opposite sides of the keel catwalk. Their function was to drive generators supplying current for lighting, heating, cooking and air conditioning. Water for 12 passenger cabins and for the cooking range was heated by using the cooling water from the engines.

Ways of keeping airships in equilibrium in order to compensate for the consumption of fuel were essential for long-distance flights, but particularly for helium-inflated airships as helium was expensive and still not easy to obtain. In her early flights the *Graf Zeppelin* carried an apparatus which condensed the vapour of the engine-exhaust gas into water. But it was heavy, and it increased the drag.[37] Goodyear Zeppelin improved on this system by locating the condensers for *Akron* and *Macon* on the surface of the hull, thereby eliminating drag and the equivalent load of extra fuel required to overcome it.

Luftschiffbau Zeppelin, meanwhile, began to use fuel gas (otherwise

M

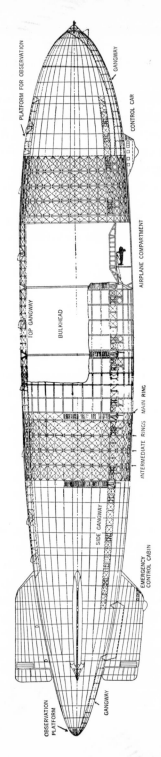

USS *Akron*

known as blaugas after its inventor Dr Hermann Blau). It was a mixture of hydrocarbons (made by cracking petroleum) and, compared with air, had a specific gravity of about 1·2. It was stored in fabric gas bags and was, therefore, always at atmospheric pressure. As blaugas was consumed, being really the same density as air, there was no reduction in the load of the ship because of the consumption of fuel. It had two disadvantages. Firstly, having a slightly greater density than air, there was a danger of leakage from the gas bags which could easily be the cause of a fire. On the other hand, it had a distinctive smell of bitter almonds, making it quickly identifiable. Secondly, if all the fuel was in the form of gas, in the event of an emergency it could not be used as ballast.[38] The ship was therefore equipped with 21 aluminium tanks of benzine which could be dropped in the event of gas bags deflating. The shift from blaugas to benzine was quite easy as the Maybach engines were equipped with a simple mixing valve which readily permitted the change.

As *Hindenburg* and *LZ 130* were fitted with diesels, the Germans reverted to a water-recovery apparatus. Again, drag ensued because the propellers sucked in air from the recovery system. In *LZ 130* this was solved by putting the propeller at the back of the engine, converting it from a tractor into a pusher.

The elevators and rudders were probably the weakest elements in the rigid airships of the 1930s; the rudders, in particular, were subject to strain during turning movements, while several accidents occurred when fabric was torn off a fin during bad weather. The most original arrangement of elevators and rudders was that of *R 101*.[39] They were not only much shorter than was usual, but also dispensed with the normal king posts and cables supporting them which added to the drag of the ship. The rudder fixed on a hinge at the extremity of the vertical fin could be operated by a servo mechanism located in the bottom fin, but after the initial trial flights this was discarded, thereby adding about ½ ton to the useful lift. However, investigation by Luftschiffbau Zeppelin on models after the *R 101* disaster revealed that the fins were prone to stalling and quickly became unable to provide the lever-like action required to extricate the ship from a steep dive.[40]

Hindenburg and *LZ 130* also had servo motors to operate the controls, but they also could be worked manually by cable. In the American ships there was a reserve control cabin situated in the lower fin. After the fatal accident to *Macon*, which was purported to have been due partly to the weakness of a fin, special care was taken to reinforce the fin structure of *Hindenburg*.[41] Care was also taken, as in all German ships, to eliminate drag in the fins as far as possible.

The air traveller of today, squeezed into a narrow seat, and with his meals deposited on a small tray in front of him, would look with envy at the spacious accommodation provided in the airships of the 1930s. The comfort provided by the British ships and the *Hindenburg* lay somewhere between an ocean liner and the Pullman train. In *R 101* two decks were slung within the hull, taking up two bays under the centre of buoyancy. On the upper deck was a lounge, a dining-room for 50 people and 26 two-berth cabins. The walls of the state rooms consisted of light duralumin girder work, across which fabric was stretched. A façade of balsa wood prevented the passengers coming into contact with the fabric of the envelope.[42] *R 100* was built to hold as many as 100 passengers and a crew of 40. The so-called 'coach' was divided into three decks, the lowest forming the crew's quarters, while the two upper decks were devoted to the passengers. A double wall enclosed the living quarters, and was generously ventilated to eliminate the possibility of any inflammable gas or vapour from penetrating within. Compared with *R 101*, the passengers enjoyed a better view, for a promenade well provided with windows ran down each side of the ship. Electricity generated in one of the engine cars provided the power for the kitchen, heating and lighting.[43]

The *Graf Zeppelin*, limited by size, could only take 20 passengers in 10 double cabins. There was a crew of 40. In the centre of the coach there was a small but comfortable lounge and dining-room. Beyond, going forward, were the kitchen and radio cabin; farther forward was the control room.[44] In *Hindenburg* and *LZ 130*, however, much more attention was paid to space and decor, involving in the former an extra 10 to 12 tons of weight.[45] In *Hindenburg*, two decks were built into the structure of the hull, which was specially stiffened for this purpose. The lower deck contained the kitchen, a mess for the officers, and a smoking-room (an innovation for Zeppelins) with walls of golden yellow leather for safety. On the upper deck was the dining-room and bar; the lounge (even equipped with an aluminium Bluthner baby grand piano!), and a writing and reading-room. Like *R 100*, promenades ran down the sides of the hull, with windows providing a view. At a pinch *Hindenburg* could accommodate 70 passengers, but the ship was more comfortable when only three-quarters of that number were carried. The cabins for the officers lay near the bow of the ship, while the crew's quarters lay aft of the passengers' cabins. *LZ 130* could only carry 40 passengers, because it was intended that she should be inflated with helium; the accommodation was therefore rather less spacious than in *Hindenburg*.

Although twice the size of the *Graf Zeppelin* and 35 per cent larger than the British ships, more austere accommodation, approximately equivalent to that of a destroyer, was found in the naval ships *Akron* and *Macon*. But instead of sleeping in the walkway, as was customary in the wartime ships, the crew occupied light, well-ventilated bunk rooms amidships. They had an ingenious galley stove combining water-heater and coffee urn to sustain them on their long-range scouting flights.[46]

Ultimately, the efficiency of a rigid airship was found in the amount of its useful lift. The Germans were well ahead of other countries in this respect, as the table below shows.[47]

	Percentage of useful to total lift
R 100 (with minor alterations)	36
R 101 (with new bay)	35
R 101 (with minor alterations)	32
Los Angeles	39
Akron	45
R 34	43
Graf Zeppelin	47

In the case of the *Graf Zeppelin*, the weight of blaugas *in vacuo* was $34\frac{1}{2}$ tons; her actual lift was 81 tons and total gross lift was therefore $81 + 34\frac{1}{2}$ tons $= 115\frac{1}{2}$ tons. She could carry a payload of 5 tons freight and 20 passengers at a range of 6,500 miles, twice as far as the British ships, and she could cruise at 75mph at 1,508rpm. *Hindenburg* had a fixed weight of 118 tons and a payload of 20 tons, though it should be remembered that if she had been inflated with helium her buoyancy and margin of lift would have been reduced by 14 tons.

The two experimental British ships did not come up to the expectations of their designers. They needed 45 per cent of useful-to-total lift to be commercially profitable. Only *R 100* could have carried a payload on the east-to-west voyage across the Atlantic! The maximum fixed weight for both ships was intended to be 90 tons, yet *R 101* rose to 117 tons and *R 100* to 105 tons. The useful lift of *R 101*, even after the insertion of the extra bay, was only 49 tons, instead of the specified 60 tons, and her larger successor, if she had been built, would have had a useful lift of not more than 53 tons. This was only a ton less than the useful lift of *R 100*. These details show that a long period of trials and modifications would have been necessary before British airships could have established routine flights from England to, say, Egypt, or between England and Canada. In the event, too much was expected of them.

The two American ships with a fixed weight of 107 tons and a useful lift of just under 72 tons, were adequate for a military role; they had a maximum range of 4,760 miles flying at a speed of 80mph. They, too, would probably have had to be modified for commercial operation. And this was the crux of the matter. Even the Germans, in building larger ships which would have been necessary in time, would have had to have faced the problem of weight, while there were other matters, such as corrosion and metal fatigue, which had hardly been taken into account.

CHAPTER 8

Achievement and Tragedy

'Airships today include the whole world in their range. No other transport specialist thinks so habitually in terms of continents as does the airship navigator.' Fritz Sturm, 'Zeitschrift des Vereins Deutsche Ingenieure', 14 Sept 1929

LZ *127* was completed by mid-summer of 1928, and was named *Graf Zeppelin* by the daughter of the Count on 8 July, the anniversary of her father's birthday. Six trial flights were then made over Germany and the North Sea, the fifth causing a flutter in the British press as the ship passed over the East Coast. The object of the flights was not only to test the ship's manoeuvrability, but also to discover the efficiency of the ventilation system which was essential if the volatile blaugas was to be used permanently. The ship was now ready to make her maiden voyage across the Atlantic.

With Eckener as Führer, Capt Flemming in charge of the ship, and Lehmann and von Schiller as watch-keeping officers, *Graf Zeppelin* left Friedrichshafen on 11 October.[1] Apart from the crew of 37, she carried 25 passengers, including Lieut Cdr Rosendahl, official observer of the US navy, several journalists, and Lady Grace Drummond Hay, an ornament of London society who earned the distinction of being the first woman to fly the Atlantic; she became an inveterate airship traveller. Stowed in the keel were 25 sacks of mail.

The ship had certain disadvantages. While the saloon was heated by radiators fed with hot water from the auxiliary engine, the cabins were unheated; smoking was prohibited; and the washing facilities, though well-arranged, were inadequate. The smell of blaugas tended to permeate the saloon. But the food, cooked by electricity, was excellent. So were the wines.

A bad-weather forecast compelled Eckener to head towards Gibraltar, instead of due west across the Atlantic as he had planned; he flew down the Rhône valley and along the coast of eastern Spain. After

Gibraltar the ship made towards Bermuda. On the third day out, in mid-Atlantic, she flew into an unsuspected storm, which tore away the cotton cover of the 60ft-long horizontal elevator. A small party of riggers, led by Knut Eckener, son of the Doctor, climbed out along the girders to rig up a makeshift cover of sheets and mattresses to stop the rain from driving into the hull and damaging the vulnerable gas bags. While the work was in progress a sudden rain squall struck the ship, driving her down to about 500ft from the sea. The riggers had to be withdrawn into the safety of the hull before the order was given to speed up the engines and regain height. The ship now had to fly at reduced speed to prevent further damage to the fin.

Another storm was encountered off Bermuda, but on 15 October the mainland was sighted and a safe descent was made at Lakehurst after a journey of 111hr 43min. In spite of the circuitous route that had been followed, *Graf Zeppelin* still had enough fuel for her to have gone on for another 65hr. That would have enabled her to have reached the Pacific—testimony to the great endurance powers of the rigid airship.

Eckener and his colleagues were given an enthusiastic welcome in New York, and, being skilled publicity men, seized the opportunity to advance the Zeppelin venture. The return journey (with a stowaway on board) did not begin until 29 October because of the repairs to the fin and delays due to cross-winds blowing outside the shed at Lakehurst. The ship ran into fog off Newfoundland, and later into a line squall. The engines were throttled down. Eckener, who was a first-class navigator, steered his charge along the edge of the squall until he came into less turbulent air. No damage was incurred and the passengers felt surprisingly little of the buffeting received by the ship (in weather like this, a man standing in the walkway could see her bend up to 5ft, thus demonstrating her flexibility). *Graf Zeppelin* landed at Friedrichshafen in the early hours of 1 November after a flight of 71hr 51min. Eckener now appreciated that for a regular passenger service a larger, more powerful, ship would be needed, one which would contain more comfortable passenger accommodation.

During that winter and the spring of 1929, *Graf Zeppelin* made a number of flights for the German Institute for Aeronautical Research, as well as two cruises over the Mediterranean. The first cruise began on 25 March 1929. The ship flew down the Rhône valley, across Corsica

and Elba, then over Rome to the Aegean, and then to Palestine, dropping mail by parachute at El Ramleh. In moonlight, *Graf Zeppelin*
flew only 500ft above the Dead Sea. As the Dead Sea is 1,300ft below
sea level, the airship was flying 800ft below the level of the Mediterranean. The return journey was made up the Adriatic and thence via
Vienna, Friedrichshafen being reached on 28 March. She had flown
4,971 miles in 81hr 29min. During the second cruise flight in April,
Egypt was included in the itinerary.

On 16 May 1929 *Graf Zeppelin* began her second voyage to the
United States, carrying 18 passengers—and a gorilla named Susie
destined for sale to an American zoo. By now the ship had flown
30,000 miles, and the engines had run for some 500hr. Weather fore-
casts compelled Eckener to fly down the Rhône valley again and along
the east coast of Spain. *Graf Zeppelin* had been flying for about 11hr
when first one engine, and then a second, broke down due to torsional
resonance in the crankshaft. By this time she was not far from Cape
Nao. Eckener decided to abandon the flight and return home. But
after crossing the Rhône delta *Graf Zeppelin* encountered the treacherous
mistral, blowing at different speeds at different altitudes. Two more
engines had failed by this time, leaving only one for propulsion. There
was no other course than to make an emergency landing, saving the
passengers if not the ship. According to one of the passengers, about
twelve attempts were made to land, during which most of the ballast
was consumed, while the lifting gas was getting low. But, throughout,
the crew remained calm, the ship rode steadily, and her routine continued to run normally.

The French, forgetting old animosities, responded to Eckener's request to land at the disused airship base at Cuers, towards which *Graf
Zeppelin* was being blown. By the time she was over the airfield a large
detachment of troops had appeared. The soldiers seized the ropes,
brought the airship safely to ground, and took her into the shed, where
the crew observed with chagrin a solitary transverse frame hanging, for
that was all that remained of the former *Nordstern*. There is no doubt
that without the co-operation of the French, the *Graf Zeppelin* would
have been seriously, if not irretrievably, damaged.

The cause of the breakdowns was found to be the too fine adjustment of an elastic coupling between propellers and engine shafts.[2]

This was discovered by two scientists (one of whom, Geiger, achieved fame for other research) after *Graf Zeppelin* equipped with new engines, had returned to base a week later.

The mishap demonstrated an important characteristic of the rigid airship, namely, that engine trouble, as with a structural accident, did not necessarily mean total failure, for *Graf Zeppelin* had made a safe landing on the power of only one engine. No further mechanical changes were necessary.

Graf Zeppelin needed further continental flying experience; above all she needed financial support, and for that further publicity was required. Eckener found a patron in Randolph Hearst, the publicity-minded American newspaper owner. Hearst sponsored a round-the-world flight of *Graf Zeppelin*, but stipulated that it should start from the USA.[3] On 8 August 1929, therefore, *Graf Zeppelin* left Lakehurst with 20 passengers, including the Australian explorer, Sir Hubert Wilkins, with Rosendahl again flying as official US observer. Proceeding east she arrived 55hr 22min later in Friedrichshafen without incident.

The second longest and most difficult leg of the journey was the non-stop flight from Friedrichshafen to Tokyo. Heavy rain and thunderstorms at that time of the year ruled out a passage over south-east Siberia and Manchuria and the airship therefore had to cross the Urals, in central, and the Stanovoy range, in eastern Russia. *Graf Zeppelin* set out on 15 August in fine weather, but apparently had to cross the Urals far south of the original plan because of a widespread depression and, as a result, had to shed much of her ballast. As it was essential to have ballast in hand, or alternatively to valve gas, to avoid making a heavy landing at Tokyo, Eckener was forced to hazard his ship at heights between 2,300 to 5,500ft through the canyons of the Stanovoy mountains and was at one time as low as 300ft from the ground. On the 19th, after tailing a typhoon, *Graf Zeppelin* landed at the air base of Kasumigaura, near Tokyo, having made the journey of 6,973 miles in 101hr 49min at an average speed of 68·5mph. As it was difficult to produce and transport blaugas, *Graf Zeppelin* was refuelled with an American commercial product called Pyrofax, which had been found to be a suitable alternative. Pyrofax was liquified propane containing some butane and had been shipped to Tokyo in bottles, there to be mixed with hydrogen to obtain the correct density. No problems arose.

Four days later *Graf Zeppelin*, taking advantage, as always, of the prevalent westerly winds, and tailing tropical storms, flew across the Pacific to Los Angeles in 79hr 54min. There she was refuelled for the second time with Pyrofax, now mixed with natural gas instead of hydrogen. Taking off heavy after a hot day, the ship, cleverly steered by Knut Eckener, just cleared high tension wires passing the airfield. The final stage of the airship's journey lay across the continent of North America. She completed the world-wide circuit at Lakehurst, 51hr 13min after leaving Los Angeles. While the time taken for the global voyage was 20 days, 14hr 4min, the actual flying time was 12 days, 12hr 40min, for a distance of 21,150 miles, meaning an average speed of 70·23mph. Blaugas proved its value, for in the entire flight only 200,000cu ft of lifting gas was required. In contrast, when *R 100* made her transatlantic trip she needed 1 million cubic feet of hydrogen after little more than 3,000 miles.

In the pre-1914 years Graf Zeppelin had conceived the idea of an airship flight over the Arctic. By the summer of 1931 his dream had become a reality. Although the Italian semi-rigid *Norge* had flown over the North Pole (see page 235), an airship of such small capacity was not suitable for prolonged scientific observation, and flying boats, an alternative type of aircraft, had not yet reached a stage of development for such a task.[4] Luftschiffbau Zeppelin initially raised objections to the flight because of the climatic conditions, such as fog, snow and the possibility of ice accumulating on the cover, but Eckener finally agreed when German financiers offered to pay for the expedition after Hearst, an earlier sponsor, had withdrawn his offer. Hearst had proposed a less scientific, though perhaps more spectacular, motive for the flight. This was to be a rendezvous between the airship and a submarine, which Sir Hubert Wilkins had obtained from the US navy, at the North Pole. A breakdown to the submarine made it impossible for Wilkins to keep to schedule.

The scientific programme for the polar flight was drawn up by the Aero-Arctic Society, an international body presided over by the veteran polar explorer, Nansen, but with a majority of Germans and Russians in its membership. It included research into polar air currents, valuable for meteorological forecasting, the magnetic pole, and the exploration of the land distribution. *Graf Zeppelin* underwent a number of modifications for the expedition, including the fixing of bumpers on the control and after engine cars, and the making of them watertight so that the ship could alight on the sea; special hatches were made for vertical photography and for the release of weather balloons; anti-freeze was put into the radiators and ballast bags; and the passenger coach was stripped of its fittings to hold equipment. That equipment included rubber boats, two Eskimo canoes, hunting weapons, tents, and iron rations in the event of a forced landing on the ice—only the essential fur coats were missing because they were the most expensive item. The full complement, numbering 46, included the scientific party, under Professor Samoilowitsch, and the American polar ex-plorer, Lincoln Ellsworth. Arthur Koestler, then a young scientific correspondent for a German newspaper, reported the flight by wireless and, much later, vividly in his memoirs 'Arrow in the Blue'.

Graf Zeppelin began her outward flight from Friedrichshafen on 24 July 1931, but soon landed at Berlin to take on more fuel. The explana-tion was that as Berlin is at a lower altitude than the airship's base, more lift was therefore available. While refuelling was in progress, members of the expedition enthralled Berliners by walking about in their polar clothing, for they possessed no other in order to keep total weight to the minimum. On the next day the ship left for Leningrad, where she was fêted by the Russians. On the 26th she left for the arctic wastes, the intention first being to rendezvous with the Soviet icebreaker *Malygin*. By the afternoon of the following day *Graf Zeppelin* had crossed the 78th parallel, Eckener having decided to fly above the fog. Wireless contact had been established with the *Malygin*, and that evening she was sighted off Hooker Island, part of the cluster of islands known as Franz Josef Land. *Graf Zeppelin*'s engines were stopped, and the ship began to descend after valving gas. At about 300ft above the sea two canvas buckets were let down at the end of ropes to act as anchors. A hose was then lowered into the sea and water pumped into the hull to serve as ballast. The ship landed well away from the icebreaker to avoid sparks from the vessel's funnel igniting her. In a few minutes a boatload of excited Russians and the airship designer, Umberto Nobile (see Chapter 9) were clinging to the rail of the car. A little over a quarter-of-an-hour, the mail handed over, the airship rose rapidly again; she had been resting on a current that would have carried her against large blocks of drift ice which would have crushed the car like matchwood.

The scientists and cartographers now got down to the serious business of surveying and mapping, first over the nebulous Franz Josef Land, and on the following day over the still only partially mapped Severnaya Zemlya, which provided magnificent views of mist-capped glaciers. Further mapping took the ship over a corner of Siberia. On the return journey the ship flew over Noyava Zemlya in the Kara Sea. On 30 July *Graf Zeppelin* returned to Leningrad, landing in Berlin in the hot summer sunshine at 5.30pm after 71hr unbroken flight.

The airship had proved an admirable scientific observatory. In three days data had been collected and mapping achieved which would probably have taken a combined land/sea expedition two years to produce comparable results. From the aeronautical point of view the flight proved that an airship, properly handled, could operate in arctic regions equally as well as in a temperate climate. It would have been possible to have flown over the Pole, but the insurance companies had misgivings about the potential dangers. Eckener prudently abstained from seizing the opportunity, even though it would only have entailed a short detour.

After further flights which took *Graf Zeppelin* to Cardington, Spain, Holland and the Balkans, she settled down to the steady, unspectacular routine of a South American regular-service run, which had been the aim of Eckener and Colsman since the end of the war. North-easterly trade winds determined the airship's route. A slow steamer service, which took 14 days from Germany to Rio de Janeiro, provided an incentive for airships to fill the gap, and there was a reservoir of potential passengers in the emigrant German population resident in South America.

Graf Zeppelin's operations were confined to the summer months. During that time, on Saturday once a fortnight, she left Friedrichshafen, arriving at Pernambuco, in Brazil, on the following Tuesday evening. She was moored at a light mast. On the Thursday, having reprovisioned, re-gassed and refuelled, she flew on to Rio, where a base was constructed. She then returned via Reçife (Pernambuco) to Friedrichshafen. The time taken for the outward journey was usually four to four-and-a-half days, with four-and-a-half to five days for the return trip. With growing experience, by 1935 flying time had progressively been reduced by about 12hr on the outward journey, and by 18hr on the return journey. If there were four or more passengers who required it, a stop was made at Barcelona on the last leg home. A single through fare cost £143, which compared favourably with the surface ship, especially considering the novelty of air travel. Freight cost 6s 6d (33p) per lb.

The inaugural voyage was made between 18 May and 6 June 1930 when the ship made a double crossing of the Atlantic, south and north.[5] She landed at Seville on the 19th to take on 12 tons of reserve fuel, as she had left with only 5 tons of benzine on leaving Friedrichshafen in order to have the maximum lift for crossing the Alps. She arrived at Pernambuco on the 22nd. Two days later she made an excursion to Rio, returning to Pernambuco on the 26th. On the 28th she left for Lakehurst, arriving on 31 May. She set off again across the Atlantic on 3 June, alighting at Seville on the 5th and arriving home on the evening of the following day. She had covered a total distance of 18,100 miles.

One of the features of these spectacular flights was the policy of applying elaborate cachets to mail carried by the ship, a practice begun by DELAG.[6] Souvenir mail was also thrown overboard to be postmarked from the place of recovery. The German Government issued special postage stamps for the first crossing of the Atlantic, which were reissued for the first South American and Arctic flights. In her first five years of service *Graf Zeppelin*'s flights led to the production of nearly a thousand different souvenir covers, postcards and cachets, all helping with publicity and producing revenue for the company.

By the end of 1933 she had crossed the Atlantic 51 times, and during the final trip of that year visited Chicago, where the World Fair was being held. She had carried a total of 9,543 passengers, 38,561kg of freight and 2,863kg of mail. She was paying her way, as only 15 per cent of running costs were subsidised,[7] the remaining costs being met from receipts, of which 75 per cent were coming from abroad.

Just before *Graf Zeppelin* began her spectacular round-the-world voyage in August 1929, *R 100* completed her lift-and-trim trials, two months ahead of her sister ship *R 101*. The total programme had cost nearly 2 million pounds by the end of 1929, an overspending of over ½ million pounds from the original estimate. By today's standards that is a paltry figure, but in days of the depression it was a significant slice of public expenditure. R 101's cost had escalated from £275,000 to £438,000 in March 1930; R 100 was built to a fixed price, but Burney declared that Vickers had had to put in extra money and the final cost was £340,366.[8]

The construction of both ships had given rise to much criticism, most of it uninformed. At a slightly more technical level a retired naval architect named E. F. Spanner conducted a lone campaign in aeronautical and engineering societies against what he called 'This Airship Business', and which reached a wider audience in a series of books which he himself had published. His arguments against the British airships were that their shape was wrong, that they were structurally unsound, that they were uneconomical in regard to fuel consumption, and that their safety factor was too low. He prophesied that they would be unable to pay their way.[9] Spanner's arguments were vitiated by his lack of knowledge of aerodynamic theory, but some of his shafts struck uncomfortably near the truth.

For instance, it became clear during her lift-and-trim trials that the useful lift of R 100 was no more than 57 tons. Various discrepancies, though, such as temperature variations in the shed, accumulation of dust and so on on the outer cover, and errors of weighing and observation had to be taken into account. But the useful lift of R 101 was discovered to be even lower—35 tons. There were many glum faces at the Royal Airship Works when this became known.[10]

R 100 was already giving trouble before she left her shed at Howden. Once outside, she could not return to the shed because of its narrowness. The outer cover split; then a 10ft hole ripped by the radial wires appeared in No 5 gas bag.[11] By the time the ship had been repaired, the first series of trial flights of R 101 were about to begin. As there was only one mooring tower, R 100 had to wait her turn.

The lift-and-trim trials of R 101 took place at the end of September 1929. They proved to be very disappointing. Most of the water ballast had to be removed to make her airborne in the shed. Her low useful lift made it impossible for her to be given an airworthiness certificate. Worse still, in her current condition it was found that she would be unable to operate on the Indian route because of the heat at Karachi. That would cause her to lose 11 tons of useful lift and she would be restricted to a load of about 7 tons of fuel. The engine tests, on the other hand, proved to be satisfactory. But engine trouble was not far away.[12]

R 101's first flight was made on 14 October. It was remarkable for its smoothness and lack of vibration. Thereafter, she made another seven flights. The last, on 17 November, was an endurance test lasting 30hr. During it the ship made a thousand-mile circuit over northern England, Scotland and Ireland. But the engines gave trouble on each flight, varying from minor breakdowns to a big-end going. While the ship manoeuvred well, and so far the outer cover and the gas bag wiring system were satisfactory, the ship was tail heavy and dismally lacking in lift for a long voyage. Other defects were the poor ballasting arrangements; the long time taken for gassing; and the indifferent communications system within the hull.

It was therefore decided that R 101 should be refitted.[13] The gas bag wiring was to be let out to increase her capacity; the servo motor operating the controls was to be taken out to save weight; two Beardmore reversible engines were ordered to enable five engines to drive ahead instead of only four. But the major change which was proposed, though not implemented for the time being, was the insertion of an additional bay, a redesign which would bring the useful lift to 55 tons. There was nothing novel in parting the ship, of course, for as has been seen, Zeppelins were treated to the same process on several occasions. In this case the improvement was to be left to a dangerously late hour, while R 101 was kept in reserve for a possible flight to Canada instead of R 100.

Before going into the shed, R 101 rode out at the tower a gale which reached 83mph. Apart from holes in the gas bags caused by surging, she suffered no damage. But a serious accident could have happened when the Air Ministry decided to invite 100 Members of Parliament for luncheon on board ship. The meal was to be followed by a short flight. Fortunately, poor weather put a flight out of question. But the general lack of lift, pointed out by the ship's officers, made no impression on the director of airship development and the luncheon took place on the moored ship which had been drastically, and illegally, lightened to take the load.[14] When on 3 November R 101 was taken into the shed, the tower was free to receive R 100.

At last, on the dawn of 16 December, the weather permitted *R 100* to leave her own shed.[15] She circled slowly over Howden before turning south to join her sister ship at Cardington. While cruising at about 55mph, there was plenty to occupy her crew—a crack in the water jacket immobilised the port engine, then the outer cover split near the passenger corridor. No trouble was experienced with mooring and this operation was completed by midday. The following day she ascended again. The intention was to find out how the outer cover behaved at speed. But further teething troubles were encountered; the engines were still unsatisfactory, and Norway discovered that a strip sealing the fabric across the rudder hinge was coming unstuck. *R 100* therefore only cruised over the airfield several times before again tying up at the mast as a preliminary to entering the shed for repairs.

However, the grounding was short, for on 16 January she was out again to embark on speed tests and turning trials. The first full speed run was made in bright sunshine above fog and cloud. With Scott in command, she reached a speed of 81·5mph, but for not more than 20min, for the reason that bulges and undulations were forming on the outer cover. A large number of small holes were also discovered in the cover. More serious was a slit found beneath one of the petrol tanks, caused by the cover flapping against the side of the tank. Fortunately that fault was spotted and repaired before the damage got any worse. No turning trials took place because of the unfavourable weather. After just over 13hr flying the ship moored at Cardington late that evening.

The next flight was designed to test modifications to the cover, and photographs of it were taken from an aeroplane over the Royal Aircraft Establishment at Farnborough while the airship flew at various speeds. Ripples still formed on the cover, especially near the propellers on the engine cars.

An endurance flight was made on 27 January, during which the wireless equipment was tested. *R 100* flew up and down the Channel in the fog (as a wireless message received en route from Air Ministry had forbidden her to fly west of a line Ushant–Fastnet Rock), and over East Anglia. The postponed turning trials were made in the vicinity of the Eddystone lighthouse. The height maintained was from 1,500 to 2,000ft. When near the Scillies a fix was requested over the wireless, the reply came that the ship was 2 miles south-west of Guildford. Scott, tongue in cheek, replied, 'Many thanks for position; sea very rough at Guildford!' The ship was in the air for 54hr. She covered 2,050 miles. Her main trouble was in connection with the engines, and an exhaust pipe extension was damaged. According to the official report the revolutions of the propellers varied considerably above and below the 1,900rpm which was their planned speed.[16] The engines were much noisier than those of R 101, but their total power was greater, and there was no vibration in the gear structure—a common failing in engines of rigids.

R 100 was now redoped on top of her outer cover, and further modifications were made to it as it had been leaking again; there was a danger that the gas bags would get wet, an occurrence against which they were not proof.[17] Auxiliary panels were fitted to prevent the cover from flapping. The ship did not fly again until 21 May, as her starboard elevator had been damaged while being brought out of the shed several weeks before. It was intended to test the cover and the engines again, as well as her general powers of endurance. But ill fortune still attended the ship. This time the rear 15ft of the stern structure collapsed while the ship was travelling at just under 80mph. The outer cover was still flapping. On return to base it was decided to cut 25ft off the end of the stern and to round it off in the hope that one alteration would enable one cover to withstand aerodynamic pressures more effectively.

As R 100 was equipped with petrol engines she was deemed unsafe to moor in high tropical temperatures (though this had been disproved by Graf Zeppelin). Instead of flying on the India route she was to make a flight to Canada that summer and moor at Montreal. But as the Canadian Parliament was dissolved at the end of May and a general election fell on 28 July, the flight could not take place until the new Parliament had reassembled and MPs could be present at Montreal to watch the airship's arrival.

On 25 July she left the Cardington tower for her seventh and final trial flight the object being to test the troublesome outer cover again, the wireless equipment, and a water-recovery system, which had recently been added. The ship cruised over England, Wales and the Channel Isles for 24hr and at the end Scott expressed himself satisfied, although the outer cover and the gas bags were still causing anxiety.

R 100 had now flown a total of 7,000 miles. Was a risk being taken to embark on a long-distance flight? With hindsight and the application of contemporary aeronautical standards the answer is 'yes'. Yet the two Zeppelins which had to date crossed the Atlantic had not made more thorough preparations. Nor, indeed, had *R 34*.

At all events, *R 100* cast off from the tower at Cardington in the early hours of 29 July. The British copied the German system of a 'Commodore', in this case Scott. He advised how much fuel and water ballast should be carried, and, during the flight, helped to plan the route.[18] But the ship was in the charge of the captain, Sqdn Leader R. S. Booth, who was responsible for preparing the ship for flight and for keeping her in trim during the voyage. He also kept watch with the chief navigator, Sqdn Leader E. L. Johnson and the first and second officers. An expert meteorologist, Capt M. A. Giblett, supplemented radio reports from the Air Ministry. Altogether 44 persons were aboard, including Colmore (director of airship development), Burney, Norway (who kept a diary), and a naval officer from the Admiralty. The ship carried 34 tons of petrol (22 per cent of the gross lift); 1 ton of engine oil; 5 tons of ballast; 1 ton of provisions; 2 tons of drinking water, and so on—altogether 53 tons of useful lift, or 34 per cent of gross lift.

On account of a depression west of Ireland, it was decided to fly to the north of that island, rather than to take the southerly route via the Azores which the Germans usually followed.[19] All went well for the crossing; the engines were at last behaving, and occasionally speeds of up to 80mph were reached. One of the chores, in which the passengers shared, was pumping petrol by hand to the gravity tanks above the cars. Booth carried out some scientific experiments for the Cambridge School of Agriculture, which wanted to discover whether living organisms could float across the Atlantic in the upper air.

R 100 reached the mainland at Belle Isle, north of Newfoundland early on 31 July. She then began to fly up the valley of the St Lawrence. Some anxiety was caused by holes which appeared in two of the gas bags, and a party of riggers under the chief coxswain climbed along the radial wires between the bags to repair them.[20] There was some risk in this work as the hydrogen gas took effect on the human frame stealthily and quickly, and the best counter-measure was to keep up a flow of chatter, whistling, or song; the presence of gas was detected when the voice became high-pitched. It had been intended to land before dark that day. But the ship ran into what was called a 'white' squall, caused by a cool wind from the mountains being sucked into the warm air of the valley and creating turbulence; unlike a 'black', or storm, squall, it was invisible. For once, the ship began to roll heavily. Scott unwisely, in the event, prevailed upon Booth to increase speed, and this, added to the effect of the gusts, split the cover on the port fin, leaving, according to Meager, the first officer, a hole through which a double-decker bus could have been driven. The ship now had to slow down to 20mph to enable the riggers to make good the damage using reserve sheets of cotton fabric carried for such emergencies. This involved the hazardous job of crawling along the outer edge of the fin or along one of the longitudinal girders at a height of some 1,500ft above the St Lawrence.

Instead of the planned arrival at Montreal, Quebec was reached that evening. As the overdue ship now made south for Montreal she was again thwarted, this time by thunderstorms. Scott now made a second error of judgement for he decided to fly through the storm instead of avoiding it. R 100 ran into a vertical gust similar to that which destroyed *Shenandoah*. She was rapidly swept up, with the bow downwards at an angle of 20°, despite the elevators being depressed hard down. Like a cork in a bottle, she rose nearly 2,000ft in a minute; the supper which had just been laid in the saloon slid down the corridor, some of it reaching the second frame in the bow. Two splits about 20ft long appeared in the starboard fin; again repairs had to be carried out at once. R 100 spent the rest of the night dodging the thunderstorms, finally mooring to the mast at St Hubert airport outside Montreal at dawn, after a flight which had lasted 79hr from Cardington, eight of which were spent in repairing the damaged fin. As 5 tons of rainwater had been collected through the recovery system, there was no need to valve much hydrogen before mooring. After a voyage of some 3,300 miles there was still about 5 tons of petrol left.

The crew of the R 100 received a great welcome. In addition to representatives of the Canadian Government, American airshipmen such as Moffett and Rosendahl, and designers such as Arnstein and Hunsaker, watched the arrival of the ship. The damage incurred during the latter part of the flight was made good at the mast.[21] Even so, there was more trouble with splitting gas bags. And the engines gave trouble, too. But *R 100* was able to show her paces in a series of local flights. Some 3,000 people visited the ship while at her moorings.

Shortly after midnight on 14 August she left for home carrying a total of 56 people, including 11 Canadians. The return trip, with favourable winds urging the ship along, was uneventful. She tied up at Cardington at 11.0 am on 16 August, after a flight of 57hr 36min. Over 3,000gal of petrol was unconsumed. In contrast to the reception at Montreal, *R 100*'s homecoming aroused little interest, exactly as had happened on the return of *R 34* from America. She moored with no more than a couple of hundred people watching. *R 100* never flew again.

Although the outward flight of *R 100* had been hazardous at times it was an achievement and, even more, held out a challenge to *R 101* to prove her worth. On 22 July, the Labour Secretary of State for Air, Lord Thomson, whose party had returned to power in 1929, and whose enthusiasm for the two rigids was as strong as when last in office, instructed that work should begin at once on parting *R 101* in order to insert the new bay.[22] Lord Thomson indicated that he intended to travel on the ship to India. There are reasons for thinking that he was destined to be the next Viceroy of India, and what better for someone so earmarked than to arrive in his future suzerainty by such a novel form of transport? But time was short for an Imperial Conference was to be held in London in mid-October. It would be attended by the Dominions Prime Ministers. Lord Thomson had to be present too. Therefore at the latest he had to leave for India by the last week in September. 'I must insist,' wrote Thomson to the air member for supply and research on 14 July, 'on the programme for the Indian flight being adhered to, as I have made my plans accordingly.' Colmore warned officials nearest Lord Thomson that his people would have to observe a very tight schedule if they were to complete the modifications and the subsequent trial flights. He suggested abandoning the Canadian flight of *R 100*, and postponing the Indian flight of *R 101* until later in the year. This more realistic approach was overruled. The air member for supply and research, Air Mshl Sir John Higgins, however, clearly told Lord Thomson that while every endeavour would be made to keep to the programme, there was little margin for unforeseen circumstances. Yet at the same time he did not consider that more than one trial flight was necessary after the modifications were completed.

Yet the heaviness and consequent difficulty of handling R 101 was clearly demonstrated in June. The chief of the air staff decided that the ship should appear at the RAF display at Hendon at the end of that month. But when she was taken out of the shed before the rehearsal her outer cover was rent on two successive days while moored to the mast. (She had weathered the November gale without a tear.) She was patched up with strengthening bands, put on with rubber solution, in time for the rehearsal (the cover was very brittle and, as described on page 186, had been doped before being put on the ship, the intention being to save weight).

Worse than this, both during the rehearsal and on the day of the display, the ship pitched heavily.

Meager, temporarily acting as first officer, described how, on returning from Hendon, he began to worry about the ship's behaviour. 'She would go into a short, sharp dive, and then the cox'n would get her nose up and we would make a long slow climb back to our flying height.'[23] It was as much as the coxswain in control of the elevators could do to keep her level, though Meager ordered a ton of ballast to be released which helped. But nearly 10 tons of ballast and oil had to be cast off in order to get the ship into equilibrium before mooring. A number of small holes were found in the gas bags, but they could not have entirely been responsible for the increase in the ship's weight for during the war Zeppelins had returned to base with gas bags riddled with bullets. It is hard to establish the cause. There is no doubt that R 101 was less easy to handle than R 100 and, during the Hendon flights, both Meager and the coxswain at the helm were unfamiliar with this ship's characteristics. Moreover, if the ship really was being flown heavy, according to the experts at the NPL, her stern rather than the bow should have gone down. Booth considered that the bow dropped from 'some design factor'.[24] It was later pointed out that L 59 and Graf Zeppelin had emerged safely from similar dives.

Another theory is that the novel automatic pressure-relief valves allowed gas to escape at a rate of about 30,000cu ft an hour. This view is supported by the fact that gas did not escape while the ship was moored. It is also possible that the gas bags were allowed to surge excessively because of the expanded wiring. One of Rope's self-adjusting bulkhead bridles was carried away after a Hendon flight. It was found that the pulleys were too small in diameter. Short lengths of chain were therefore introduced into all bridles of this type.

Whatever was the cause, *R 101* was now parted amidships for the long-planned insertion of the extra bay. A large part of the outer cover was also renewed, though not near the bow, as it had been discovered that temporary patching of tears with rubber solution had rotted the fabric. This time the cover was doped in situ after the German practice, and indeed, ordinary aeroplane practice. Finally, the ship was fitted with the two new Beardmore reversible engines, 150lb lighter than the non-reversible one, which enabled her to use all five engines for flying ahead, thus giving a much wider margin of power and making the mooring operation easier.

She left her shed early on 1 October and the same afternoon cast off from the masthead for a 16hr flight over the East Coast to test stability and control and to see how the new cover behaved. All seemed to be satisfactory. A speed test was to have been made, but an oil cooler for one of the forward reversible engines burst, putting that engine out of action for the rest of the flight.

On return to Cardington the following morning, Colmore discussed with Cave-Brown-Cave whether they should permit the ship to go on the Indian voyage, due to begin in two days time, without a full speed test. Lord Thomson, in the last discussion on the flight, put the onus of deciding the date of departure on Colmore. According to Cave-Brown-Cave, it was appreciated that if the Secretary of State was not brought home in time for the Imperial Conference, no money for the ship would be forthcoming and none could be asked for.[25] This feeling was reflected in the tension that mounted in the short time that was left for the crew to prepare for the flight. Lieut Cdr Atherstone, the first officer, wrote in his diary for 3 October: 'Everybody is rather keyed up now, as we all feel that the future of airships very largely depends on what sort of show we put up. There are very many unknown factors and I feel that that thing called luck will figure rather conspicuously in our flight.'[26]

Another disturbing factor was that in spite of the extra bay, and other modifications which increased the gross lift to 167·2 tons, the disposable lift was still only 49 tons—an increase of 14 tons (the total gain from lightening was 5·7 tons and an extra 8·6 tons was gained from the additional gas). But the steel crankcases of the engines which had not yet been replaced with aluminium were still too heavy. Moreover, despite the efforts to reduce weight a carpet weighing 1,000lb which invariably formed part of Lord Thomson's kit on special journeys since World War I was installed at the last moment. Fifty per cent more fuel than was necessary for the flight to Egypt was taken, in order to reduce the time needed for refuelling at Ismailia, where a state dinner party was to be given in the airship at her moorings.

Nevertheless, Colmore decided to ignore the risks. His decision was reinforced by the certificate of airworthiness obtained on the strength of the one test flight. At 6.36 pm on 4 October, with a promise of rain and wind which would clear on the following morning, *R 101*, only 0·5 tons light, just managed to lift away from the tower. On board in addition to Lord Thomson, were the director of civil aviation, Air Mshl Sir Sefton Brancker, Colmore and Richmond; while Scott acted in the same capacity as he had done on the flight of *R 100* to Canada. The captain of the ship was Flt Lieut H. C. Irwin.

The airship flew low over southern England in order to carry what must have been an excessive load (there is conflicting evidence on the break down of *R 101*'s weight at take-off; no authentic load sheet prepared for departure has ever been found), crossing the coast at Hastings.[27] It was now raining quite hard and soon she had to fly against a headwind which may well have been blowing at 30mph. After crossing the Channel she seems to have set a course along the line of Paris–Tours–Toulouse–Narbonne, well to the west of the Rhône valley which had been one of the alternate routes proposed. By midnight the passengers, well-dined, and having smoked a last cigar, retired to bed and the crew 'settled down to watch-keeping routine'. The ship was near Poix at 1.0 am, when she asked for her true bearing. Yet she was making heavy going, for an hour later she had only covered 20 miles. At 2.9 am she dived into the hillside in undulating country 3 miles south-east of Beauvais, and only 359ft above sea level. Several of the local inhabitants saw her descend. On touching the ground there was an explosion setting the hydrogen on fire and the ship was consumed in flames. Of the complement of 44, only 8 of the crew survived; 2 later died of their injuries.

The crash was regarded as a national disaster, particularly on account of the notable passengers who perished. The victims were given a state funeral, and later a court of inquiry was held under the Attorney-General, Sir John Simon. It rejected either weakness of structure, failure in the control gear, or abnormal weather as being in any way responsible for the accident. It concluded that the immediate cause was loss of gas from the bags in the forward part of the ship; chafing of the gas bags against the padded nuts of the longitudinals may also have worn the fabric and caused leakage; so could have involuntary opening of the valves due to the pitching of the ship. It was believed that the more serious and sudden loss of gas was connected with the ripping of the fore part of the outer cover.

A number of neutral, competent airship authorities were, however, not convinced by the conclusions, which to them smacked of 'white-washing'. Their views were to some extent borne out by a Cabinet paper written after the findings of the court had been published, and which stated, with perhaps more truth, that the precise cause of the disaster would never be known.[28] The paper concluded that there was no evidence that non-completion of trials contributed to the accident. (There had been greater risks involved in the R 100's voyage to Canada.) A number of the witnesses summoned by the court were, of course, not disinterested, having been closely concerned with the building of the ship, while it was to be expected that the views of those associated with the building of the sister ship R 100 would be critical.

All that is certain is that the gusts of wind were fairly strong, and that R 101 was caught in one of them. Shortly after the watch had been changed, meaning a new height coxswain taking the wheel, the order to 'up-elevator' was given; the ship recovered slightly, though the bow was still pointing downward. At the same time engines were run to half-speed, and (this is especially significant) warning that the ship was coming down was given by the chief coxswain, who left his post in the control-room for this purpose. The angle of dive now increased with the pressure of the wind. In a few seconds the bow struck the ground and the ship burst into flames.

There have been a number of theories about the cause of the crash including failure of an electrical circuit in the ship while in mid-air; surging of the gas bags due to the unbraced transverse frames, thus causing undue instability; failure of the girders in mid-air; inexperience of the crew; and so on. The reasoning of the court is difficult to reconcile with one of the principal characteristics of a rigid airship which was that serious structural damage would not prevent a ship from returning to base and this had been proved by both *R 33* and *R 36*. It is unlikely that the back of *R 101* broke in mid-air (only one airship's loss has been ascribed to this cause—the *Shenandoah*).[29]

It is also improbable that the cause of the accident was due to the inexperience of the crew, although it is possible that the coxswain who had come on duty a few minutes before the crash may have failed to appreciate the airship's lack of height, bearing in mind her heaviness. There is no doubt that the disaster was largely due to the heaviness of the ship, her tendency to pitch, and her lack of disposable lift—in itself attributable to errors in design. These errors amounted to 5–10 per cent and Professor A. F. Lindemann (later Lord Cherwell) pointed out, at an aeronautical research committee meeting on airships in 1931, that a 10 per cent error in design was the difference between the lift of helium and hydrogen.[30]

So much for the technical reasons. Regarding the experiment as a whole, it is clear that it was subjected to unwarranted political pressure. Of the two air staff officers who were responsible, neither Higgins nor Dowding (who succeeded the former shortly before the *R 101* disaster) were airshipmen. Otherwise the air staff ought to have prevented the ship from being sent on her premature and fatal flight.

The effect of all this on British airship development was malignant, although its demise was delayed. Plans for *R 102*, which was to have a capacity of 7 million cubic feet, a gross lift of 226 tons and a disposable lift of 85 tons, had already been drawn up.[31] But Dowding, after the publication of the Simon inquiry report, decided that a new ship should not be built before thorough research had been carried out on *R 100*.[32] For it was at last recognised that the estimates for the first two ships had been far too optimistic. (The ratio of disposable lift to gross weight for *R 100* was only 33 per cent, while that for *R 101* was lower still at 25 per cent, but was increased to 38 per cent when the ship was enlarged.) To be commercially viable an efficiency of 45 per cent was required.[33] *R 100* was therefore to be given an extra bay, while further thought was to be given to the effect on the airship of climatic conditions on the India route. For example, the effect of varying changes in temperature on lift were to be considered. Experiments were also to be made with gaseous fuels.

None of these plans came to fruition. In August 1931, the recently formed National Government, in the grip of economic crisis, for the second time in ten years, decided to scrap the airship programme. Apart from a bay which was kept for experimental purposes,[34] *R 100* was broken up and sold for scrap; and although a skeleton staff in the Royal Airship Works survived for a few more years, observing foreign airship development, the Government took no more interest in the potentiality of the rigid airship.[35]

The cancellation of the British programme also had a dispiriting effect on the Goodyear Zeppelin works at Akron. They feared that it would only encourage the anti-airship faction in the USA, then suffering acutely from the economic depression.[36] However, *Akron*, as she was named, was the first of the two ships to be launched, in August 1931. Twice the size of *Graf Zeppelin*, and 35 per cent larger than *R 100* and *R 101*, she made her first flight on 23 September carrying 112 persons, including Adm Moffett and the Secretary of the navy. After ten flights in which the controls, and the swivelling propellers, able to give thrust in four directions (ahead, astern, upwards and downwards), were tested, speed runs made and dynamic lift tests carried out, the ship was accepted by the navy and was based at Lakehurst. Her commissioning was celebrated on 2 November by a special press flight with no fewer than 207 people on board, including Adm Moffett—a world record for passengers carried in a single aircraft. (Arnstein would have increased the total to 300 but the authorities forbade it.)[37] Her formal acceptance trials were completed by May of the following year.

In January 1932, having carried out successfully a number of cross-country flights, *Akron* took part in a three-day exercise with the scouting fleet off the coast of the Carolinas and north-east of the Bahamas.[38] She operated without her aeroplanes, as the launching equipment was not yet ready. After arriving at the rendezvous, having tailed a storm and collected some 8 tons of snow and ice on the outer cover, her military performance was judged to be a qualified success. Shortly afterwards she moored to the mast of the *Patoka* in Hampton Roads.

Public opinion, ever eager to exploit any mishap to the airship, was presented with a good opportunity when *Akron* was hauled out of her shed to enable a party of Congressmen to fly in her and form an opinion of her airworthiness.[39] Outside the shed a cross-wind caught the ship and one of the holding ropes broke away. The ship slewed round, while the tail first swung up in the air and then hit the ground with a bump. The politicians were apparently not too disconcerted, but extended repairs compelled *Akron* to miss the annual fleet exercise in the Pacific. It was admitted later that the ship should have not been taken out of the shed in such weather conditions. However, not long after when the ship completed her acceptance trials, the Congressmen took a further trip and exonerated her from all the allegations made against her. But her speed fell short of the required 85mph, and this was largely due to the two-bladed wooden propellers.

Akron now set out on her first trans-continental flight to the new airship base at Sunnyvale, California. The ship had to fly through a series of violent gusts and after 77hr in the air her captain, Rosendahl, decided to land at the airfield at San Diego, which had neither the proper facilities nor trained landing party to receive the ship.[40] The two aeroplanes, now on board, were released and one of the pilots took command of the raw landing party.

As there were no bollards for the side guys, the latter had to be held by the landing party. But while the main wire was being dropped, a violent gust blew the ship across the landing ground, carrying her up, in spite of the action of the swivelling propellers, and before the main wire had been connected. The side ropes were torn out of the hands of the landing party who all let go except three, two of whom were killed. The third man was laboriously winched aboard the ship. But in endeavouring to save the men, *Akron* had valved a lot of gas. The aeroplanes therefore flew independently to Sunnyvale. For this incident Rosendahl received a reprimand as he had sufficient fuel to reach Sunnyvale where a trained landing party was in readiness.

Akron moored to *Patoka* in San Francisco Bay and, although short of helium, joined the scouting fleet in an exercise off the Californian coast. She twice located 'enemy' cruisers, but the latter retaliated with seaplanes and *Akron*'s aeroplanes were not on board to provide defence. As the ship was again light, one of her aeroplanes was flown aboard to act as ballast. The usual practice was for the airship to ascend light and the aeroplanes would later take off and hook on to the ship. An unfavourable assessment of the ship's performance in the exercise was given by the officer in command, who added that in his opinion no more money should be spent on airships.

Akron returned to Lakehurst, but while over Arizona a propeller was damaged, and in order to reduce weight the aeroplanes were ordered to fly on to Lakehurst on their own. Later, while crossing a mountain range near Douglas, Arizona, at pressure height, there was a loss of gas through the automatic valves.

During the later months of 1932 six Curtiss F9C-2 hook-on aeroplanes were accepted, and a number of practice flights were made with them using the trapeze, both by day and by night.

There were no specialist officers in the US navy. On 22 June 1932 Rosendahl had been relieved as captain of *Akron* by Cdr Alger H. Dresel. Early in 1933 the captain was changed again; the newcomer was Cdr Frank C. Wood. Irrespective of the personal qualities of the officers concerned here and elsewhere, that system of posting men has been criticised as being one which did not help to make experienced airship officers.[41]

One of *Akron*'s tasks was to assist in the calibration of radio-direction finding stations on the East Coast. But *Akron* also appeared in ceremonial guise over Washington during the inauguration ceremony of the new President—Franklin D. Roosevelt.

On the evening of 3 April 1933, with orders to calibrate radio-direction finding stations off the New Jersey coast, *Akron* took off with a complement of 73, including Moffett.[42] The ship was in good form, but the forecast was unpromising with a low-pressure front to the south-west. Radio aerials were reeled in because of lightning. Shortly after midnight, after the ship had manoeuvred in a number of directions, a thunderstorm was encountered. Suddenly *Akron* began to fall. Ballast was dropped and the bow came up. The ship was now at a dangerously low altitude—about 800ft above the sea, so that when struck by a sharp gust, the lower vertical fin struck the water. *Akron* made one desperate attempt to rise, but it was too late. With a strong wind blowing on the port side, the hull hit the water and broke up at once. Only three men survived, including the executive officer, Lieut Cdr H. V. Wiley. They were picked up by a ship. It was the heaviest loss of life due to an air crash to date. But, in spite of a revulsion of feeling against airships, a Congressional committee recommended that airship operations should continue and that the second rigid should go into service. It seems that *Akron*'s altimeter was faulty—had she been 100ft higher when she pulled out of her last dive she would have been saved. Earlier appreciation of the storm area would also have saved her. *Akron* made a total of 62 flights and had been airborne for 1,695hr.

Less than a month before *Akron*'s unhappy end, Adm Moffett's wife christened the new airship *Macon*. Her completion was delayed because the men feared that because of the depression a third ship would never be built. She closely resembled her sister ship, but certain improvements were incorporated and she cost less to build. A series of trials, during which she was based at Lakehurst, took place during the summer of 1933. She was a faster ship than *Akron* achieving 87mph. (*Akron*'s best speed was 79·4mph), due to better streamlining of the hull and to the use of three-bladed variable pitch propellers.[43]

On 12 October she left Lakehurst for Sunnyvale, now named Moffett Field, in memory of the leading airship protagonist, under command of Dresel. For the next 12 months *Macon* operated with the Pacific Fleet. On several occasions she was judged to have been shot down by 'enemy' aircraft, but she was admittedly vulnerable, and she may have been mishandled.

On 20 April 1934 she was ordered to join the Atlantic Fleet off Florida. On her way across the continent she flew into a strong gust over the San Gorgonio Pass in California. On the 21st, with all eight engines at full speed, she negotiated a turbulent patch over Texas and pockets of disturbance made her pitch up and down in rapid succession. Several girders buckled and it looked at the time as if the port horizontal fin might be carried away. But temporary mid-air repairs were made and she flew on to moor at an expeditionary mast at Opa-Locker, Florida. Here more permanent repairs were effected in order that the ship might take part in a fleet exercise. *Macon* was 'shot down' by six fighters from the aircraft carrier *Lexington*, but not before she had reported the carrier's position. After a second exercise *Macon* flew back to Moffett Field, her aeroplanes proceeding independently. Her performance in the exercise, like that of *Akron* on a previous occasion, failed to convince the commander-in-chief that rigid airships were an asset to the fleet.

Lieut Cdr Herbert V. Wiley, probably the most experienced American airship pilot, now took command of *Macon*, and for the next seven months she resumed operating with the Pacific fleet. One of the features of this period was the use of a 'spy basket', similar to those used by Zeppelins during World War I. The main disadvantage was that while the 'spy basket' was unreeled the ship's aeroplanes were unable to operate.

It had been agreed that several transverse frames and the fins needed reinforcing because of the April accident, but observance of the scheduled operational programme meant that nothing had been done by the autumn of 1934. Burgess reported to the Bureau of Aeronautics that nobody seemed unduly worried.

Macon continued to exercise with the Pacific fleet with the repairs still outstanding. Early on the morning of 11 February 1935 she left Moffett Field to take part in a minor fleet tactical exercise off the Santa Barbara Islands. During the day she made good use of her four aeroplanes. The following evening, while returning to base in boisterous weather, including rain and thick cloud, she was caught in a gust and fell from 2,700ft to 1,700ft. The upper vertical fin was carried away. The damage spread to the stern part, which collapsed, deflating the stern gas bags. Loss of gas made the bow tilt upwards. During the efforts to bring the ship to an even keel, too much ballast was dropped. Consequently she rose above pressure height. That meant that her automatic valves opened, releasing the small margin of lift that remained. Twenty-four minutes after the accident, *Macon* landed like a free balloon on the Pacific. She sank after 30min, carrying her aeroplanes with her. Distress signals from the crew, who fortunately had had time to don lifejackets or to board rubber rafts, brought help from a cruiser, and so 81 of the 83 persons on board were saved. Petrol which streamed from broken tanks, now deep under water, was ignited by flares dropped during the rescue operation. *Macon* had made 54 flights and had traversed 90,546 miles.

Thus a relatively minor structural failure had precipitated a critical situation. At the subsequent inquiry an attempt was made to discover an inherent defect in the fin structure, but it also transpired that if No 17.5 main transverse frame had been reinforced at its junction with the upper fin all would have been well. With hindsight it could be said that it ought to have been possible to bring back *Macon* to base after its fin and stern damage by using one rudder and making a redistribution of weight; Zeppelins had been nursed home during the war in worse shape.

The loss of *Macon* might not have been the end of US naval use of rigid airships.[44] In 1936 the Secretary of the navy set up a committee of distinguished scientists under Dr William F. Durand to investigate whether it was worth while continuing development, as opposed to whether airships had any military value. The committee concluded unanimously that there was a future both in the military and the commercial role for large airships. It recommended that development should not be brought to a halt, though it felt that further research and more training of crew were both necessary. Such views were reinforced by two other committees, one of which was appointed by President Roosevelt.

But airships continued to lose favour and the destruction of *Hindenburg* by fire in May 1937 merely confirmed the prejudice of the anti-airship faction. The pro-airship men, such as Garland Fulton, on the other hand tried to promote the rigid as an aircraft carrier, and prepared a design for a ship of $9\frac{1}{2}$ million cubic feet capacity, which would carry nine dive-bomber aeroplanes. An airship of more modest dimensions—3 million cubic feet capacity—under the designation *ZRN* was approved, but the design was not properly worked out largely because the President stipulated that her length should not exceed 325ft. By 1940 the possibility of becoming involved in a fresh world war was absorbing the naval authorities. The need was for aeroplanes—in quantity—and it was inevitable that the claims of the rigid airship should be forgotten. Meanwhile *Los Angeles* had been sold for scrap, and on 16 December 1940 the Goodyear Zeppelin Corporation was liquidated.

The successor to *Graf Zeppelin* started under the designation *LZ 128*. She underwent a number of changes in the light of the accidents to

R 101 and to *Akron* and *Macon*. Those changes included the installation of diesel engines and the strengthening of her fins. But the engine development, which had been put out to tender (Daimler Benz coming nearest the requirement), took much longer than anticipated. So although 70 per cent completed in 1933, *LZ 129* (as she now was) had still not been finished by the autumn of 1935.[45] It will be recalled that the ship was to be inflated with helium because of the *R 101* disaster. However, on account of the depression, Eckener failed to obtain the non-inflammable gas.[46] Few modifications were needed, though, to inflate the ship solely with hydrogen, and the gas-pressure valves did not require changing.

In anticipation of a regular transatlantic service a new company called Deutsche Zeppelin Luft Reederei was set up jointly with Lufthansa at Frankfurt am Main, which was to be the new terminal for the North American service. A shed large enough to accommodate *LZ 129* was constructed there.

LZ 129, now named *Hindenburg* after the aged soldier-president of the German Republic, made her maiden flight on 4 March 1936. Further flights were made on 5 and 19 March, including a 30hr endurance test starting on the latter date. On the 26th, in company with *Graf Zeppelin*, she made a four-day flight over Germany, dropping leaflets and broadcasting by loudspeaker, as part of the Nazi Party's propaganda campaign for the elections, held on the 29th to vindicate Hitler's recent reoccupation of the Rhineland. Her controls were slightly damaged on take off for this flight, but she was able to cruise for 3hr before landing for quick repairs.[47]

At the beginning of the following month, the new ship made her first voyage to South America under command of Ernst Lehmann. On return she began a series of ten round trips from Frankfurt to Lakehurst under Capts Lehmann or Pruss. Seven more trips were made to South America.

As usual the voyage was planned on the weather map. On one North Atlantic flight, for example, Lehmann navigated across the top side of two depressions, one off the north-west coast of Ireland, and the other moving to mid-Atlantic from Newfoundland. This enabled the ship to take advantage of following winds which, off the southern tip of Greenland, added 102mph to the ship's own speed. The ground

O

speed at this moment was averaging 180mph, possibly the fastest known speed accomplished by a rigid airship. While at Lakehurst on this occasion only 6hr were spent in refuelling, gassing, provisioning and taking on a fresh complement of passengers.[48]

As noted in the previous chapter, there was more luxury in *Hindenburg* than on *Graf Zeppelin*. The cuisine was excellent and the promenade deck was equal to a stroll from port to starboard across the deck of a 27,560-ton ocean-going liner. Ten tons of mail could be carried in the keel, and, in order to expedite delivery of that mail, it was proposed to launch a light aeroplane from under the hull. In March 1937 launching and pick-up trials were carried out by Ernst Udet, later to become chief of the German air staff. Apart from mail, a variety of freight was carried, including a circus horse, antelopes and cars. But a line was drawn at taking an elephant.

At last it seemed that the long-range airship had a future, for even if the aeroplane caught up with it in terms of endurance, the airship had greater comfort, smoother operation, no noise or vibration, and was reckoned to be cheaper to operate. For the outward trip to North America *Hindenburg* averaged 65hr, and for the return trip she averaged 50hr, and she soon acquired a reputation for punctuality. By the end of 1936 she had made over 55 flights, flown 2,764hr, cruised 191,583 miles, carried 2,798 passengers, and handled 160 tons of freight. She had recovered 75 per cent of her operating costs in spite of the short season.[49]

Then tragedy struck. On 3 May 1937, after returning from the initial scheduled flight of the year to South America, and fitting in a round-Germany publicity journey, *Hindenburg* set out over the Atlantic on the first of the summer season's crossings to the USA. It was her 63rd flight. Persistent head winds delayed her arrival over Lakehurst on 6 May. Rosendahl, in charge of the airfield, radioed the ship not to land until a rainstorm had dispersed. Pruss, the ship's captain, agreed. About an hour later, at 5.12 pm (Eastern standard time) the airfield was clear, although an occasional flash of lightning was visible on the horizon. At 5.22 pm Rosendahl advised Pruss to land. What was known as the 'high landing' procedure now took place, the ship dropping ropes from the bow. The only thing watchers noted unusual about *Hindenburg* was that she was tail heavy even after dropping ballast and valving gas, and an extra precaution was taken by sending six men forward to equalise the weight. As the ship began to land rain started to fall gently. Evidence at this point is confused. According to some witnesses, *Hindenburg* made a short turn, approaching the mooring area quite rapidly. At 6.25 pm, while she was being held by one of the hemp bow ropes, and was still about 700ft up, fire broke out near the stern at the top of the hull. The flames spread towards the stern, which sank to the ground, inclining the bow upwards at a sharp angle. Flames rapidly ran along the full length of the ship, and within a minute *Hindenburg* was a blazing mass on the ground. Miraculously, out of 61 people on board, 39, including Pruss, though he was severely burned, were saved. Of the 36 passengers, 13 died, the first passenger casualties in commercial Zeppelin operations. One of them was Ernst Lehmann, the veteran airship pilot.

The cause of the fire remains a mystery.[50] The US Bureau of Commerce committee which thoroughly investigated the accident ruled out the possibility of sabotage, a theory avidly seized on by authors of popular books on airships. It also considered, but dismissed, the possibility of a leaking gas bag causing a combustible mixture of gas and air within the hull; the accumulation of gas in the ship's ventilating system; the breaking of a propeller, fragments of which might have punctured a gas bag; the ripping of a gas bag by a circumferential wire; a structural failure in the stern of the ship causing hydrogen to be set free by puncturing a gas bag while the accidental breaking of an electric lead or metal part produced a spark; ignition of gas by sparks from an engine; the heat of exhaust gases causing ignition; and the ignition of a pocket of gas by an electrical short in the keel, the fire travelling upwards setting alight the hydrogen below the outer cover at the top of the ship. Finally, there was the possibility of ignition by brush discharge whereby electricity would be attracted to the top points of the ship when the mooring ropes touched the ground, and, because the ropes were damp a spark could have jumped across the mixture of hydrogen and air.

Basing their conclusions on the evidence that there had been a leak in Nos 4 and 5 gas bags in the stern, and that the first appearance of fire was just forward of the upper vertical fin, the committee maintained that a brush discharge probably ignited the hydrogen and air. In reaching this conclusion, they ignored other evidence which contended that there was a muffled explosion, like turning on a gas ring, within the ship.

The destruction of *Hindenburg* by fire, coming so close after the burning of *R 101*, compelled Eckener to cancel the reliable *Graf Zeppelin* South American service. In her last years this veteran airship not only broke a number of time records by cutting down the outward journey from Germany to South America to 71hr and bringing the return journey down to 61hr, but she also established a new record for endurance. This was caused by a revolution which prevented the ship from landing at Reçife (Pernambuco), Brazil. Her first duty was to drop mail by parachute at a suitable spot. The ship then cruised offshore. There was sufficient fuel and oil for another four days; food was the problem, but even this was solved by lowering a net on to the deck of a German steamer and taking on provisions. Eventually the airship landed safely at Reçife after being airborne for 119hr.

In sum, *Graf Zeppelin* paid for herself and helped to finance the construction of her two successors. She had crossed the South Atlantic 140 times, the North Atlantic seven times, and the Pacific once. By the end of her last commercial trip, she had flown over 16,000hr, covering a total distance of 1,060,000 miles, and carried without injury 13,100 passengers.

Germany's last rigid, *LZ 130*, was to have been inflated with helium.[51] Eckener doggedly maintained that even with this more expensive gas, by pre-heating, thereby helping to conserve gas, it would be possible to run a cheaper, though slower (but more comfortable) transoceanic service than one operated by flying boat or aeroplane. But although Congress had assented to the sale of helium to Eckener, with Hitler in power in Germany, the Secretary of the Interior, Harold Ickes, intervened on the grounds that helium was of potential military value.

This was the final blow against a regular commercial service. Named by Eckener, *Graf Zeppelin II*, and the 119th Zeppelin to be built, she passed under control of the German air force despite Eckener's disapproval. She was, in any case, forbidden to operate commercially outside Germany. Her spacious saloon was fitted with radio interception gear, and her first duty was to fly reconnaissances near the Czech border in the autumn of 1938, in the hope that radio transmissions from the Czech forces would be picked up.[52] In the summer of 1939, under command of Capt Albert Sammt, but with senior air force signals officers on board, she made history by being the first aircraft to carry out an electronic countermeasures mission. She was flown off the English east coast, her state rooms crammed with electronic equipment, in an endeavour to discover the function of the high towers set up at Bawdsey. Those towers were early signs of the British radar chain, already in operation. Imagine the surprise of the radar operators to see the unmistakeable 'blip' of a great airship on their cathode ray tubes! But on the three occasions on which reconnaissances were flown the crackling noises produced by the electronic gear in *Graf Zeppelin II* failed to elucidate the true function of the towers. The signals officers concluded that they were connected with radio transmissions.[53] So by a strange turn of fate the last flight of a Zeppelin was designed to fulfil one of the original functions of rigid airships as conceived by Count Zeppelin.

In the meantime, with international tension growing and the inability of the Deutsche Zeppelin Reederi to use helium, the construction of two more large rigids was abruptly terminated. One of these ships was to have been sold to a Dutch shipping firm which wanted to start an airship service between Holland and the Dutch Far East possessions. Another proposal was for a route linking New York and the Dutch East Indies, touching down in Spain and in the Middle East en route.[54]

Graf Zeppelin I and *Graf Zeppelin II (LZ 130)*, once the pride of Germany, were to suffer greater humiliation. In March 1940 Reichs-Marshal Goering, head of the German air force, who had ensured that Lufthansa was the dominant partner in Deutsche Luftschiff Reederei, ordered that both ships should be broken up for scrap. Goering was an ex Luftwaffe pilot, too, and naturally antipathetic to airships. He also instructed that the new airship shed at Frankfurt was to be demolished. The girders of the elder ship were used to construct a radar tower in Holland. Luftschiffbau Zeppelin was turned over to war production, making, in the final stages of the war, radar equipment and parts for *V 2* rockets. By the end of 1944 the sheds at Friedrichshafen had been devastated by Allied bombing. So, at least for the time being, Count Zeppelin's dream of the trans-oceanic airship was incapable of fulfilment.

But the dream had already become tarnished despite the enthusiasm of Eckener, Arnstein, Hunsaker, and others to turn it into a reality. The rapid progress being made by heavier-than-air craft was putting the airship into the shade. Ironically, duralumin and aluminium, which the airship had originally exploited, were now being used to make aeroplanes, such as the Junkers and the Douglas, more efficient in design while more powerful engines enabled a greater payload to be carried. Although still not able to compete in range, aeroplanes could now fly 1,000 miles without a stop, and they were reaching speeds of 200mph. They were also becoming safer. On the second anniversary of Charles Lindbergh's flight across the Atlantic (20 May 1928), out of 18 attempts to fly the Atlantic from America to Europe only 7 had succeeded and the failures had cost 12 lives. Out of 13 flights from Europe only 3 succeeded, and 5 men and 3 women were killed. By 1945 transatlantic flights had become routine, not only with flying boats but with four-engined aeroplanes.

Aeroplanes were cheaper to build than airships; they could fly at higher altitudes and so escape poor weather; they could operate comfortably over sea and land, whereas the airship performed best over the ocean; and their total flying hours were greater.

In order to survive and improve its performance the airship had to be bigger. Inflated with helium, *Hindenburg* would have lost two-thirds of her payload; *R 101* would have been unable to ascend. But size presented problems which designers were then unable to solve; girders would have to be even stronger than before; gas bags would have to be contained within larger bays; engines would have to be more powerful and economical in fuel consumption; and outer covers would have to be stronger and at the same time light. The problems of mooring, helium, radio, radar, and fuel systems were of lesser importance.

CHAPTER 9

Further Developments in Non- and Semi-Rigids

Italy led the world in the development of semi-rigid airships from the end of World War I until 1927. She exported ten ships of the type. Four went to Spain, two to the USA, two to Argentina, and one each to Holland and Japan.[1] They were all constructed by the Stabilimento di Construzione Aeronautiche (SCA), in Rome, or at outlying factories. For instance, the metal structure was usually assembled at Turin. SCA had had a wartime start, being founded by four engineers—Crocco, Nobile, Celestino Usuelli and Prassone. Umberto Nobile, a brilliant young engineer who had been trained by Crocco, but who had been found unfit for military service, was the brains of the group.

However, unlike his colleagues, Nobile believed that the future lay with the semi-rigid rather than with the rigid.[2] In particular, although unable to carry such a heavy load as rigids, semi-rigids were easier to design because they contained the minimum amount of rigid material required for the critical areas of the envelope. These stresses centred mainly on the strong keel which had, at the same time, considerable elasticity. Semi-rigids could be built more cheaply, more easily, and more quickly than rigids; and they were easily dismantled and re-assembled; while the metal parts could be inspected more easily than in a rigid airship. In one respect only did Nobile concede that the rigid was superior—that it was capable of greater streamlining and therefore had less drag than the semi-rigid.

In the early days the group worked harmoniously on *Roma* (see page 53), but Crocco wanted to build a much larger ship of a capacity of 4 million cu ft and of a rigid design. The group now split up, and while Crocco's rigid was never built, Nobile who was favourably regarded by the recently formed Fascist Government, and was given military rank, designed the smaller *N* ship.

N 1 had a capacity of 654,000cu ft; she was 347ft long: her maximum diameter was 60ft: her gross weight was 17 tons, and she had a useful lift of 8 tons. Her power consisted of three 260hp reversible Maybach engines, suspended from the keel.[3] They were capable of propelling the ship at a cruising speed of 53mph, while a maximum speed of over 60mph was obtainable. The passenger car could hold 20. There was a kitchen, and hot as well as cold running water. The envelope was more streamlined than *Roma,* and the control car had ample visibility for navigation. The envelope was divided into ten compartments to hold the gas; the keel was strong enough to withstand the stresses should one of the cells be deflated. The shape of the fins was cruciform with large control surfaces. Two of these ships were to be used for arctic exploration. The third, *N 3,* of 274,700cu ft capacity, was bought by the Japanese navy, but was destroyed after making a forced landing during manoeuvres.

Nobile also designed *O–1,* of the *O* type, mentioned on page 126, with a volume of 127,000cu ft and sold her to the US navy. But she had a brief, inglorious career, for she was flown into an orchard shortly after delivery. His other ships built between 1922 and 1924 were the *SCA* (named after the airship works), with a capacity of 53,000cu ft, to be used either for scouting in a military role, or as a sporting ship. Two similar crafts were sold to the Spanish Government. Next was the *PM,* alike to the *SCA.* Finally, *Mr,* a baby airship with a capacity of only 33,885cu ft and a useful lift of 990lb, was produced.

In Milan Enrico Forlanini continued to design semi-rigid airships, though none appear to have been built. In the early 1920s he planned the *FV* of 813,000cu ft capacity, with two cars instead of one. Each car was to contain two engines driving two independent propellers; at the stern were to be cruciform fins like a rigid airship.[4] A larger vessel would have had a capacity of nearly $1\frac{1}{2}$ million cubic feet.

Shortly before his death in 1930, however, Forlanini designed a much more revolutionary craft called *Omnia Dir,* with a capacity of 143,500cu ft powered by a 150hp engine. He intended this small experimental semi-rigid to be capable of manoeuvring in any direction at its lowest speed or when hovering, and it could also be kept on a definite course. The declutched engine was to drive air through vertical and horizontal jets arranged at either end of the envelope. The

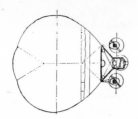

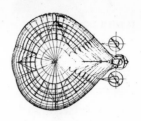

Cross-section

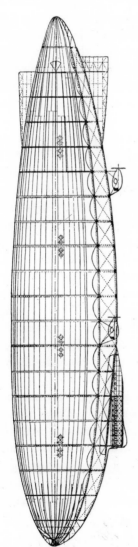

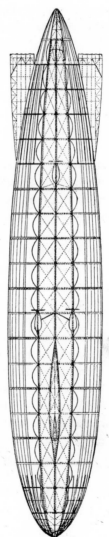

Italian *N* type semi-rigid (*Norge*)

Upper: side elevation. Lower: plan

airship was also to carry its own mooring mast—an inverted pyramid of light struts which could be anchored to a securing link on the ground. Lack of funds prevented development of this unusual design; and, by 1930, airships were no longer regarded favourably by the Italian Government.

The north passage across the North Pole from the Atlantic to the Pacific—the historic short route from Europe to China and the Indies —had eluded explorers since 1527 until the early 1900s. Capt Roald Amundsen had negotiated the north-east and north-west passages in 1903–6 and 1918–20 respectively. On both occasions he entered from the Atlantic side.

In the 1920s both heavier- and lighter-than-air craft were used to penetrate still farther into the Arctic. On 19 May 1925 Amundsen and the American explorer, Lincoln Ellsworth, made a reconnaissance in two Dornier-Wal flying boats, coming to within 90 miles of the North Pole.[5] After a spell of 25 days on the ice, they abandoned one flying boat and flew back to Spitzbergen in the other. On 29 April of the following year, Cdr Richard Byrd, of the US navy, arrived in King's Bay, Spitzbergen. On 9 May, flying a three-engined Fokker mono-plane, he and his pilot, Floyd Bennett, made the first flight over the North Pole, returning to their starting point after just under 16hr absence.

However, Amundsen and Ellsworth appreciated that at that time airships were more suitable than flying boats for long-distance flights and for scientific observations. Sponsored by the Aero Club of Norway, they therefore purchased *N 1* from the Italian Government, although a second and larger ship, *N 2* was under construction. It was agreed that the Italians should be responsible for flying the ship, while the Norwegians would supply provisions and clothing, plus the requirements for an emergency landing on the ice.

On 29 March, 1926 *N 1* was renamed *Norge*. Two months later, watched by Benito Mussolini, she took off for King's Bay, Spitzbergen. Nobile commanded the ship; under him was a polyglot crew of Italians, Americans, Norwegians, Swedes and Russians, not forgetting Nobile's dog Titinia. Maj Scott flew on the first leg of the voyage from Rome to Pulham, where a brief landing was made to refuel. The ship was proving to be very heavy. Nobile, for that reason, rejected a proposal of Amundsen's to postpone the flight until June, when there would be less chance of ice forming on the envelope. Nobile pointed out that the warmer weather would only reduce the lift.

Norge arrived at King's Bay in 103hr flying time, having covered about 5,000 miles. At this improvised base a mast had been erected, and while the ship was moored a new port engine was installed to replace one with a broken crankshaft. Nobile now had to work out how much petrol he should carry in the event of meeting strong head-winds.

All was ready by 11 May. That morning *Norge* took off for the transpolar flight, carrying 16 people. They included Amundsen and Ellsworth, the joint leaders of the expedition.[6] Making her way by wireless and magnetic compass direction, and by solar observations, *Norge* reached the North Pole at 11.30 am on 12 May. Speed was reduced while Amundsen, Ellsworth and Nobile dropped their respective countries' flags. At 6.30 am the following day *Norge* reached the location of the 'ice pole' (the centre of the polar ice pack) and confirmed Peary's belief that no land existed in that region; she continued on her way until the 80° north latitude. She then changed course to a westerly direction, sighting Port Barrow on the coast of Alaska at 6.30 pm (GMT) on 13 May, 46hr 45min after leaving King's Bay. Fortunately she had a following wind for the latter part of the flight.

The main hazard which the airship had encountered was fog, particularly prevalent in the Arctic during the summer months. Luckily, the fog never rose above 3,000ft, and consequently Nobile was usually able to fly his ship over it and so avoid the danger of ice encrustation. But the fog became thicker as *Norge* followed the Alaskan coastline. For much of the way she actually flew under the fog, thus making navigation both dangerous and difficult. At about 8 am on 14 May Nobile decided to land at the settlement of Teller, Alaska. He ordered the landing ballast buoy, or weighted sack, to be thrown out at the end of a hemp rope to act as an anchor.

Once on the ground *Norge* was deflated. Designed to fly in the relatively calm atmosphere of the Mediterranean, she had been in the arctic air for 71hr. She had made history by flying over the north passage, bisecting a million square miles of unknown arctic territory by a trail of about 100 miles in width. Apart from this feat much astronomical, magnetic, meteorological and zoological data had been accumulated; while the navigation entirely on meridian was a record for all types of vessel. A surface expedition operating by land and sea at that time would have taken two years to achieve the same purpose, spending a couple of winters on the ice cap.

The fear that the ship would become too heavy because of the formation of ice proved to be unfounded. In fact, while the ship was flying through the fog, ice did form in some depth on the propellers, but only to a small extent on the envelope. The real danger came when ice, falling in the path of the propeller blades, was hurled against the keel. Perforation of the envelope would have placed the ship in jeopardy. It was a problem that could be overcome, either by smearing special grease over the outer metallic parts, or by protecting the propellers from the flying ice. Snowstorms proved to be no problem as the snow was blown away by the wind before it had a chance to form on the envelope.

Norge's flight showed, as already described in Chapter 8, that the airship was an admirable vehicle for arctic exploration. It could hover, stand at anchor in favourable conditions, and there was ample room for equipment and for making observations. Nobile was therefore keen to continue such flights. But, as sharp disagreements had arisen between him and Amundsen and the Norwegians, the Italians decided to go it alone, the next expedition being financed by the city of Milan.

The party was to embark on *N 2*, named *Italia*. She was similar in most respects to *Norge*, except that the keel was stronger and made watertight; the control car was fitted with a double wall of canvas covering for better insulation against the cold; the bow stiffening was increased; the envelope was reinforced as protection against ice being thrown off the propellers; more fuel tanks were accommodated.[7]

On this occasion two scientists were included in the expedition, while experienced navigators and wireless operators were taken. It was intended to land the scientists as near to the Pole as possible so that they could carry out observations and research over a long period. Therefore, equipment such as an inflatable raft, dinghies, sledges, tents, and special arctic clothing was carried in the airship. Finally, a wooden cross, blessed by the Pope, was to be dropped on the Pole. The total load amounted to 1½ tons while 2 tons of ballast had to be taken—a heavy weight for such a small ship.

Thus heavily laden, at 1.15 am on 15 April 1927, *Italia* rose slowly into the air. Avoiding the Alps, she flew eastwards over Hungary and Czecho-Slovakia, before making towards Poland. The weather was far from perfect, storms and strong headwinds being met; much of the ballast had to be thrown overboard. Finally, a radio message was received advising Nobile to increase speed to Vadsö, on the edge of the Barents Sea, where there were mooring facilities. *Italia* reached Vadsö just 30hr after leaving Milan, having covered a distance of 1,200 miles.

After 23hr of unpleasant buffeting at the mast at Vadsö, Nobile cast off on the last leg of the outward flight to King's Bay, Spitzbergen. The wind had changed at last to a more favourable quarter, and *Italia* arrived at her destination at 11.30 am on 6 May. Here, supposed to provide succour, was the Italian base ship *Citta di Milano*, another mooring mast, and an inadequate shed without a roof to accommodate *Italia* while she was being prepared for the flight over the Pole.

Nobile decided to make a number of test flights to see how his airship behaved. But, on return from the first flight, snow fell heavily on the vulnerable envelope, threatening to crush it. The crew, working desperately, swept the snow off the top, without damaging the fabric with their heavy boots.

The weather cleared after four days and enabled rehearsals for lowering the pneumatic raft which was to carry the scientists to take place. A tent, sleeping-bags, and provisions were to be lowered with the raft in case the airship dragged her anchor and drifted away. Before the big flight Nobile carried out a 69hr survey in the direction of Nicholas II Land. That trip, in the event, proved to be the most successful part of the programme. About 25,000 square miles of arctic territory were explored and valuable meteorological data acquired. On 18 May *Italia* was back at King's Bay, having logged 2,500 miles.

Early on the morning of 23 May Nobile judged that all was in order and the ship cast off for the North Pole with 16 on board. The route which took her via the north tip of Greenland was impeded by fog, but still more serious was the forecast of two cyclonic areas. Rather than risk headwinds on the return journey from the Pole, Nobile was in favour of continuing the flight either to Alaska, as with *Norge*, or to Siberia. But the scientists were loath to give up their programme, and the navigator was optimistic that the tail-wind would cease. These anxieties were temporarily allayed when the ship passed over the Pole and the wooden cross and Italian flag were cast out on to the ice.

Nobile now decided to return to base because *Italia* was having to face strong cross-winds from the south-west. In order to avoid flying against the wind he chose an indirect approach to King's Bay. But the ship continued to be dogged by cross-winds, and the dreaded fog thickened. Members of the crew now reported that the cross-braces of the forward part of the ship were giving way. Then ice from the propellers began to plaster the envelope and soon small holes were formed. Two men were set to work to repair these rents. However, the Swedish meteorologist, Dr Finn Malmgren, was still confident that the wind would drop. He urged Nobile to increase speed to the maximum even at the danger of running short of fuel.

But the wind did not abate, and the ship's speed, in spite of the exertions of the engineers, began to drop. Finally, the elevator wheel jammed. Nobile ordered engines to be stopped, allowing the ship to drift. One of the crew released the elevator control with a blow from a light hammer. Temporarily, all went well again. It was 10 am on 25 May and they reckoned they were about 180 miles from King's Bay. The ship then went down by the stern. This was her final agony. Appreciating a crash was inevitable, Nobile ordered the engines to be stopped, and for ballast to be discharged and for the ballast chain thrown out with the object of reducing the ship's rate of descent. But, her nose high in the air, the stricken airship fell on to the ice at a speed of about 60mph. Ten men, including Nobile, with his dog, were thrown out; the airship thus lightened, shortly after rose up, carrying with her six of the crew. She vanished, never to be seen again. One man was killed on impact with the ice cap, and Nobile and several others were seriously injured. However, due to the presence of mind of the chief engineer who managed to throw out a tent, radio equipment and fuel before the ship drifted away, their condition was not yet desperate.

The subsequent marooning of Nobile and his party of survivors in their tent stained red with dye from the special bombs carried in the airship and used for estimating height (the time was taken from the moment a bomb left the ship until the dye was scattered on the ground), is a familiar story as are the attempts by Russians, Norwegians and Swedes to rescue them. It is an unhappy story: Amundsen who, in spite of his recent quarrel with Nobile, set out to search for him in a hydroplane, was lost. When Nobile was finally rescued by a Swedish aircraft on 23 June, it was said that he insisted on being taken off before the others. In fact, it was the pilot who had insisted on taking Nobile first. Earlier the Italians had said that Nobile should be taken off first so he could locate the missing men. Moreover, Italian aeronautical circles turned against Nobile and airships in general. A new semi-rigid *N* of 1,800,000cu ft capacity under construction, and which would have been even larger than Roma was abandoned; this was due in no small measure to the Italian air force officer, Gen Balbo, who was making a reputation with flying boats.

Nevertheless, the question remains whether *Italia* could have been saved. Unfortunately, the court of inquiry, which included Nobile's ex-colleague Crocco among its members, and who had severed relations with the former on account of his predilection for rigid airships, was tainted by political intrigue generated by the Fascists. In such an atmosphere Nobile moved as an innocent. Crocco held that Nobile had failed to handle the ship correctly, although he (Crocco) was personally unacquainted with either *Norge* or *Italia*.[8] Yet while Nobile in practice had undoubtedly distinguished himself in his handling of *Norge*, he was primarily a designer rather than a pilot and leader.

An unbiased and convincing explanation of the accident has been offered by the experienced airshipman, Knut Eckener.[9] He pointed out that while the elevator was being repaired the airship was floating in the fog as a free balloon, but soon she gained altitude, with a consequent expansion of gas, culminating in blowing off through the automatic valves. *Italia* was now once more in equilibrium, but was floating in the sunshine above the fog. Superheating therefore occurred, and more gas escaped through the valves. The repairs were completed and the engines started up. But Nobile, in order to get back on course, had to descend through the fog in order to get his bearings.

Now the loss of gas proved to be fatal. The small amount remaining in the envelope cooled quickly, thus diminishing the lift. The efforts of the crew to lighten the ship by throwing out ballast and every disposable article was to no avail. A crash was quite inevitable. If Nobile had immediately released enough gas in the first place by opening the manoeuvring valves so that the ship did not rise above the fog, the accident might well have been averted. Again, in retrospect, *Italia* was too small for the task of carrying a scientific expedition. A rigid airship, like *Graf Zeppelin*, would have been far more effective for the purpose.

All this does not excuse the shabby treatment meted out to Nobile, and it is some consolation that he was exonerated from blame after the end of World War II. His final act in the affair was to resign from his official appointment as airship designer and he retired into semiseclusion, though under surveillance by the secret police. In 1931, however, a new phase in his life began.

The Soviet Government had followed the flights of *Norge* and *Italia* with considerable interest, and, as Nobile was no longer holding any official Italian appointment, he was invited to the Soviet Union as technical adviser on semi-rigids. He remained in Russian employment until 1935, and is believed to have been responsible for the design of nine semi-rigid airships.

It will be recalled that Russia was one of the pioneer nations in non-rigid airship development, but that since the Revolution this interest had waned. However, by 1931 the Soviet Union's plans for developing the great tracts of Siberia, with its poor or non-existent communications, and her interest in polar research, provoked a revival of interest in airships, especially semi-rigids. The visit of *Graf Zeppelin* to Moscow also helped to stimulate interest in lighter-than-air craft.[10]

Semi-rigids were particularly appropriate for underdeveloped areas as they could be moored out in the open without difficulty, were easily deflatable, and had greater speed than river steamers, the alternative form of transport. The Russians intended to use them for carrying freight of a perishable nature, medical supplies, instruments, machinery and provisions, and for surveying and photography.

Very little information is available on Soviet airship development. It appears that there were two large works. One was at Leningrad, and the other near Moscow, at which was already situated the smaller, and older, airship factory and experimental centre of Zagi, where the well-known physicist, Tsiolkovski, was designing metalclad airships. The programme included the construction of 94 airships, but it is not known how many were actually built. Several semi-rigids, known as the *BV* class, were probably modelled on the *Italia*. They had a capacity of 700,000cu ft, were powered by three engines, possessed a maximum speed of 68mph, and had a maximum range of 2,000 miles. They were able to carry 16 passengers as well as a crew of the same size. In 1937 one of these ships (probably *BV 6*), claimed an endurance record of 130hr 26min, covering a distance of 3,107 miles. The ship was destroyed in the following year while attempting an arctic rescue.

Around 1937 about four non-rigids were constructed and were probably used mainly for experimental purposes. They were classified by the initials *VK* or *V*. The first was known as *First of May* and had a capacity of 78,000cu ft. Her two 75hp engines gave a maximum speed of 55mph. She carried a crew of seven and was able by using special equipment to pick up passengers from the ground without landing. Her endurance capability was 12hr. *V 2*, also a product of the Zagi Works, had double the capacity. She was given two 230hp engines and was able to carry 8 passengers in addition to the crew. On one occasion she broke loose from the handling party during a sudden storm with 13 aboard. The captain and two of the ground party were swept off their feet hanging on to ropes; the ground party men let go some 15ft off the ground, but the captain pulled himself up to the control-car. Meanwhile, the ship was steered by a helmswoman under the direction of the captain. After a tough struggle against gusts of wind, the ship was brought safely to the ground.[11]

V 3 and *V 4* were still larger than *V 2*, with capacities of 230,000cu ft to 250,000cu ft and a range of 750 miles. The flurry of airship construction of the early 1930s seems to have ceased after the crash of the semi-rigid, *BV 6*, and development was not revived until the 1960s.

Today the USSR is probably the only nation using airships commercially.[12] As before World War II, non-rigids are being used in the far north and east, principally for geological prospecting and for logging. In respect of the former, it has been estimated that two small airships of modest range with a complement of 15 surveyors and their assistants can cover in one year an area which would otherwise require 2,000 men with helicopters to investigate. The carriage of timber by airship has been estimated as being 60 per cent cheaper than lifting by helicopter. The Russians are evidently making use of modern technology in airship construction, for details are to hand of *B 1*, a non-rigid, made of glass fibre with a tricycle undercarriage.

The other nation to continue both military and commercial development of airships in recent years has been the USA. The US army operated a small number of non-rigid airships in the inter-war years until they were taken over by the US navy in 1937. The main role of these airships was coastal defence, but the army also initiated experiments in hooking-on and launching small aeroplanes from airships. Their airships were also intended to be used for transport duties.

The first post-war army non-rigid was *A–4*, built as a naval airship of one of the *E* and *F* types; she had a volume of 95,000cu ft and was inflated with hydrogen. The *MA*, *MB* and *OB* types followed, all with small volumes; the first was an adaptation of the small *Pony Blimp*, while the *MB* and *OB* types could be used either as dirigibles or as observation balloons. The MB was used to exterminate the gypsy moth in New England by spraying crops. All these craft, apart from *MB–1** were built by the Goodyear Tire and Rubber Company.[13]

In 1922, however, the army ruled that all airships should be inflated with helium and this at once made airships of small capacity impracticable. *TA–1*, a modification of *A–4*, was the first to conform to the new ruling, her capacity being enlarged to 130,000cu ft.

A series of larger ships known by the initials *TC* followed from 1922 until 1935. *TC–4* and *TC–5*, built in 1923–4, had a capacity of 200,000cu ft. They were fitted with double, instead of two single, ballonets, with the object of preventing the stern from drooping, and increasing the lift in the area of the fins. An air compartment was inserted directly above the engine and propeller to prevent loss of helium should the envelope accidentally be torn by the propeller. Radio was installed in the rear cockpit of the car. However, *TC–7*, *TC–8* and *TC–9* reverted to two single ballonets, as difficulties were experienced with the double ballonet and its compartments.

TC–13 and *TC–14* were the largest army airships to be built. The former was 200ft long with a car 40ft in length.[14] Her gross lift was 11

---

* Built by Airships Inc, New York, which also constructed *TA–1*, *TA–2*, *TA–3*, *TA–4* and *TA–5*, distinguished by tractor engines.

tons and she had a useful lift of 4½ tons. She carried a crew of six; equipped with bombs and a machine-gun, she could remain airborne for five days. She was powered by two 375hp engines. In some respects she was the equivalent of the British *North Sea* airship. *TC–14*, completed in 1934, was still larger, with a capacity of 400,000cu ft; she was 248ft long and 50ft in diameter. Intended for use as a scout and for training observers, she carried a crew of 16.

The US navy took over in toto *TC–10*, *TC–11*, *TC–13* and *TC–14*, and a miscellaneous collection of envelopes, control cars, fins, engines and spare parts.[15] Only *TC–13* and *TC–14* were comparable to the naval *K–1* (see page 244) and were thought worth while putting into commission. Both ships took part in World War II. *TC–13* was deflated in 1942; *TC–14* continued to fly until 1943.

The US army was experimenting with hook-on aeroplanes several years before it was decided that they should form part of the complement of *Akron* and *Macon*. Lawrence B. Sperry,* president of the Sperry Aircraft Company, designed a hook-on apparatus located above the centre of a 60hp Sperry Messenger aeroplane weighing just under 1,000lb. A trapeze was fitted underneath *TC–3*.[16] The role of this tiny aeroplane was threefold. It was to act as a scout to the parent ship, to carry messages back to base when the airship was operating far out to sea; and to land to supervise the descent of the airship. The first release from the airship was accomplished on 3 October 1924 at 1,500ft over Dayton, Ohio, while the first hook-on and unhooking in mid-air took place over Scott Field that December. No difficulty was experienced with hooking-on, provided the airship could maintain a speed approximately 5mph faster than the stalling speed of the aeroplane. In the event, the plane was flying at full speed at 62mph and the airship at 51mph.

Goodyear Tire and Rubber began building non-rigids in 1912 and continued after World War I with the development of a number of small ships, starting with *Pony Blimp* in 1919; she had a capacity of only 35,050cu ft.[17] Types *A* and *AA* were driven by 40 and 50hp engines respectively; and they were fitted with one ballonet instead of two. They were used for mapping deep-sea fishing areas, photography, and

* Sperry was killed flying the English Channel before seeing his device in operation.

even for carrying passengers between Los Angeles and the Gulf of Catalina. But the blunt form made the little ships unstable.

Next came *Pilgrim* and *Puritan*, of 50,000 and 86,000cu ft capacity respectively. They were the first American non-rigids to use an internal suspension system, thus eliminating the drag of the car-suspension cables. They were used for carrying passengers, advertising, and for training pilots for rigid airships. *Puritan* flew 8,000 miles on her first trip, which lasted for ten days. In 1929 a number of larger ships of 186,000cu ft capacity were built, and named after the America Cup yachts—*Volunteer, Mayflower, Rainbow, Vigilant* and *Defender*.

Goodyear developed the technique of flying a non-rigid off the ground like an aeroplane, using a wheel attached to the car. The airship could now ascend in a 'heavy' condition (about 2,000lb), and it was possible to conserve the expensive helium. In order to do this, it was necessary to fill the ballonets with air so as to cope with high altitudes and with superheating. The only drawback to the manoeuvre was that more space for ascent was required. A portable mooring mast attached to the top of a bus was also used by ground crews.

Although its main interest in lighter-than-air craft in the 1920s and 1930s centred on the rigid, the US navy had not altogether lost sight of the non-rigid. In 1929, the Bureau of Aeronautics, interested in the possibilities of blaugas, began to develop a non-rigid of 319,000cu ft capacity. The envelope was bought from Goodyear and the car was obtained from the Naval Aircraft Factory rather than be sought by tender, non-rigids being still the responsibility of the army. This non-rigid, known as *K-1*, the first of a series of *K* types, made her first flight on 3 October 1931. She had an internal suspension and was fitted with a taxying wheel. Her envelope contained a special ballonet for holding fuel gas.[18] The problem was that there was no way of purifying the helium after being contaminated by air and by a combustible gas. The helium therefore had to be thrown away when its purity deteriorated—an expensive procedure considering the high cost of supplies.

Most of the operational non-rigids used by the US navy in World War II were provided by the Goodyear Aircraft Company, which had absorbed the airship element of Goodyear Zeppelin. The prototype for this fleet was *K-2*, a ship of 416,000cu ft capacity, 248ft long and

57·85ft at the maximum diameter. With two 400hp Pratt and Whitney engines, it had a range of 2,245 miles when flying at 57·6mph, and could remain airborne for 39hr. It was a great advance on previous non-rigids. This ship was taken over by the navy in December 1938.

A gap of about two years followed before *K–3* to *K–8* appeared. By then it was becoming increasingly probable that the USA could well be involved in World War II before long and various modifications were proposed. One of them concerned the replacement of the heavy-geared Pratt and Whitney engines by the lighter Curtiss-Wright engines, only to find that there was a decrease in performance and an unacceptable increase in propeller noise. On the day after the Japanese attack on Pearl Harbour it was decided to revert to the Pratt and Whitneys as soon as possible.[19]

The outbreak of war found the US navy hard pressed to defend American coastal waters, either in the western Atlantic or in the Pacific. Almost immediately the eastern US seaboard and the Caribbean became the hunting ground of German U-boats, and in 1942, especially that spring, they reaped a terrible harvest of undefended merchant shipping; a total of 454 ships were sunk in American waters during the year.

The Americans could only deploy a defence force of older destroyers and armed yachts, with a few aeroplanes and flying boats, which were supplemented by six sea-going airships.[20] The latter were only able to operate from one base—Lakehurst. In World War I, experience had shown that non-rigids with adequate range and speed were admirable for convoy escort and submarine hunting. But by mid-1942 only thirteen airships were available, including *K–2* to *K–8*, with their Pratt and Whitney engines, and with a capacity and endurance not much greater than the British *North Sea* airships of World War I.

Equally important for an expanding airship fleet was the training of crews to man the airships, never an easy task. For this purpose the five Goodyear ships were taken over by the navy after Pearl Harbour to supplement the *L*-type blimps, originally ordered in 1937, but only to be delivered in quantity in 1943. They had a capacity of 123,000cu ft, but no armament. Altogether, twenty-two were procured for training between 1937 and 1943.

During 1943 the U-boat threat had largely been brought under control, due in no small measure to the introduction of better radar equipment, which led to increased detection and sinkings. Sinkings of Allied ships in east American coastal waters were reduced to sixty-five. At the same time a larger type of *K* ship was coming into service, starting with *K–14* and continuing to *K–135*. They had an increased capacity of 425,000cu ft; more powerful engines of 425hp; and an increased range of 1,910 miles. They were able to operate for about 38hr at a stretch. Some of these blimps were further enlarged to make them at least competitive in range with the Catalina flying boat and very-long-range land-based aeroplanes. For this purpose, they were equipped with a new envelope of 456,000cu ft capacity adapted to the existing control car.

As the U-boats had extended their operations to the South Atlantic, it became necessary to deploy airships into equatorial waters, radiating as far south as Rio de Janeiro. For these areas, where high temperatures reduced lift, the *M*-type blimp was designed. The first had a capacity of 625,000cu ft. She made her maiden flight on 16 October 1943. But only three more ships of this class were built—*M 2*, *M 3* and *M 4*. They were delivered in the spring of 1944.[21] As constructed the capacity was 647,500cu ft, but, in due course, all the *M* ships were fitted with envelopes able to contain 725,000cu ft of helium. On account of their size *M* ships were equipped with four ballonets; the 117ft-long control car was built in three articulated sections so that it could flex with the envelope. Although clumsy-looking, this long car was superior to later car designs, as it kept catenary loads almost wholly at 90°, thereby preventing the incidence of wrinkles in the envelope. The airships were powered by two 550hp Pratt and Whitney engines. A machine-gun was carried and 2,400lb of bombs.

Several of the *M* ships contained a retractable tricycle landing gear— an idea first put into practice by Cdr F. L. M. Boothby, RN, in a *Coastal* airship in the earlier war. This device enabled the ship to take off 'heavy', thereby enabling it to carry more fuel and equipment. But the landing gear gave a lot of trouble. It is worth note when considering the *M* class that on 2 November 1946, *M 1* set up an endurance record of 170hr 17min. The *K* ships, although unsuitable for operating in the South Atlantic, performed this role in lieu of the *M* ships and proved to be adequate for the task.

By 1944, airship bases had been formed at Richmond in Florida, Trinidad and Reçife, in addition to Lakehurst. But the blimps were also able to operate from bases of the most rudimentary nature, often in jungle, where there were no sheds or other facilities, save a wooden stick mast (bow mooring had been greatly improved over the war years and mechanical 'mules' developed). Moreover, it was found that the blimps were able to operate despite tropical deluges and the fierce equatorial sun.

Airships were organised into 15 squadrons, or 'blimprons'. A squadron usually consisted of five blimps. Much of the escort work and submarine hunting amounted, as an airship pilot expressed it, to 'hours and hours of sheer boredom for 15 seconds of terror once in a while'.[22] While patrolling a shipping lane, patrols took a zigzag course to cover a corridor. Such patrols were not without inter-ship incidents. One night the pilot first quoted pursued a radar blip at the edge of his corridor. Closing in, he found that a searchlight suddenly opened in front. He pulled up his airship sharply, thereby avoiding a collision with another naval airship patrolling a parallel corridor. Each airship had seen the other on radar. After that episode, orders were issued for airships patrolling adjacent areas to fly at different altitudes.

In the summer of 1944, No 14 Squadron equipped with K ships of a capacity of 425,000cu ft and carrying magnetic anomaly detection (MAD) gear, which was intended to enable the crew to detect disturbances in the earth's magnetic field even though deep in the sea, was ordered to operate against U-boats in the Straits of Gibraltar and along the North African coast. These airships were first based in French Morocco (later using the old French airship base at Cuers), and flying in pairs, made the transatlantic voyage in two hops via Newfoundland and the Azores. They were so useful, being steadier than flying boats and able to fly at very low altitudes and low speeds at night while their quietness suited the not very reliable MAD equipment, that the British navy requested the Americans to provide a squadron for the south-west approaches to Britain. The idea was that the blimps would be used especially for convoy escort, releasing long-range aeroplanes for use farther out at sea.[23] They would have been based at Chivenor, in South Devon, with a maintenance unit located at Cardington, the old Royal Airship Works. The war ended before the plans came to fruition.

The blimps also had a 'general utility' role, which included the recovery of torpedoes during firing trials, aerial photography, calibration of special equipment, such as radar, air-sea rescue operations, spotting minefields, and other types of operation which required flying at low altitudes and at low speed for extended periods of time.

At the end of the war, US naval non-rigids, first commanded by Vice-Adm Rosendahl, the veteran airshipman, and subsequently by Vice-Adm T. G. W. Settle, who had been inspector of airships at Akron, had escorted 89,000 surface craft and made some 35,000 operational flights over the Atlantic, and 170,000 flights over the Pacific.[24] No airship-escorted vessel was lost to an enemy submarine, though that statement should be qualified by observing that while the submarine menace reached its peak in 1942, airships were not operating in strength until 1943. Of the blimps assigned to fleet units, 87 per cent were in operational readiness at all times. The only airship lost as a result of enemy action was *K–74*, shot down by a U-boat on 18 July 1943 off the Florida coast, and that was only after the blimp's bomb-release gear had failed to operate, leaving her defenceless to the surfaced submarine. The non-inflammable helium proved to be a valuable asset; only one of the crew was killed.

At the end of the war the non-rigids were decommissioned with the exception of two *K* ship squadrons. In September 1945 nine airships and three sheds full of equipment were destroyed in a hurricane at Richmond.

The outbreak of the Korean war in 1950, and the tension between the USA and the Western World, and the USSR and her satellites, and, in particular, the growth of the Russian navy, revived interest in the blimp. The new types were designated *ZP2K*, *ZP3K* and *ZP4K*,* all of them improvements on the wartime *K* class.[25] Fourteen *ZP4K* ships were actually delivered to the navy. About seventeen to eighteen *ZP5K* ships were built in 1955 with capacities of 650,000cu ft, but were later redesignated as *ZS2G* ships as they bore little resemblance to the original *K* class.

A more modern type of non-rigid began with the *ZPN–1*, later

* In 1947 the US navy finally decided to abandon the rigid airship; there was no longer any need to distinguish between Rigid and Non Rigid. The *N* was dropped, blimps simply using the *Z*. *ZP* indicated a lighter-than-air craft for patrol service.

redesignated as *ZPG–1*, and the first of a new class.[26] She was delivered by Goodyear to Lakehurst in June 1951. She had a capacity of 875,000cu ft and four ballonets. Her overall length was 324ft, her maximum diameter being 73ft; she was powered by two Wright 800hp engines; her gross lift was 56,822lb and she had a useful lift of 12,470lb. She was able to remain airborne for 85hr and had a range of 1,360 nautical miles. She was the first naval blimp to have engines installed inside the control car, and she disposed of the usual cruciform arrangement of fins in favour of a multiple arrangement, while the controls in the car were similar to those of an aeroplane. A double crew of 14 was carried. But only one ship of this class was built.

Following on *ZPG–1* were twelve *ZPG–2* ships, completed between 1953 and 1957. They had a capacity of 975,000cu ft and two engines totalling 1,400hp.[27] Designed for anti-submarine warfare (ASW), they could carry an optional load of three types of torpedoes and two types of depth charges, but no more than two units of each. They were equipped with radio, radar, MAD gear, sonar, a searchlight, and facilities for in-flight refuelling at sea from surface ships. The two engines were again installed inside the control car and could be cross-connected, ie the starboard engine could drive the port propeller. The control car was double-decked, the upper deck (inside the envelope) enclosing a bunkroom for the crew, normally numbering 14.

These airships had varying performances. For instance, the four airships of the 1951 contract used a three-ply envelope and had an official useful lift of 12,800lb. The first ship of the 1952 contract had a three-ply envelope and a useful lift of 11,500lb, while the other three had two-ply envelopes, the useful lift being increased to 13,600lb. The 1955 ships had two-ply envelopes and a useful lift of 14,700lb. Thus there was a considerable discrepancy between the ships. It is believed that the three-ply envelopes used the old cotton-rayon base, and the later two-ply types employed Dacron which was stronger, more gas-tight, and more durable.

An intensive programme of flight testing and evaluation of the all-weather capability of airships for use in airborne early-warning and anti-submarine warfare began in January 1957 when five *ZPG–2s* maintained an early-warning station 200 miles off the New England coast during bad-weather conditions. In March a *ZPG–2* ship, commanded by Cdr J. R. Hunt, made a non-stop double Atlantic crossing without refuelling, flying along the coasts of Portugal and West Africa and returning to Key West via the West Indies. The airship covered 9,448 miles in 264·2hr (11 days).[28] This was a record for any type of aircraft, one which easily beat the 1929 performance of *Graf Zeppelin* for 6,980 miles in 101hr on the Friedrichshafen–Tokyo leg of her round-the-world flight. The vulnerability of the USA to air attack in the 1950s, both from conventional and nuclear weapons, led to the navy being given an air defence commitment; for this purpose the *ZPG–2* was modified for the airborne early-warning service. Five new airships were obtained between 1955 and 1957.[29] Classified as *ZPG–2Ws*, they were in most respects similar to the *ZPG–2*, except for the large radar assembly, which included a radome for height-finding, located on top of the envelope. The radome was manned in flight and entrance was effected by climbing up a shaft through the envelope from the control car.

Next came four *ZPG–3W* ships specifically designed for the early-warning role; the first was delivered to the navy in June 1959 and the last in March 1960. This type was the largest non-rigid ever built and had a capacity of 1,500,000cu ft;* it was 403ft long with a maximum diameter of 85ft and a fineness ratio of 4·7; it was propelled by two 1,525hp Curtiss-Wright engines and was manned by a crew of 25. The envelope was of cotton neoprene. These airships operated off the east coast of America with safety until the summer of 1960, having proved themselves in severe endurance tests during the previous winter. But on 6 July one of the ships (*3W* No 144242) crashed into the sea within sight of the New Jersey coast. She had been searching for a missing yacht; 18 of the crew were killed.[30] The other ships were grounded from then on.

As usual, there was no unanimous view as to the cause of the accident, opinion veering between, on the one hand, the possibility of the envelope failing and the gas being expelled; and, on the other, failure of the forward ballonets causing the bow to collapse and the envelope to become entangled with the propellers; the airship then being flown inadvertently into the sea. Recovery of the envelope from the sea

---

*A four-engined O type blimp designed in 1943 to carry a single aeroplane, but never built, would have had the same capacity.

revealed a rent 133ft long; but if witnesses of the accident from nearby boats are to be trusted, the tear was caused by the airship's impact with the sea.

Distrust of lighter-than-air craft, seemingly never far below the surface, particularly from ex-carrier officers now holding naval senior appointments; demands on the helium supply by the space industry, thus increasing operating costs; and government requirements for economies in expenditure, led to the *ZPG-3*s being reduced to two in 1961. The airship service was finally terminated in 1962, though the deflated blimps were stored against 'war mobilisation'.

Loss of the *ZPG-3W* ship indicated that possibly there were ways of improving airship design, which has, after all, in principle, hardly deviated from the original conceptions of Meusnier and Zeppelin. Yet in the 1920s, Ralph Upson, balloonist and aeronautical engineer, appreciating that as the all-metal aeroplane had become a reality, the same principle could be applied to lighter-than-air craft. It will make them able to withstand stresses better, be more fireproof and weatherproof, and to be even lighter and cheaper to build than had been possible with rigid airships.

The forerunner to Upson's proposal had been Schwartz's experimental—but unsuccessful—sheet aluminium airship of 1897. But there was an even earlier antecedent of Francesco de Lana, a Jesuit priest who, in 1670, proposed a car supported by four hollow spheres of very thin copper from which the air was to be expelled, thus making them lighter than air. A vacuum airship was, so far, impossible to realise because no known material could withstand the outside pressure on the airship's hull. There was, however, a design for a vacuum airship that came from Alexandre Vaugean, of Milan, in the early 1920s.[31] This was known as an 'airship with variable rarefaction', and the lift was to be obtained within its walls by the creation of a partial vacuum, variable at will, which, it was claimed, would give subtleness of control and make an appreciable saving in cost of production. By filling the hull with hydrogen, or helium, thereby replacing the intense compressive stresses with mainly tensile stresses, the metal airship, Upson believed, became feasible.

The US Naval Bureau of Aeronautics had, it has been seen on page 60, shown interest in the metalclad which was being developed by

Upson and the Aircraft Development Corporation of Detroit. Upson's first design was for an airship of 1,600,000cu ft capacity, as he then believed that this was the smallest metalclad unit which was practicable.[32] However, he discovered that the airship would be actually lighter in gross weight than a fabric-covered rigid, and stronger and more efficient than the contemporary *Shenandoah*. For the meantime, it was decided to build a small prototype of 202,200cu ft of helium, with two ballonets holding 50,600cu ft of air; it was to be 150ft long with a maximum diameter of 53ft, the hull being covered by duralumin sheeting of 0·0095in thickness. The airship was to be propelled by two Curtiss-Wright engines giving a total of 440hp. Upson, however, visualised building metalclads of up to 5,400,000 and 7,250,000cu ft capacity with a gross lift of 200 tons. In daytime passengers would be accommodated in a large streamlined external car, withdrawing into the hull at night to sleep.

Essentially, *ZMC-2*, as the experimental metalclad was called, was a single structure in which the surface sheeting carried a large part of the direct stresses. As in other non-rigids, the envelope had to retain the lifting gas. Thus its success depended entirely on the permanence of its leak-proof shell, and the simplicity of the automatic and mechanical means to attain and hold the necessary pressure as soon as, and as long as, required by the variable conditions. The method of construction was unique. The duralumin was laid on in sheets, each sheet being long enough for a complete circumference of the hull. A specially designed riveting machine inserted 40,000 small rivets in 8hr, literally sewing the metal covering on to 12 circular transverse frames. Five of these frames were built-on girders with wire bracing and carried the weight of the car, fins and engines. The rest of the structure was built of very light sections, primarily designed to keep the shape of the hull and to support the envelope when the airship was deflated. Three air and two gas valves were used; and several manholes provided access to the interior of the envelope. The fins were an innovation as they were equally placed round the circumference, four acting as vertical surfaces and four as horizontal surfaces. The principal defect when flying seems to have been that when the ship began to yaw, the surfaces became ineffective, but this may have been due to the tubby shape of the airship—she had a fineness ratio of 1 to 2·83.

The numerous qualities ascribed to the metalcald were challenged by the rigid airship protagonists. They contended that cotton fabrics, provided they were doped properly, were equally weatherproof and durable, and they maintained that metal sheeting was not fireproof. In regard to the more important matters of strength and weight, they believed the metalclad to be especially vulnerable to inter-crystalline corrosion; moreover, the ship would have to be deflated for any repair or maintenance work, a condition from which the rigid was fortunately free; finally, the metal hull would be just as brittle as fabric.

Yet, it has been shown that, apart from the Zeppelins, the outer covers of rigid airships, particularly the British, had given a lot of trouble with flapping and tearing. And Upson asserted that corrosion in the gas space, where there was no oxygen and little moisture, would be inconsiderable and could be contained by covering with a protective film. He pointed out that the major deteriorating effect on fabric was not moisture but sunlight and sunlight had no effect on metal; in respect to the chances of being struck by lightning, he quoted the contention of the celebrated physicist, R. A. Millikan, that, provided the ship was unconnected with the earth by metal connections, no harm would be likely to occur.

On completion, *ZMC-2* was found to be 127lb under the weight of the original specification—a very unusual event in a prototype airship. The maiden flight was made from Detroit on 20 August 1929.[33] The pilot, who later confessed that he was most worried about whether the envelope would hold the gas, took her up without engine power to some height before starting the engines so that should any defect in control have become evident, the airship could have been brought back to earth as a free balloon. After four flights testing the controls and ensuring that the metal skin held gas (which it did), *ZMC-2* was flown to Lakehurst, travelling overnight. At an early stage in the flight a speed run was made and 52mph achieved. The airship also had to be refuelled in mid-journey and the crew let down a rope and hooked up petrol cans from a truck on the ground. In the dawn mist the little ship was skimming along just above the tree-tops, and after arriving at Lakehurst 13hr since taking off, a 0·45 calibre bullet hole was found in the envelope; evidently a hunter had taken a pot shot at this unusual object in the sky, unknown to the crew. At least the incident proved that the riveting was strong enough to withstand the strain and the skin did not tear any further.

But the naval airshipmen did not take kindly to *ZMC-2*, known as the 'Tin Balloon' or the 'Tin Blimp'. Although the Bureau of Aeronautics would have liked a larger version, funds were not forthcoming. However, the metalclad remained in commission for 12 years, making 752 flights. In the summer of 1942 she was finally scrapped to make room for wartime blimps. The main structural fault of the ship was that the asphalt-like mixture coating the seams inside the hull to make it gastight had begun to crack and it was not considered worth while to renew it.[34]

The Russians also contemplated building a slightly larger metalclad in the 1930s; it was the design of Tsiolkovski, who, like Upson, believed that there was a future for this kind of airship construction; but the project never left the drawing-board.

Today with new materials for building airships to hand, a monocoque hull has possibilities which would repay study; and it is the impact of modern technology on future airship design that will be discussed in Chapter 10.

CHAPTER 10

A Role for the Future?

'The large family of aeronautical stepchildren which in past years has included such promising infants as the helicopter, jet-propelled plane, and guided missiles, also includes a long-neglected member—the airship.' Paul W. Litchfield, President, Goodyear Aircraft Corporation, 1948

Over thirty-five years have elapsed since the transatlantic service of Deutsche Zeppelin Reederei was so abruptly curtailed by the disaster to *Hindenberg*. In the interval revolutionary and unforeseen changes have been made by heavier-than-air craft; jet propulsion has been introduced, followed by supersonic flight; while a gamut of space vehicles, having landed man on the moon, are penetrating further into the unknown. Yet in the last decade or so there has been a revival of interest in lighter-than-air craft—particularly in the large rigid airship.

Why is this? Earlier chapters have attempted to show that the benefits conferred by aerostatic lift, which include the saving of power and the ability to carry great weight, have never been fully exploited. Both materials and engine power were inadequate for the big volume required to carry an acceptable size of useful load. Now, it would be possible to build the members of the hull with glass-fibres and carbon-fibres, or of corrosion-resistant alloys of titanium and aluminium; impermeable synthetic films might be used for the lining of the gas bags and nylon fabrics employed for the outer cover. Helium which, in the inter-war years, was a rare commodity, has been used extensively in the space and atomic-energy programmes, but although it has been discovered in North Sea and in Algerian natural gas, it is cheaper for European countries to import supplies (approximately £1 per 1,000cu ft) from North America—still the richest source of helium.

So much for materials. Why should the present time be propitious for a revival of the airship? Heavier-than-air craft have until recently been designed mainly to carry passengers; the criterion has been speed at the expense of comfort; while the economics of the airline business usually require that the maximum number of passengers be carried in every aeroplane.[1]

Yet the movement of heavy, indivisible loads is increasing. In Britain, for example, during 1971, the number of loads on the roads weighing over 50 tons, such as generators, transformers, earth-moving equipment, nuclear and petro-chemical engineering plant, either within or out of the country amounted to nearly 4,000. There is probably an annual increase of 5 per cent, particularly since Britain's entry into the EEC. It is not hard to imagine the difficulties of handling, the special routing required, the police escorts, the loading and unloading at docks at the beginning and end of a sea journey, not to mention the expense entailed on account of these inevitable activities. For this type of cargo the large airship is ideal, and increases in size do not limit its efficiency. Further, it has the advantage of flexibility, for provided the approaches are not obstructed by high buildings, chimneys, pylons or cables it will be able to lift a load direct from the place of manufacture and convey it direct to its destination. By contrast, heavier-than-air craft, though increasingly able to carry heavy loads, are still restricted to terminals which may be some distance from the load's point of arrival. The airship has the additional asset of generating far less noise than large jet aircraft, and there would be less pollution of the atmosphere. The ability of airships to ferry cars, people, or cars and people, the latter being particularly relevant to the tourist industry, should not be overlooked. But it is essential to appreciate that these roles are not necessarily competitive with heavier-than-air craft. They are complementary, and employ entirely different techniques—such as had always been envisaged by protagonists, like Eckener and Arnstein, of the large airship.

It does not need to be stated that airship operating costs will have to be appreciably lower than those of conventional air transport, and comparable with the costs of surface systems of transport. Technical problems—the control of the airship while hovering close to the ground in order to pick up a load; control of aerostatic lift without exhausting gas or ballast; the provision of buoyancy while ascending with a heavy load; dealing with height pressure and temperature variations—all still require satisfactory solution: a challenge indeed to the technological age.

A great rigid airship has still to take shape, though this has not been for lack of proposals which have, however, still to attract capital from government or private enterprise. The art of airship construction has fortunately been kept alive by the Goodyear Airspace Corporation. No sooner than World War II had ended than the indefatigable Arnstein was advocating a rigid airship of 9,750,000cu ft capacity, similar in design to the pre-war rigids, with accommodation for 112 passengers equivalent in standard to that of an ocean liner, but also able to compete with aeroplanes; by eliminating a dining-room with accommodation for 60 passengers at a time and converting the whole interior to Pullman-type compartments it could carry 232 passengers; while using reclining chairs, similar to those used on domestic airlines, the airship could carry 288 passengers. A design speed of 75mph was given, though Arnstein foresaw that, using stern propulsion and other refinements in design, cruising speeds of 100mph might be reached.[2]

However, it was the problem of fitting a nuclear propulsion unit into a heavier-than-air craft for military purposes in the 1950s that revived interest in the rigid airship; and nuclear propulsion seemed particularly appropriate to the latter as it eliminated the problems of fuel displacement. A team under Prof Francis Morse, of Boston University, concluded that the weight of a reactor would be substantially less than the weight of fuel required by a conventionally powered ship of 12·5 million cubic feet capacity.[3] They also believed that the vast space enclosed by the hull would ensure adequate security for the reactor in the event of an accident.

Morse designed an airship to be used either as a cargo carrier, or as a passenger-cargo carrier with a capacity of 400 passengers. He estimated the length of his airship would be 980 ft and would have a useful lift of 300,000lb and a payload of 180,000lb. The nuclear power plant would drive three engines at the stern—a 4,000hp gas-turbine revolving 60ft-long dual-rotation propellers and two 1,000hp turbofans which would also help to eliminate the reduction of drag. In order to balance the weight in the stern, Morse proposed a control bridge inside the hull near the bow of the ship, but it has been pointed out that this would afford little vision to those controlling the movements of the ship.

Otherwise the structure of the hull would be along traditional Zeppelin lines, with a hotel section located in two bays of the hull and containing a dining-room with a capacity for 200 persons as well as a cinema and promenades. Room would be found for a shuttle aeroplane able to carry 18 passengers to and from the ship while in full flight. But no money was forthcoming for this project.

A larger nuclear-powered airship was designed by the late Erich von Veress, of Graz, Austria.[4] Known as *ALV-1*, it was to have a volume of about 14 million cubic feet, carry 500 passengers and 100 crew, and handle 100 tons of freight; it was to be propelled by a nuclear-powered turbine with two propellers in tandem inside the hull near the bow; the air for propulsion would be driven through vents in the bow outside the hull, where the airflow would prevent surface turbulence and drag. This would eliminate any protuberance on the hull exterior. In addition, the reactor would be able to heat or cool the helium in order to gain extra lift, or, alternatively, to increase weight, thereby avoiding valving of gas. Veress contemplated a light metal structure to form the hull, but the outer cover of synthetic fibres would be self-supporting.

Veress produced his design primarily to carry passengers, special attention being paid to giving adequate space for comfort. The planned speed would enable a westerly crossing of the North Atlantic to be made in 22hr, the return trip taking 18hr. The ship would be constructed in covered-over shipyards or partially built in the open, using turntables, though out-of-doors construction for large airships has never been attempted before.

There are a number of serious disadvantages to both the Morse and Veress designs. Firstly, both are too small in capacity to enable them to carry an adequate payload in addition to their means of propulsion. Secondly, insufficient attention has been paid to the crucial problem in airships—the spreading of the total load over the ship, which the designers of the Zeppelins so successfully achieved. In these two nuclear-engined designs the weights are concentrated either in the bow or in the stern. This is not to say that nuclear power would not be used in what may be termed the 'second generation' of airships. The latest type of isotope generators, it has been pointed out by Frank Hyde, of Airfloat Transport Ltd, are component units of 100kW which can be distributed evenly throughout the ship, thereby solving the weight problem. As very little shielding would be required, special precautions would not be needed for the generating machinery. Alternatively, an in-core unit of achieving power levels over 100kW could be used.

Two other possible difficulties regarding nuclear airships have been noted by Gerhard Hoffman, one of the engineers engaged in the construction of *Hindenburg*.[5] He is sceptical about Veress's claim of being able to cope with superheating, as allowance would have to be made for a heavy air-conditioning apparatus. Finally, Hoffman states that it has been assumed that crews to man rigid airships could be found easily. On the contrary, crews would require a long period of training, for while flights, on the whole, would be of a routine nature, there was always the possibility of the unexpected happening and need rapid attention. The Germans long ago found that the best crews usually had a maritime background.

More realistic in conception, and relying more on traditional Zeppelin design, at least in the early stages, is one of two British rigid airship schemes which have been made public—that for a freight-carrying rigid airship designed by a team headed by Edwin Mowforth, of Airfloat Transport Ltd.[6] They appreciate that an initial design will inevitably be restricted by lack of finance, but at the same time they believe it necessary for the airship to be large enough to prove that it can carry a heavier load than currently operating cargo aircraft, and capable of operating in varying weather conditions. They therefore propose an 'interim airship'. This has been designed to operate in a 'short-range' category, ie covering Britain and western Europe, rarely exceeding a radius of 1,000 to 1,500 miles.

An adequate payload of an indivisible kind, has been estimated as being in the region of 400 tons, and for that weight the Airfloat airship would need a capacity of over 40 million cubic feet. This figure allows for a hoisting gear located in the belly of the ship and the carriage of water ballast to compensate for loss of lift caused by a damaged gas bag. Its overall length would be 1,345ft and its maximum diameter would be 263ft. Power would be provided by six Proteus gas turbines driving 21ft propellers. All the engines would be self-reversing, and four would be able to provide thrust in any direction. All operation would be automatic, with sensors supplying information to a computer

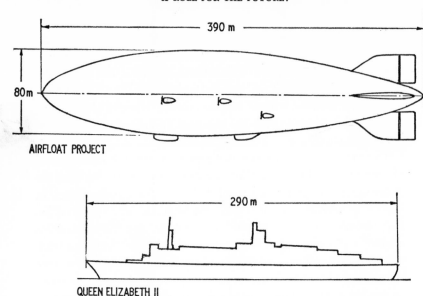

AIRFLOAT PROJECT

QUEEN ELIZABETH II

Airfloat projected rigid airship (special load carrier, 1971 design)

controlling among other things lift-and-trim operations and gust evasion. The designers claim that their ship will be able to cope with all the eventualities that proved to be the undoing of so many large rigids of the past. Their ship would be able to rotate on its own vertical axis, and to move backwards or sideways. Its hovering ability would be such that it could be flown to a standstill, while release and get-away conditions would present no problem.

As only the vulnerable components would need to be built under cover, the construction of the hull could take place in the open, thereby reducing expenditure. Sections would be mounted on a turn-table, similar to that forming part of the Jodrell Bank radio telescope, and assembly could be still further facilitated by partially inflating the gas bags within the structure. The hull would be made of welded steel to avoid the joining difficulties of light-alloy frames which charac-terised the rigid airships of the 1930s. The outer cover would be of fabric using synthetic fibres. In general, the structural design would be built with the same high margins of safety which were found in *R 100*, particularly in relation to gusting in a vertical direction.

Perhaps the most interesting feature in the Mowforth design is the ingenious winching arrangement for load transfer executed in hovering flight, thus avoiding the need for a wide landing area. This system also provides the best way of attaching loads to the ship. For loading from the ground involves internal accommodation, whereas hoisting permits external carriage with less structural complication and dimensional restriction.

The carriage of such a heavy load demands that the weight should at all times be balanced by the lift in addition to the familiar need for balancing fuel consumption, and for this reason ballast must be deposited when picking up a load and recovered when the load has been delivered at the destination. It is essential that the location has suitable approaches. Apart from this, picking up and delivering loads must be conducted very quickly (in 20min) because of the need to keep the airship stable. The design included a hoist mounted on a turntable so that the ship could hover into wind regardless of the orientation on the ground. From the hoist would be suspended the load frame comprising a pair of parallel frames 200ft long and 35ft apart on which the load would be hung; also hanging at the ends of the frames would be two ballast packs. The load would be hooked on to the frame and the ballast packs detached. The airship would then move off to its destination.

Capital costs, including construction of hull, gas, engines, research and development have been estimated to amount to £5.300 million; approximate cost per annum would be £2.228 million, but the all-important cost per-capacity-ton-mile would be as little as 1.5 pence.

Detailed plans are not yet available for the project of Aerospace Developments Ltd, in which the feasibility of carrying natural gas in great airships 1,800ft long and 300ft in diameter, with mainly parallel midship sections, is being investigated on behalf of Shell International Gas Ltd.[7] The hull is intended to be of rigid monocoque construction, using honeycomb material which would require no maintenance. The interior would contain 100 million cubic feet of gas, of which 90 per cent would constitute cargo, the remaining 10 per cent being helium to lift the empty hull for the return trip to the loading point.

This aerial tanker would be driven by four Russian Kutznetsov fan-jet gas turbines, each totalling 12,000hp and driving 30ft reversible propellers; the engines would be fitted in pairs parallel to each other and hang in pods from the horizontal tail fins on either side of the hull, where they would be reached by walking inside the 10ft-thick fins. It has been proposed that the two sheds at Cardington should be converted into one for the purpose of building this airship.

The advantage of this scheme is that it avoids the construction of expensive liquifaction plants at the terminals and pipe lines and tankers to carry the liquified gas. A bonus of the scheme is that several of the currently operated natural gas fields lie in areas where the political situation is potentially explosive, and where it would be an advantage not to have to rely on extensive ground installations. Basic development and construction costs are reckoned to be in the region of £450 million, but this would be a substantial cost advantage over conventional systems and would also reduce the impact of the political uncertainties associated with them.

Compared with the self-contained load, which can be lifted into the airship as a whole, individual containers are not practicable. Loading them merely increases the vulnerable period when the airship is hovering near the ground; they create problems of lift (eg in the case of partially filled containers) which are, as already described, related to fuel consumption. Moreover, forms of surface transport carry containers more efficiently.

Containers are usually associated with proposals to load airships by large helicopters which would land on a pad on the hull. But such an operation is time and manpower-consuming, as well as being dangerous to the airship. These ideas may stem from a misconception of the role of the aeroplane-carrying *Akron* and *Macon*, and a failure to appreciate that their small aeroplanes were intended to be scouts, units capable of flying at very low speeds to enable them to re-enter the airship.

Finally, in the rigid class, designs for a hybrid airship appear from time to time. Such, for example, was the Dutchman Arno Boerner's plan in the early 1920s for a ship of some 10 million cubic feet capacity. Fitted with twin keels, her engines generating 6,000hp, driving swivelling propellers. She was intended to land without assistance from handling parties. The idea attracted some attention in Germany when airship construction was prohibited. An obvious disadvantage of the hybrid airship is its increase of drag compared with the orthodox

Zeppelin shape, while the necessity to fly aerodynamically, thereby requiring a runway, robs the airship of one of its chief assets.

One small prototype in the hybrid airship class has actually been built.[8] This is the American *Aereon III*. Her designer, John Fitzpatrick, an ex-US navy airship officer, based his plan on the catamaran principle of three hulls, with a volume of 340,000cu ft, an overall length of 86ft, a width of 53ft, and height of 18ft. Inflated, the airship was really a buoyant wing. It had the advantage of being able to lift heavy loads without distorting the ship, and the framework was constructed so that stresses were distributed in a new way and opposed one another; the three hulls could be pressurised and so added considerably more strength. The ship was propelled by a two-bladed helicopter type rotor, 21ft in diameter on a horizontal axis at the stern of the central hull. Heat resulting from cooling the engine warmed the helium in the hulls and provided controlled lift without having recourse to disposable ballast. This is the first time that such controlled lift has been built into an airship. *Aereon III* also conveyed her own mooring mast in the form of a 20ft retractable strut carrying the front landing wheel. Unfortunately the airship, intended by the Rev Monroe Drew Jnr, of Trenton, New Jersey, to play a part in bringing assistance to the underdeveloped countries, was smashed by a gust of wind while being handled outside her shed.

Non-rigids have, in recent years, been used for advertising, for geological surveys, and for lumber work in Canada and Russia. In the future they would be used for refuelling, and generally maintaining, large rigid airships. They might also provide feeder services for passenger aircraft, being quieter than helicopters, and able to make a powerless ascent.[9]

Germany, despite the interruption of two world wars, continues to maintain the tradition of building and operating non-rigids that goes back to the first Parsevals, built at the beginning of the century. In the 1930s H. Naatz, the chief engineer of the Wasser und Luftfahrzeug Gesellschaft, of Berlin, builders of Parseval airships, developed what was virtually a semi-rigid. The envelope was sustained by a fine steel mesh which was secured to girders at top and bottom of the envelope. The keel girder also held a walkway. This *PN* type of over 90,000cu ft capacity, and 151ft in length, was used to advertise the products of

Trumpf, the chocolate manufacturers. Construction of these small airships depended on revenue from sales promotion and advertising, and two other firms, Underberg and Schwab, also employed *PN*-type ships with capacities of 123,000 to 157,000cu ft and equipped with automatic pressure control.

Since 1969 non-rigid airship construction and operation has been kept alive by Theodor Wüllenkemper, owner, manager and pilot of West Deutsche Luftwerbung.[10] He planned to build four helium-inflated non-rigids increasing in volume from 210,000 to 444,000cu ft, powered by engines developing totals of 370 to 1,400hp and able to carry payloads varying from 1 to 30 tons. In the autumn of 1972 the shed at the airship base at Mulheim-Ruhr was destroyed in a gale; one of the two airships constructed, which was successfully riding out the storm at a mast, was destroyed by flying debris from the shed. Nevertheless, the future of the non-rigid in West Germany seems secure by concentrating on advertising and special tasks, including even the carriage of containers.

It is recognised that the USSR is the most airship-minded nation today (page 240) in spite of opposition from the Soviet Ministry of Aviation. On the other hand, in the USA the only airship practitioners are Goodyear, which still has four non-rigids in operation. *Europa*, of 202,700cu ft capacity, is the latest (and the 300th to be built by this firm, and was assembled in England in the airship shed at Cardington); she operates, like her sister ships, in a publicity role. She is equipped to operate television cameras and she can be illuminated for night advertising.

This study has traced the progress of the 'airship era', a period spanning little more than the first half of the twentieth century, and has indicated the possible form of a rigid airship revival. But there are arguments against such a revival which cannot be ignored. Some of these are voiced by old airshipmen, like von Schiller,[11] and by Sir Barnes Wallis, possibly Britain's most successful airship designer. Yet before them even Count Zeppelin in his last years lost interest in his brainchild; and a disillusioned Eckener, after two world wars, believed that the airship had no future because aeroplanes were more adaptable to a military role. Experienced voices argue, firstly, that the handling of airships can only be learnt by experience. Secondly, other critics maintain that the cost of an airship programme will be immense (£300 million is one estimate, to which would be added annual running costs of £3 million). These factors might require future construction and operation to be put in the hands of an international group. Thirdly, other critics contend that such a slow-moving unit as an airship has no place in the modern world, and a revival is only an excuse for a nostalgic excursion into outmoded, but attractive, means of transport like coal-fired locomotives, luxury ocean liners and steam-driven yachts.

But these last-named critics regard the airship as a rival to heavier-than-air craft. Airships, it has been emphasised, have a role of their own to play; and the strength and lightness of new materials and modes of propulsion, such as gas turbines, endow them with a greater chance of success than their vulnerable predecessors of the 1920s and 1930s.[12]

The answer to the critics must wait, assuming the money is available, until a prototype airship is built and tested, and crews provided with the opportunity of live handling for which simulators are no substitute. The success of such a ship will at last dispel the image of disaster which has, for so long, dogged the airship endeavour.

In the 1920s British airship promoters used the theme of imperial communications to attract governmental interest. A defeated Germany saw the Zeppelin as a new symbol of prestige and it became the first vehicle designed for non-stop inter-continental air travel. The case for an airship revival today must ultimately depend on the recognition that transport, in one form or another, is one of the keys to alleviating over-centralisation and traffic congestion, to name only two environmental problems.

Between the privileged handful of travellers in the *Graf Zeppelin*, and the package tourists in the jumbo jet aeroplane, lies a revolution not only in technology but in social change and habit. Current (1974) anxieties over the sources of energy provide another argument for the airship with its economical consumption of fuel. But further change must come, and speed may, in the future, no longer be such a desirable criterion. The air which, to stress the obvious, covers ten-tenths of the world, may at last be fully utilised as a medium for transport as much as the sea in former centuries, vindicating Sir George Cayley's prophetic words, written in 1816: 'An uninterrupted navigable ocean, that comes to the threshold of everyman's door, ought not to be neglected as a source of human gratification and advantage.'[13]

SELECT BIBLIOGRAPHY

Arnstein, K. *The Development of Large Commercial Airships*, Trans ASME, January/April 1928.

Blakemore, T. L. and Pagon, W. W. *Pressure Airships*, New York, 1927.

Burgess, C. P. *Airship Design*, New York, 1927.

Dürr, Ludwig, *25 Jahre Zeppelin-Luftschiffbau*, Berlin, 1924.

Eckener, Hugo. *My Zeppelins*, (trans by Robinson, Douglas), 1958.

Higham, Robin D. S. *The British Rigid Airship, 1908–1931*, 1961.

Kirschner, Edward J. *The Zeppelin in the Atomic Age*, Urbana, University of Illinois Press, 1957.

Lehmann, E. A. *Zeppelin. The Story of Lighter-than-Air Craft*, 1937.

Lewitt, E. H. *The Rigid Airship*, 1925.

Nobile, Umberto. *My Polar Flights*, 1961.

Pratt, H. B. *Commercial Airships*, 1920.

Robinson, Douglas H. *The Zeppelin in Combat*, 1962.

Robinson, Douglas H. *Giants in the Sky*, 1973.

Sinclair, J. A. *Airships in Peace and War*, 1934.

Smith, Richard, K. *The Airships Akron and Macon*, Annapolis, Maryland US Naval Institute, 1965.

Sprigg, C. *The Airship, Its Design, History, Operation and Future*, 1931.

Schiller, Hans von. *Zeppelin Wegbereiter des Luftverkehrs*, Bad Godesberg, 1967.

Vaeth, J. Gordon. *Graf Zeppelin*, 1959.

Whale, George. *British Airships: Past, Present and Future*, 1919.

REFERENCES

Abbreviations

Aircraft Engineering: Aircraft Engng.
American Society of Mechanical Engineers Transactions: ASME Trans.
Journal of the American Society of Naval Engineers: J Amer Soc Nav Engrs.
Bulletin Wingfoot Lighter-than-Air Society, now called *Buoyant Flight,* Bulletin Lighter-than-Air Society: Bull Wingfoot LTA.
Cave-Brown-Cave Papers Collection, Imperial War Museum: CBC Papers.
Engineering: Engng.
Institution of Naval Architects Proceedings: Proc Instn Nav Arch.
Public Record Office: PRO/AIR (Branch of Air Staff); PRO/DSIR (Department of Scientific and Industrial Research) followed by document number.
Aeronautical Journal of the Royal Aeronautical Society: J Roy Aeron Soc.
Royal Engineers' Journal: RE Jnl.
Scientific American: Sci Amer.
Society of Automotive Engineers, Journal and Transactions: SAE Jnl Trans.
Zeitschrift für Flugtechnik und Motorluftschiffahrt: ZFM.

Chapter 1

1 Scott, G. H. 'Airship Piloting', J Roy Aeron Soc, 2 Dec 1920; Lewitt, E. H. *The Rigid Airship,* 1925; Cave-Brown-Cave, T. R. 'Airships', Lecture to Brit Assn, 1919. Published in *Engng,* 12 Sept 1919.

2 Campbell, C. I. R. 'Development of Airship Construction', Proc Instn Nav Arch, Vol LXI, 10 April 1919.

3 Upson, Ralph H. 'Metalclad Rigid Airship Development', SAE Jnl, Feb 1926.

4 Arnstein, Karl. 'The Development of Large Commercial Airships', Trans ASME, Vol 49–50, 1927–8; Pritchard, J. E. M. 'Rigid Airships and Their Development', J Roy Aeron Soc, 1920; Campbell, C. I. R. 'The Effect of Size in the Performance of Rigid Airships', Procs Instn Nav Arch, Vol LXII, 1920.

5 Hovgaard, William. 'Deformation and Stress Distribution in the Performance of Rigid Airships', Procs Instn Nav Arch, Vol LXIX, 14 July 1927.

Chapter 2

1 Hildebrandt, A. *Airships Past and Present*, 1908; Davy, M. J. B. *Aeronautics: Lighter-Than-Air Craft*, 1950.

2 Berget, Alphonse. *The Conquest of the Air*, 1909; Dollfuss & Bouché. *Histoire de L'Aeronautique*, Paris 1932.

3 Rolt, L. T. C. *The Aeronauts: A History of Ballooning, 1783-1903*, 1966, pp 215-20.

4 Wykeham, Peter. *Santos Dumont. A Study in Obsession*, 1962.

5 Berget, op cit, p 96.

6 *L'Aerophile*, XIII, pp 151-9 and 272-82, July 1905; Blakemore, Thos L & Pagon, W. Watters. *Pressure Airships*, New York, 1927, pp 187-8.

7 Sci Mus Library, London. Alexander, P. J. 'Collection of Aeronautical Cuttings', 1903.

8 Krogh, Christopher von. *In Die Lufte Empor! Entwicklung und Technik der Luftschiffahrt*, Charlottenburg, 1908.

9 Berget, op cit; Kingston, Capt Lucius A. 'Military Aeronautics', Jnl Instn Automob Engrs, 1910, pp 16-18.

10 Sci Mus Lib, op cit, Rolls, S. C. *Daily Mail*, 30 Nov 1907.

11 *The Airship*, Nos 3-4, 1934-5.

12 Ibid. *The Story of the Societé Zodiac*, Vol 7, No 1, Spring 1948, pp 10-11.

13 *Sci Amer*, 'German-French Airship Rivalry', 24 Aug 1913; ibid, 'Comparison of French and German Strength in Dirigible Airships', 16 Aug 1913; PRO/AIR 1/2477.

14 Kriegswissenschaftliche Abteilung der Luftwaffe. *Die Militärluftfahrt bis zum Beginn der Weltkrieges*, Frankfurt-am-Main, 1965.

15 Eisenlohr, Roland. 'History of Development of Parseval Airship', *Flugwelt*, 19 Nov 1919; PRO/AIR 2/196; *Engng*, 'The Parseval Airship', 10 Sept 1909.

16 Koreuber, Hauptman. 'Development of German Airships of the Semi Rigid and Non Rigid Type', *Illustrierte Flugwelt*, 27 Oct 1920.

17 PRO/AIR 2/196; PRO/AIR 1/2493.

Chapter 3

1 *L'Aerophile*, Aug 1905, pp 173-4.

2 Giacomelli, R. 'An Historical Survey of Italian Aeronautics', J Roy Aeron Soc, Vol XXXIII, Sept 1929; Blakemore & Pagan, op cit, pp 190-8.

3 Sci Mus Lib, op cit, *Spectator*, 22 June 1912; PRO/AIR 1/2518.

4 Blakemore & Pagan, op cit, p 198.

5 *Flight*, 24 Jan 1914.

6 *The Engineer*, 'The Forlanini Airship', 17 April 1914.

7 Gibbs-Smith, Charles (Ed). *Sir George Cayley's Aeronautics 1796–1855*, 1962.

8 Sci Mus Lib, op cit, 21 March 1903.

9 McKinty, Alec. *The Father of British Airships. Biography of E. T. Willows*, 1972.

10 Walker, Percy B. *Early Aviation at Farnborough, Vol 1, Balloons, Kites and Airships*, 1971; Broke-Smith, P. W. L. 'The History of Early British Aeronautics', RE Jnl, 1952 (Academic Reprint, 1968); Waterlow, C. M. 'History of British Army Airships', *The Airship*, Vol 7, Nos 4–6, 1948.

11 Sci Mus Lib, op cit, 22 July 1905.

12 Roskill, S. W. (Ed). 'Documents Relating to the Naval Air Service', Vol I, 1908–18, Doc No 22, Navy Records Soc, 1969.

13 PRO/AIR 2/1.

14 PRO/AIR 1/2517.

15 Bull Wingfoot LTA Soc, Woodward, Donald. 'Lighter-than-Air in Japan', Vol 9, Nos 5–7, 1961–2.

16 PRO/AIR 2/197.

17 Wellman, Walter. *The Aerial Age*, New York, 1911.

Chapter 4

1 Eckener, Hugo. *Count Zeppelin*, 1938; Schiller, Hans. *von Zeppelin Wegbereiter des Weltluftverkehrs*, Bad Godesberg, 1967; *Die Militärluftfahrt*, op cit.

2 Stahl, Friedrich. 'Rigid Airships', *Illustrierte Flugwoche*, Jan–June 1921; Robinson, Douglas. *Giants in the Sky*, 1973, Chaps I–II.

3 Sci Mus Lib, op cit. Wolf, Eugen. 'Count Zeppelin's Airship', *Windsor Magazine*, June 1901.

4 Stahl, op cit; Robinson, op cit, pp 36–9.

5 *Die Militärluftfahrt*, op cit, p 66.

6 Robinson, op cit, p 58.

7 Dienstbach, Karl. 'A Journey in a Zeppelin', *Sci Amer*, 17 May 1912.

8 Dürr, Ludwig. *25 Jahre Zeppelin-Luftschiffbau*, Berlin, 1924.

9 *Die Militärluftfahrt*, op cit, p 212 and Robinson, Douglas. *The Zeppelin in Combat. History of the German Naval Airship Division, 1912–18*, 1962, p 20.

10 Robinson. *The Zeppelin in Combat*, op cit, p 24.

11 Robinson. *Giants in the Sky*, op cit, p 81.

12 Rühl, D. (Chief Engineer, Luftschiffbau Schütte-Lanz). 'The Importance of the Schütte-Lanz Airship', Aircraft Technical Note, No 204, 15 Aug

1921, US Navy Dept, Bureau of Inspection and Repair; Dick, Adm Karl. 'Luftschiffbau Zeppelin v Luftschiffbau Schütte-Lanz', *Der Luftweg*, 19 May 1921.

13 Dürr, Ludwig. 'Comments on Adml Dick Article', *Der Luftweg*, 30 June 1921.

14 Roskill, op cit, Doc No 2; Sueter, Murray F. *Airmen or Noahs*, 1928.

15 PRO/AIR 1/2488.

16 PRO/AIR 3/1; PRO/DSIR 23/124.

17 PRO/AIR 1/2444; PRO/DSIR 23/140.

18 Roskill, op cit, Doc No 17.

19 PRO/AIR 1/2456.

20 Murray, D. G. 'British Rigid Airships', Prelim Draft for Sir Walter Raleigh, *War in the Air*, 1921 (CBC Papers).

21 Roskill, op cit, Doc No 27.

22 Murray, op cit.

23 PRO/AIR 1/2477; PRO/AIR 1/2518; PRO/AIR 1/2519.

24 Giacomelli, op cit.

25 Eckener, Hugo. 'The Zeppelin Crisis', *The Airship*, Vol 5, Nos 17–20, 1938.

Chapter 5

1 PRO/AIR 2/196; Robinson. *The Zeppelin in Combat*, op cit and *Giants in the Sky*, op cit, Chap IV passim; Cuneo, John R. *Winged Mars. The Air Weapon, 1914–16*, Harrisburg, Pa, 1942.

2 Stahl, op cit; PRO/AIR 11/50.

3 Robinson. *The Zeppelin in Combat*, op cit, p 69.

4 Stahl, op cit.

5 Stahl, op cit.

6 Jones, H. A. *The War in the Air*, op cit, Vol III, p 237.

7 Stahl, op cit.

8 Jones, H. A., op cit, Vol V, 1935, pp 152–9.

9 Hezlet, Sir Arthur. *Aircraft and Sea Power*, 1970, p 34.

10 Marder, A. J. *From the Dreadnought to Scapa Flow*, Vol III, 1966, p 151; Marder, ibid, Vol IV, 1969, Chap 1.

11 Marder, op cit, Vol III, pp 247–9; Hezlet, op cit, pp 61–3.

12 Mielke, Otto. *Verwegener Flug nach Afrika*, Munich, 1958.

13 D'Orcy, Ladislas. 'The Case for the Airship', SAE Jnl, 7 March 1919.

14 Murray, op cit.

15 Murray, op cit; Norris, Capt David to 5th Sea Lord, Mem 'Delays in

Prodn of Rigids', 28 Feb 1917 (CBC Papers); Graham Greene, Sir W. to Director Air Services, Mem 28 Dec 1915 (CBC Papers).

16 Rigid Airship Cttee Mtg, Mins 2 May 1916 (CBC Papers).

17 Murray, op cit.

18 Rigid Airship Cttee Mtgs, 23 May, 9 June 1916; Marsh, W. Lockwood. 'Rigid Airship Design', *Air Annual British Empire*, 1930.

19 Murray, op cit.

20 Rigid Airship Cttee Mtg, 23 May 1916.

21 Roskill, op cit, Doc No 185.

22 Roskill, op cit, Doc No 158.

23 Norris to 5th Sea Lord (Comm Godfrey Paine), 28 Feb 1917.

24 Murray, D. G. 'The Development of Non-Rigid Airships', Draft for Raleigh's *War in the Air*, passim.

25 Author's interview with Air Mshl Sir Victor Goddard, 26 Sept 1970.

26 Rosser, S. J., Letter to Author, 11 Sept 1970.

27 Maitland, Air Mshl P. E., Typescript on North Sea Airships.

28 PRO/AIR 3/42.

29 Secretary to the Admiralty. 'Development of the Airship Service', 1 Nov 1918 (CBC Papers).

30 Fletcher, J. N. and Norris, D. 'Operational Superiority of North Sea Airship to Rigid Airship' (CBC Papers).

31 *The Aeroplane*, 20 Aug 1919; D'Arlandes. 'French Military Airships', *The Airship*, Winter 1947–8, No 2 (New Series).

32 PRO/AIR 11/55; PRO/AIR 10/176.

33 Meager, George. *My Airship Flights, 1915–30*, 1970; Williams, T. B. 'Flight of SR 1 from Italy to England', *The Airship*, Vol 1, No 3, Autumn 1934.

34 Teed, P. L. 'Report on Visit to Canada and USA' (Air/608766) 1917 (CBC Papers).

35 Hunsaker, J. C. 'The Navy's First Airships', US Naval Inst Procs, Vol 45, No 8, Aug 1919; Smith, R. K. 'An Inventory of US Navy Airships 1916–61', Xerox Copy, pp 52–65.

Chapter 6

1 Inter-Allied Aeronautical Commn of Control, Memo 15 March 1920 (CBC Papers).

2 PRO/AIR 2/268.

3 PRO/AIR 11/50.

4 Colsman to Masterman, copy of letter (CBC Papers).

5   PRO/AIR 11/50.
6   Roskill, S. W. *Naval Policy Between the Wars. The Period of Anglo-American Antagonism 1919–29*, 1968; Higham, Robin D. S. *The British Rigid Airship 1908–31*, 1961.
7   PRO/AIR 8/21; PRO/AIR 5/301.
8   PRO/DSIR 23/2187; PRO/DSIR 23/2252; PRO/AIR 11/153.
9   PRO/DSIR 23/884.
10 PRO/AIR 2/154.
11 PRO/AIR 2/125.
12 Pritchard, J. E. M. 'Transatlantic Flight of R 34' (Tech Rept); Maitland, E. M. *The Log of HMA R 34*, 1920; Turner, E. E. 'The Atlantic Cruise of HMA R 34', Soc of Engrs, Nov 1922; PRO/AIR 2/125.
13 Alcock, W. Newman. 'The Case for the Airship Today', Oct 1951, Roy Aeron Soc Award 1955. Typescript in Roy Aeron Soc Lib, p 6.
14 CBC Papers, op cit. 'Destruction of R 34', 8 March 1921.
15 Adm War Staff Int Div, CB 1265, A–B *German Rigid Airships, 1917.*
16 Butcher, F. L. C. 'Handling by Means of Landing Parties and Wind Screens', J Roy Aeron Soc, Dec 1920; PRO/DSIR 23/10314; PRO/DSIR 23/10317; PRO/DSIR 23/10322; PRO/DSIR 23/10325–6.
17 Bleistein, von W. 'Luftschiffe am Mast', ZFM, p 362, 1929; PRO/AIR 11/49; PRO/AIR 11/68; Rosendahl, C. E. 'The Mooring and Ground Handling of a Rigid Airship', ASME Trans, Vol 55, 1933.
18 Dawson, Sir Trevor. 'The Commercial Airship. Its Operation and Construction', *Engng*, 22 Oct 1920; Pratt, H. B. *Commercial Airships*, 1920.
19 Maitland, E. M. 'Modern Airships', Lecture delivered at House of Comons, 28 June 1920. Later delivered as 'The Commercial Future of Airships', Roy Soc of Arts, Vol LXVIII, p 461.
20 PRO/AIR 2/126.
21 PRO/AIR 2/210; PRO/DSIR 23/1653.
22 Aeron Res Cttee (Accidents Investigation Sub Cttee). 'Rept on Accident to *HMA R 38*', R & M, No 775 (A2), March 1922.
23 PRO/AIR 5/910.
24 Alcock, W. Newman, op cit, pp 10–12.
25 PRO/AIR 5/284.
26 Blakemore & Pagan, op cit, pp 202–7.
27 Blakemore & Pagan, op cit, pp 223–9.
28 Smith, Richard K. *Inventory of US Navy Airships*, op cit, pp 3–6; PRO/AIR 11/58; Campbell, C. I. R. 'Rept on Visit to USA', 17 Jan 1920 (CBC Papers); Burgess, C. P., Hunsaker, J. C., Truscott, Starr. 'Strength of Rigid Airships', J Roy Aeron Soc, June 1924.

29 'Technical Aspects of the Loss of USS Shenandoah', J Amer Soc Nav Engrs, Vol XXXVIII, No 3, Aug 1926.

30 Turnbull, Archibald T. & Lord, Clifford R. *History of US Naval Aviation*, Yale Univ Press, 1949, p 251.

31 Smith, Richard K., op cit, pp 9–15.

32 PRO/AIR 2/268; PRO/AIR 5/1022; PRO/AIR 11/59; Burgess, C. P. 'The Rigid Airship ZR-3', J Amer Soc Nav Engrs, Vol XXXVI, No 4, Nov 1924.

33 Smith, Richard K., op cit, p 10.

34 *L'Aerophile*, pp 1–15, Feb 1924; *Engng*, 11 Jan 1924.

35 Engberding, Dietrich & Parseval, August von. 'Tragedy of Airships (*Dixmude* Disaster)', ZFM, 26 March 1924.

Chapter 7

1 PRO/AIR 19/546.

2 PRO/AIR 19/527.

3 PRO/AIR 8/21.

4 PRO/AIR 8/74; PRO/AIR 5/1062.

5 PRO/AIR 8/21; PRO/AIR 5/1035.

6 PRO/AIR 5/381.

7 PRO/AIR 2/656.

8 Smith, Richard K. *The Airships Akron and Macon* Annapolis, Maryland US Naval Inst, 1965, Introd.

9 Eckener, Hugo. *My Zeppelins* (trans by Robinson, Douglas), 1958, pp 28–31; Vaeth, J. Gordon. *Graf Zeppelin*, 1959, Chap 3.

10 PRO/DSIR 23/1621.

11 Shute, Nevil. *Slide Rule*, 1954.

12 Author's Interview with Lord King's Norton, 22 April 1970 and Sir Alfred Pugsley, 17 Aug 1970.

13 PRO/AIR 5/1058; PRO/AIR 2/268.

14 Lawrence, T. E. *Letters*, 1938, p 704.

15 Author's Interview with Sir Barnes Wallis, 3 Sept 1970; Morpurgo, J. E. *Barnes Wallis*, 1972.

16 Burney, Sir Dennistoun. *The World, The Air, and the Future*, 1929.

17 Wingfoot LTA Soc Bull, Vol 9, No 11, 1961–2.

18 Wallis, B. N. 'Rigid Airship Design and Construction', *Aircraft Engng*, Jan 1930. Roxbee Cox, H. R. 'External Forces on an Airship Structure', J Roy Aeron Soc, Vol XXXIII, Sept 1929.

19 Dürr, Ludwig F. 'Massnahmen zur Verbesserung der Zeppelin Luft-

schiffe für den Fernverkehr', Schriften der Deutschen Akademie der Luftfahrtforschung, Heft 2, Munich, 1939. Commem of Count Zeppelin's Centenary of Birth.

20 Arnstein, Karl. 'The Development of Large Commercial Rigid Airships', ASME Trans, 1927–8, Vols 49–50.

21 Burgess, C. P. 'Progress in Airship Design from USS Shenandoah to USS Akron', J Amer Soc Nav Engrs, Aug 1931; *Aircraft Engng*, 'Modern British Airship Practice', Nov 1929.

22 PRO/AIR 11/49.

23 *Aircraft Engng*, 'The Latest Rigid Airship (Akron)', Nov 1931.

24 *The Engineer*, 'Graf Zeppelin (LZ 127)', 5 Oct 1928.

25 PRO/AIR 11/49.

26 Wallis, op cit; CBC Papers, Nixon to Cave-Brown-Cave, 27 Nov 1933.

27 Southwell, R. V. *R 101*, Nature, 14 Dec 1929.

28 Richmond, V. C. 'Some Modern Developments in Rigid Airship Construction', Procs Inst Nav Arch, Vol LXX, 30 March 1928.

29 Wallis, op cit.

30 PRO/DSIR 23/2049.

31 *Aircraft Engng*, op cit, Nov 1929.

32 PRO/DSIR 23/2673; CBC Papers, Arnstein–Cave-Brown-Cave Corresp, 17 Dec 1932–30 March 1933; Roy Aircraft Estab Eng Exptl Dept, 'Use of Hydrogen as a Fuel for Airship Engines' (Rept No E, 1739), Dec 1927.

33 CBC Papers, 'Chronology: Development of R 101 Engines, 21 May 1924–5 Dec 1928'.

34 CBC Papers, Cave-Brown-Cave-Mevill Jones. 'Corresp on *R 101* Engines', June 1929.

35 Wilkinson, P. A. *Aircraft Diesels*, 1940.

36 CBC Papers, Nixon, S. to Cave-Brown-Cave, 26 Aug 1936.

37 Dürr, *Massnahmen zur Verbesserung der Zeppelin Luftschiffe*, op cit, pp 25–30.

38 Teed, P. L. 'Airship Propulsion Methods', *Aircraft Engng*, Dec 1929.

39 'Modern British Airship Practice', *Aircraft Engng*, op cit, Nov 1929.

40 Robinson. *Giants in the Sky*, op cit, p 302.

41 CBC Papers, Nixon to Cave-Brown-Cave, 3 Oct 1935.

42 *Aircraft Engng*, op cit, Nov 1929.

43 Wallis, op cit.

44 Rosendahl, C. E. 'Inside the Graf Zeppelin', *Sci Amer*, March 1929, p 204.

45 Ehrle, Albert. *Die Entwicklung des Zeppelin-Luftschiffes zum Fernverkehr*, Schriften der Deutschen Akademie der Luftfahrtforschung, op cit, pp

44–7; Robinson, Douglas H., Famous Aircraft Series, *LZ 129 Hindenburg*, Dallas, 1964.

46 'The World's Largest Airship USS Macon', *The Airship*, Autumn 1934, Vol No 3.

47 PRO/AIR 5/987.

Chapter 8

1 Kleffel, Walther and Schulze, Wilhelm. *Im Luftschiff nach Amerika und Zuruck. Die Zeppelin Fahrt*, Berlin, 1928; PRO/AIR 11/49.

2 Kamm, Wunibald and Steiglitz, Albert. 'Investigations on the Oscillations in Power Plant of Graf Zeppelin', ZFM, Vol 20, No 18, 28 Sept 1929, pp 465–74; *Engng*, 11 Oct 1929.

3 Vaeth, op cit, Chap 7.

4 PRO/AIR 11/164.

5 Breithaupt, J. *Mit Graf Zeppelin nach Sud und Nord Amerika*, Baden, 1930.

6 Mackay, James. *Airmails 1870–1970*, 1971, pp 38–44, 145–9.

7 PRO/AIR 11/49.

8 PRO/AIR 5/7.

9 PRO/AIR 5/1018; PRO/AIR 2/324.

10 Atherstone, N. G. 'Journal R 101' (unpublished), 11 July 1929–3 Oct 1930.

11 PRO/AIR 5/974.

12 Atherstone, op cit.

13 PRO/AIR 2/349.

14 Atherstone, op cit.

15 Meager, op cit, p 154–5.

16 CBC Papers, 'R 100 Speed Trial, 16 Jan 1930'. Rept on Machinery.

17 PRO/AIR 5/983; PRO/AIR 5/1068.

18 PRO/AIR 5/13.

19 Johnston, E. L. 'Atlantic Flight of R 100', *Aircraft Engng*, Nov 1930.

20 Meager, op cit, p 207; CBC Papers, 'Canadian Flight of R 100' (Rept to Roy Airship Works), 1 Aug 1930.

21 PRO/AIR 2/364.

22 Ibid.

23 Meager, op cit, p 190.

24 PRO/AIR 5/1408.

25 Cave-Brown-Cave. 'R 101 and Other Airships. The Process of Development', J Roy Aeron Soc, Vol 66, Aug 1962.

26 Atherstone, op cit.

27 Cmd 3825. 'Rept of the R 101 Inquiry', 1931.

28 PRO/AIR 8/21.
29 PRO/AIR 5/910.
30 PRO/DSIR 23/3144.
31 PRO/AIR 5/1407.
32 PRO/DSIR 23/3144.
33 PRO/AIR 8/123.
34 PRO/DSIR 23/3345.
35 PRO/DSIR 23/3228.
36 PRO/AIR 11/168.
37 Arnstein, Karl. *Über Einige Luftschiffprobleme*, ZFM, 14 Jan 1933, p 13.
38 Smith, Richard K. *The Airships Akron and Macon*, op cit, Chaps 3–5.
39 PRO/AIR 11/168.
40 Ibid.
41 Hunsaker, Jerome C. Address to SAE, Aug 1933.
42 Smith, Richard K. *The Airships Akron and Macon*, op cit, Chap 6.
43 Ibid, Chaps 7–10.
44 Ibid, Chap 11.
45 CBC Papers, Nixon to Cave-Brown-Cave, 3 Oct 1935.
46 Robinson. *LZ 129*, op cit.
47 PRO/DSIR 23/5603.
48 Ibid.
49 Eckener. 'The Airship and Its Place in Modern Transportation', SAE Jnl,
    Vol 40, No 5, May 1937; Rept of US Bureau of Commerce Cttee, 'The
    Loss of the Hindenburg', *Aircraft Engng*, Oct 1937.
50 Ibid.
51 Eckener. 'The Zeppelin Crisis', op cit; Vaeth, op cit, Chap 16.
52 Wingfoot LTA Soc Bull. *LZ 130*, Vol 11, Nos 3–4, Feb 1962.
53 Wood, Derek & Dempster, Derek. *The Narrow Margin*, 1961, pp 17–20.
54 PRO/DSIR 23/4033.

Chapter 9

1 PRO/AIR 11/54.
2 CBC Papers, Nobile, Umberto. 'The Use of Airships in Passenger Transport', Rome, Dec 1920.
3 Blakemore & Pagan, op cit, pp 207–12.
4 PRO/AIR 11/54.
5 Woodruff, Roy V. 'The First Flight to the North Pole and the Crossing
   of the Polar Sea', Speech to the House of Representatives, 27 Feb 1927,
   Washington, 1927.

6 Nobile, Umberto. 'The Dirigible and Polar Exploration', Amer Geograph Soc Spec Pub, No 7, N York, 1928.

7 Cross, Wilbur. *Ghost Ship of the Pole*, N York, 1960; Nobile. *My Polar Flights*, 1961.

8 Commissione D'Indagini per la Spedizione Polare dell' L'Aeronare *Italia* Relazine, 'Rivista Maritima', Roma, 1928.

9 Eckener, Knut. *A Note on the Technology and Development of the Zeppelin Airship*. App to *My Zeppelins*, Eckener, Hugo, 1958, pp 187-8.

10 PRO/DSIR 23/4139; PRO/DSIR 23/3603; Mintschall, Vladimir. 'Status of the Airship in the USSR', Foreign Sci Bull, Vol 1, No 10, Oct 1963; Addinell, H. 'Russia and Her Airships', *Flight*, 1 Dec 1932.

11 *Kansas City Times*, Stalino Ukraine, 8 Sept 1938.

12 'Phoenix Newsletter', The Airship Assn, No 8, July 1972.

13 Blakemore & Pagan, op cit, pp 17-24; Swanborough, G. & Bowers, P. *US Military Aircraft since 1908*, 1971.

14 PRO/DSIR 23/4033.

15 Smith, Richard K. *Inventory of US Navy Airships*, op cit, pp 86-7.

16 PRO/DSIR 23/2100.

17 Allen, Hugh. *Story of the Airship*, Goodyear Tire & Rubber Co, 1931, Chap VII; Arnstein, Karl. 'Developments in Lighter-than-Air Craft', SAE Jnl, May 1929.

18 Smith, Richard K. *Inventory of US Navy Airships*, op cit, pp 61-73.

19 Flickinger, M. L. 'To Keep Them Flying', *Buoyant Flight*, Bull LTA Soc, Vol 20, No 2, Jan-Feb 1973.

20 Lewis, David D. *The Fight for the Sea*, Cleveland and New York, 1961, Chap 11.

21 Smith, Richard K. *Inventory of US Navy Airships*, op cit, pp 76-7.

22 Broedling, James E. 'Experiences Flying Navy Blimps', *Buoyant Flight*, Vol 19, No 2, Jan-Feb 1972.

23 PRO/AIR 20/1311.

24 Rankin, R. H. 'Goodbye to the Gasbags', US Nav Inst Procs, Vol 87, No 10, 1961.

25 Smith, Richard K. *Inventory of US Navy Airships*, op cit, p 72.

26 Ibid, p 78.

27 Ibid, pp 81-2.

28 Rankin, op cit.

29 Williams, A. H. 'A Stabilized Platform to Mount on a Non Rigid Airship Base', Aerophysics Dept, Goodyear Aircraft Corp, ASME Prep (56-AV-27), 1956; Smith, Richard K. *Inventory of US Navy Airships*, op cit, pp 83-5.

30 Wingfoot LTA Soc Bull, Vol 14, No 9, July-Aug 1967.

31 PRO/AIR 2/214.

32 Upson, Ralph H. 'Metalclad Rigid Airship Development', Automotive Inds, Vol 54, No 5, Feb 1926; Fritsche, Carl B. 'The Metalclad Airship', J Roy Aeron Soc, May 1933.

33 Upson, Ralph H. 'Past Adventures and Future Prospects of the Metalclad Airship', SAE Jnl, Vol XXVI, May 1930, pp 567–75.

34 Smith, Richard K. *Inventory of US Navy Airships*, op cit, p 88.

Chapter 10

1 Kirschner, Edwin J. *The Zeppelin in the Atomic Age*, University of Illinois Press, Urbana, 1957, pp 49–57.

2 Arnstein, Karl. 'Rigid Airship Competes for Long Range Handling', SAE Jnl, 19 Aug 1946.

3 Morse, Francis. 'The Nuclear Airship', *New Scientist*, 7 April 1966.

4 *Flugwelt 19*, No 6, 1967, pp 412–15.

5 Hoffman, Gerard. 'No Nuclear Airships Please', *Engng*, 28 Nov 1969.

6 Mowforth, E. 'A Design Study for a Freight-Carrying Airship', J Roy Aeron Soc, Vol 75, No 723, March 1971; 'The Airfloat Project', Procs of One Day Symp, 20 Sept 1971; Hyde, F. W. 'Airships Reborn', Soc of Engrs, 6 Dec 1971.

7 'Phoenix Newsletter', No 8, Jul 1972. Address by Messrs Monk & Wood of Aerospace Development Ltd, to Airship Asson.

8 Robinson. *Giants in the Sky*, op cit, pp 320–3.

9 Bodroghy, B. G. 'Airships for Noiseless Feeder Service', *Engng*, 22 July 1972.

10 Jane's *Freight Containers*, 'Future Trends (Airships)', 1971–2, pp 602–9.

11 Schiller, Hans von. *Zeppelin Wegbereiter des Weltflugverkehrs*, Deutsche Luft und Raumfahrt Mitteilung, 72–7, Stuttgart, 1972.

12 Howe, D. 'The Feasibility of the Large Rigid Airship', Cranfield Rept Aero No 5, Cranfield Inst of Tech, Coll of Aeronautics, March 1972.

13 Gibbs-Smith, Charles (Ed), op cit, p 70.

CHARACTERISTICS OF PRINCIPAL RIGID AIRSHIPS

GERMANY
ZEPPELINS

Builder's No	Owner Number built ( )	Name	Volume cu ft	Length ft in	Diameter ft in	Useful lift lb	Engines no and type	Total hp
LZ 1	Zeppelin Co		399,000	420'	38' 6"	1,430	2 Daimler	28·4
LZ 2	Zeppelin Co		366,200	414'	38' 6"	6,180	2 Daimler	170
LZ 3	Zeppelin Co		403,600	440' 3"	38' 6"	6,180	2 Daimler	170
LZ 4–	German army	Z I	430,800			6,400	2 Daimler	210
LZ 5	Zeppelin Co	Z II	530,000	446'	42' 6"	10,150	2 Daimler	210
LZ 7–	German army	Deutschland				10,250		
LZ 8	DELAG	Ersatz Deutschland	683,000	446'	46'	11,000	3 Daimler	360
LZ 10	DELAG	Schwaben	628,000	460'	46'	14,300	3 M C–X	435
LZ 12	German army	Z III						
LZ 15	German army	Ersatz Z I	690,000	466'	48' 6"	18,080	3 M C–X	510
LZ 16		Z IV				16,700		

Builder's No	Owner Number built ( )	Name	Volume cu ft	Length ft in	Diameter ft in	Useful lift lb	Engines no and type	Total hp
LZ 22	German army	Z VII	780,000	510'	48' 6"	19,500	3 M C-X	540
LZ 23		Z VIII	794,500	518' 2"	48' 6"	20,250	3 M C-X	630
LZ 24–	German navy (7)	L 3	879,500	518' 3"	52' 6"	24,365	3 M C-X	630
LZ 35	German army (6)	LZ 35	1,126,400	536' 5"	61' 4"	30,800	4 M C-X	840
LZ 36	German navy	L 9	1,264,100	585' 5"	61' 4"	34,200	4 M HSLu	960
LZ 42–	German navy (5)	LZ 72				40,100 approx	4 M HSLu	960
LZ 50	German army (4)	L 16						
LZ 59–	German navy (5)							
LZ 61 & 64– 71								
except for LZ 60 & 70	German army (6)							
LZ 72– 90 except for LZ 73	German navy (14)		1,949,600	644' 8"	78' 5"	71,600 approx	6 M HSLu	1,200
LZ 77 & 81	German army (2)							
LZ 91– 94	German navy (4)	L 42 / L 46	1,970,300	644' 8"	78' 5"	83,400	5 M HSLu	1,200
LZ 95– 99	German navy	L 48 / L 54	1,970,300	644' 8"	78' 8"	87,100 approx	5 M HSLu	1,200
LZ 100–	German navy	L 53	1,977,360	644' 8"	78' 5"	89,200	5 M HSLu	1,200
101		L 55				89,600	5 M MbIVa	1,225
LZ 104	German navy	L 59	2,418,700	743' 0"	78' 5"	114,400	5 M HSLu	1,200
LZ 106– 111	German navy	L 61 / L 65	1,977,360	644' 8"	78' 5"	86,200	5 M MbIVa	1,225

LZ 112–	German navy	*L 70*	2,418,700 approx	743' 2" approx	78' 5"	112,700 approx	6 M MbIVa	1,470
LZ 114		*L 72*	706,200	393' 4"	61' 4"	22,000 approx	4 M MbIVa	980
LZ 120	DELAG	*Bodensee*	795,000	426' 1"	61' 4"	25,350		
LZ 126	US navy	*ZR 3*	2,762,100	658' 4"	90' 8"	101,430	5 M VI-I	2,000
LZ 127	Zeppelin Co	*Graf Zeppelin*	3,995,000	775' 0"	100' 0"	66,000	5 M VI-II	2,650
LZ 129	Zeppelin Reederei	*Hindenburg*	7,062,100	803' 10"	135' 1"	224,200	4 Daimler-Benz	4,200
LZ 130	Zeppelin Reederei	*Graf Zeppelin II*	7,062,100	803' 10"	135' 1"	224,200	4 Daimler-Benz	4,200
SCHÜTTE-LANZ's								
SL 1	German army	*SL 1*	734,500 / 861,900	432' 0"	60' 5"	11,000	2 Daimler	480
SL 2 (lengthened 1915)	German army	*SL 2*	981,600	474' 0"	59' 10"	17,300	4 M C-X	780
SL 3–	German army	*SL 3*	981,600	513' 3"	59' 10"	22,800	4 M C-X	840
SL 5		*SL 5*	1,143,500	502' 4"	64' 10"	31,300	4 M C-X	840
SL 6– / SL 9	German army	*SL 6* / *SL 9*	1,240,300	534' 5"	64' 10"	34,750	4 M C-X	840
SL 10– / SL 19	German army	*SL 10* / *SL 19*	1,369,300	570' 10"	65' 11"	47,400 approx	4 M HSLu	960
SL 20– / SL 22	German army	*SL 20* / *SL 22*	1,989,700	651' 0"	75' 3"	82,600	5 M HSLu	1,200
GREAT BRITAIN								
No 9	Royal Navy	*No 9*	890,000	526'	53'	8,520	4 Wolseley-Maybach	720
No 23– / R 26	Royal Navy	*No 23* / *R 26*	940,000	535'	53'	13,400–14,050	4 Rolls-Royce	1,000
R 27 (23X) / R 29	Royal Navy	*R 27* / *R 29*	990,600	539'	53'	19,400	4 Rolls-Royce	1,000

S

Builder's No	Owner	Name	Volume cu ft	Length ft in	Diameter ft in	Useful lift lb	Engines no and type	Total hp
R 31–	Royal Navy	R 31	1,535,000	614' 8"	64' 10"	37,000	6 Rolls-Royce	1,500
R 32		R 32						1,250
R 33–	Royal Navy	R 33	1,950,000	643'	78' 9"	58,100	5 Sunbeam Maori	1,250
R 34		R 34						
R 36	Air Min	G-FAAF	2,101,000	675'	78' 9"	35,900	2 Sunbeam Cossack 2 M MbIVa	1,540
R 38	Air Min US navy	R 38 ZR 2	2,724,000	699'	85' 6"	102,144	6 Sunbeam Cossack	2,100
R 80	Air Min	R 80	1,200,000	535'	70'	39,900	4 Wolseley Maybach	920
R 100	Air Min	R 100	5,156,000	709'	133'	114,000	6 Rolls-Royce Condor	3,960
R 101	Air Min	R 101	4,998,000 5,508,800 (after lengthening)	732' 777' (after lengthening)	132'	78,500 108,000	5 Beardmore Diesel	2,925
UNITED STATES OF AMERICA								
ZR 1	US navy	Shenandoah	2,235,000	680' 3"	78' 8"	53,600 47,500	6 Packard 5 Packard	1,800 1,500
ZRS 4	US navy	Akron	6,850,000	785'	132' 11"	160,170	8 Maybach VL-II	4,480
ZRS 5	US navy	Macon	6,850,000	785'	132' 11"	173,000	8 Maybach VL-II	4,480

CHARACTERISTICS OF PRINCIPAL SEMI-RIGID AIRSHIPS

FRANCE

Builder	Owner	Name	Volume cu ft	Length ft in	Maximum diameter ft in	Useful lift lb	Engines no and type	Total hp
Lebaudy Frères	French army	Lebaudy 1 (Le Jaune)	80,000	187'	32'		1 Daimler	40
Lebaudy Frères	French army	Lebaudy 2 (Lebaudy 1 rebuilt)	105,000	197'	35'		1 Daimler	50
Lebaudy Frères	British army	Morning Post	353,166	337'	39' 6"		2 Panhard and Levassor	135

GERMANY

Prussian army	Prussian army	Ma	63,576	131'	39'		1 Daimler	20
Prussian army	Prussian army	M 1	176,500	214'	36'	3,000	2 Körting	150
Prussian army	Prussian army	M IV	476,000	323'	50'	7,050	3 Maybach	480

ITALY

Brigata Specialisti	Italian army	P	173,000	203'	41'	4,045	2 Fiat	150
SCA	Italian army	PV	183,800	203'	42'	4,360	2 Fiat	380
SCA	Italian army & navy	M	441,000	271'	55'	13,610	2 Itala	400–440

Builder	Owner	Name Number built ( )	Volume cu ft	Length ft in	Maximum diameter ft in	Useful lift lb	Engines no and type	Total hp
SCA	Italian army & navy	M (enlarged)	441,000	271'	55'	15,820	2 Itala	400–440
SCA	Italian army & navy	O	127,100	177'	35'	3,290	2 Colombo	220
SCA	US army	Roma	1,240,000	410'	74'	41,950	4 Ansaldo (changed to 4 Packard)	1,200
SCA	Aero Club of Norway	Norge	654,000	347'	63'	21,000	3 Maybach	780
SCA	City of Milan	Italia	250,000	269'	42'	7,619	3 Maybach	780
Forlanini	Forlanini	F 1	131,000	131'	46'	—	1 Antoinette	30
Forlanini	Forlanini	F 2	460,000	236'	59'	8,960	2 Isotta-Fraschini	170
Forlanini	Italian Army	F 3	530,000	295'	59'	—	4 Fiat	360
Forlanini	Italian army	F 4	672,000	295'	59'	—	2 Isotta-Fraschini	360
Forlanini	Italian army	F 5	672,000	295'	65'	—	2 Isotta-Fraschini	360
Forlanini	Italian army	F 6	672,000	295'	65'	—	4 Isotta-Fraschini	720
UNITED STATES OF AMERICA								
Goodyear Tire & Rubber Co	US army	RS 1	745,000	282'	70'	23,600	4 Liberty	1,200
Aircraft Development Corp	US navy	ZMC 2	202,200	149'5'	53'	2,700	2 Wright J 5	440

Builder	Operator	Name	Volume (cu. ft.)	Length	Diameter	Weight	Engine	H.P.
Royal Aircraft Factory	British army	*Nulli Secundus*	55,000	122'	25'	—	1 Antoinette	50

CHARACTERISTICS OF PRINCIPAL NON-RIGID AIRSHIPS

FRANCE

Builder	Operator	Name	Volume (cu. ft.)	Length	Diameter	Weight	Engine	H.P.
Aeronautical Estab Chalais Meudon	French army	*La France*	66,000	165'	27'	—	1 Gramme	9
Santos Dumont	Santos Dumont	*No 6*	22,239	108'	20'	352 approx	1 Panhard	12–16
Astra Societé de Constructions Aeronautiques	French army	*Ville de Paris*	112,000	180'	34' 6"	—	1 Chenu	75
Astra Societé	French army	*Adjutant Reau*	560,000	285'	42'	—	2 Brasier	250
Astra Societé	French army	*Astra–Torres 1–18*	222,300–339,000	224'–264'	34·6'–52·8'	5,438–9,967	2 Renault, 2 Renault	320, 500
Clement Bayard	French army	*Adjutant Vincenot*	315,000	264'	48'	5,800	2 Clement Bayard	260
Clement Bayard	French army	*Dupuy de Lôme*	315,000	264'	48'	5,800	2 Chenu	260
Chalais Meudon	French navy	*Chalais Meudon (8)*	194,000–321,000	231'–287'	37'–46'	4,930–11,098	2 Salmson, 2 Salmson	300, 500

Builder	Owner	Name	Volume cu ft	Length ft in	Maximum diameter ft in	Useful lift lb	Engines no and type	Total hp
Zodiac Societé	French army	Zodiac III	70,600	120'	25' 5"	—	1 Ballot	45
Zodiac Societé	French army	D'Arlande & Champagne	501,000	303'	52' 8"	13,896	2 Zodiac	440
Zodiac Societé	French navy	Vedette	77,600	—	—	—	2 Ansani	140
Zodiac Societé	French navy	Eclaireur	219,000	—	50'	—	2 Hispano-Suisa	440
Zodiac Societé	French navy	Croiseur	430,000	331'	50'	—	2 Zodiac	450

GERMANY

Builder	Owner	Name	Volume cu ft	Length ft in	Maximum diameter ft in	Useful lift lb	Engines no and type	Total hp
Luftfahrzeug GmbH	Imperial Aero Club	PL 1	115,000	180'	28'	—	1 Nene Automobil Gesellschaft (NAG)	100
Luftfahrzeug	Luftfahrzeug GmbH (taken over by German navy)	PL 6	315,000 (after modification)	225'	45'	6,000	2 NAG	220
Siemens Schuckert	German army	Siemens Schuckert	525,000	360'	40'	8,000	4 Daimler	480
Luftfahrzeug Gmbh	German navy	PL 25	494,400	360'	54'	11,314	2 Maybach	420

GREAT BRITAIN

Builder	Owner	Name	Volume cu ft	Length ft in	Maximum diameter ft in	Useful lift lb	Engines no and type	Total hp
Willows	Willows	Willows 1	12,500	74'	18'	—	1 Peugeot	7
Roy Aircraft Factory	British army	Beta	35,000	104'	35'	—	1 Green	35
Roy Aircraft Factory	British army	Gamma (1) (2)	75,000 / 101,000	152'	30'	—	(1) 1 Green (2) 2 Iris	80 / 90

Manufacturer	Operator	Name	Volume	Length	Diameter	Weight	Engines	Power
Roy Aircraft Factory	British army	*Delta*	175,000	150'	29'	—	2 White & Poppe	110
Armstrong Whitworth, et al	Royal Navy	*SS*	65,000	144'	28'	1,236	(1) 1 Renault (2) 1 Green	70 / 100
Armstrong Whitworth, et al	Royal Navy	*SS Zero*	70,000	143'	32'	319	1 Rolls-Royce Hawk	75
Armstrong Whitworth, et al	Royal Navy	*SS Twin*	100,000	165'	49'	1,600	2 Rolls-Royce Hawk	150
	Royal Navy	*Coastal*	170,000	196'	52'	3,467	2 Sunbeam	300
	Royal Navy	*Coastal Star*	210,000	218'	49' 3"	3,086	1 Fiat	260
	Royal Navy	*North Sea*	360,000	262'	56' 9"	7,384	2 Fiat	520
UNITED STATES OF AMERICA								
Goodyear; Goodrich	US navy	*C*	181,000	196'	42'	4,050	2 Hispano-Suisa	300
Goodyear	US army	*A 4*	95,000	262'	33·5'	2,224	1 Curtiss OX	300
Goodyear	US army	*TC 1-3*	200,600	196'	44·5'	4,116	2 Wright 'T'	300
Goodyear	US army	*TC 13*	349,600	232·25'	53·9'	9,300 (static & dynamic)	2 R-1340-2	375
Goodyear & Naval Aircraft Factory	US navy	*K 1*	319,900	219·2'	53·9'	7,684 (incl 3,929 lb fuel gas)	2 Pratt & Whitney	600
Goodyear Zeppelin Corpn	US navy	*K 2*	416,000	248·5'	57·85'	9,400	2 Pratt & Whitney	400
Goodyear Aircraft Corpn	US navy	*L*	123,000	147·5'	39·8'	2,540 (S & D)	2 Warner	290

Builder	Owner	Name	Volume cu ft	Length ft in	Maximum diameter ft in	Useful lift lb	Engines no and type	Total hp
Goodyear Aircraft Corpn	US navy	M 2	725,000	302'	69·5'	48,450 (S & D)	2 Pratt & Whitney	550
Goodyear Aircraft Corpn	US navy	ZSG4 (formerly 2P4K)	527,000	266'	69'	?	2 Wright?	1,100
Goodyear Aircraft Corpn	US navy	ZS2G	650,000	285'	75'	?	2 Wright?	1,400
Goodyear Aircraft Corpn	US navy	ZPG–2	975,000	342·65'	75·42'	66,141 (S & D)	2 Wright	800
Goodyear Aircraft Corpn	US navy	ZPG–2W	975,000	342·65'	75·42'	17,200	2 Wright	800
Goodyear Aircraft Corpn	US navy	ZPG–3W	1,465,000	403'	85'	22,907	2 Curtiss	2,550

INDEX